The European Heritage in Economics and the Social Sciences

Volume 24

The European heritage in economics and the social sciences is largely locked in languages other than English. Witness such classics as Storch's *Cours d'Economie Politique*, Wicksell's *Finanztheoretische Untersuchungen* and *Geld, Zins und Güterpreise* or Pareto's *Trattato di Sociologia Generale*. Since about 1937, partly caused by the forced exodus of many scholars from the German language countries and the international reactions to this event, English has become the undisputed primary language of economics and the social sciences. For about one generation, this language shift did not result in a loss of access to the European non-English sources. However, after foreign language requirements were dropped as entry prerequisites for receiving the PhD at major research universities, the European heritage in economics and the social sciences has become largely inaccessible to the vast majority of practicing scholars. In this series, we hope to publish works that address this problem in a threefold manner. An aspect of the European heritage in a language other than English should be critically documented and discussed, reconstructed and assessed from a modern scientific point of view, and tested with respect to its relevance for contemporary economic, social, or political discourse. We welcome submissions that fit this bill in order to make the European heritage in economics and the social sciences available to the international research community of scholars in economics and the social sciences.

More information about this series at http://www.springer.com/series/5902

Jürgen G. Backhaus • Günther Chaloupek
Hans A. Frambach
Editors

Samuel Pufendorf and the Emergence of Economics as a Social Science

Springer

Editors
Jürgen G. Backhaus
Emeritus Professor of Krupp Chair
in Public Finance and Fiscal Sociology
University of Erfurt
Erfurt, Thüringen, Germany

Günther Chaloupek
Former Director
Department of Economic Research
Austrian Chamber of Labour
Vienna, Austria

Hans A. Frambach
Department of Economics
University of Wuppertal
Wuppertal, Nordrhein-Westfalen, Germany

ISSN 1572-1744 ISSN 2197-5892 (electronic)
The European Heritage in Economics and the Social Sciences
ISBN 978-3-030-49790-3 ISBN 978-3-030-49791-0 (eBook)
https://doi.org/10.1007/978-3-030-49791-0

This Springer imprint is published by the registered company Springer Nature Switzerland AG
The registered company address is: Gewerbestrasse 11, 6330 Cham, Switzerland

Contents

Introduction

Günther Chaloupek and Hans A. Frambach

Abstract The emergence of economics as a social science, which was substantially influenced by the emancipation of thinking about economic phenomena from medieval theology, is part of the emergence of a rationalist world view with its understanding of natural phenomena in terms of cause and effect, instead of purpose inherent in the substance of things. Central to the new world view is the concept of law as a force independent of human intention applicable to external physical nature and to human nature. In the spirit of the Baconian sentence *scientia est potentia*, knowledge of such laws brings with it the power to influence the course of events according to desired goals.

Keywords Emergence of modern economic thought, Enlightenment, Natural law, Rationalism, Mercantilism

The emergence of economics as a social science, which was substantially influenced by the emancipation of thinking about economic phenomena from medieval theology, is part of the emergence of a rationalist world view with its understanding of natural phenomena in terms of cause and effect, instead of purpose inherent in the substance of things. Central to the new world view is the concept of law as a force independent of human intention applicable to external physical nature and to human nature. In the spirit of the Baconian sentence *scientia est potentia*, knowledge of such laws brings with it the power to influence the course of events according to desired goals.

In the Middle Ages, theorizing about economic phenomena, such as property, price formation, money, interest etc., which were discussed with considerable

G. Chaloupek (✉)
Former Director, Department of Economic Research,
Austrian Chamber of Labour, Vienna, Austria
e-mail: guenther@chaloupek.eu

H. A. Frambach
Universität Wuppertal, Wuppertal, Germany

J. G. Backhaus et al. (eds.), *Samuel Pufendorf and the Emergence of Economics as a Social Science*, The European Heritage in Economics and the Social Sciences 24, https://doi.org/10.1007/978-3-030-49791-0_1

analytical sophistication, was embedded in a theological context. In the Modern Age, the view of the Scholastic theologians that norms which govern social actions of men are based on divine commandments was replaced by a new philosophy of nature, which came to underlie the thinking about social and economic phenomena. Under this new perspective, social relations were considered under the aspect of causal relationships based on the physical or psychical nature of man. At the same time, the doctrine of 'natural law', in the sense of 'natural jurisprudence', came to dominate thinking about institutions and laws upon which the organization of society and the state is based. 'The distinction between laws of a causal type and laws of a normative type was, as a rule, not strictly observed' (Pribram 1983, 60).

As a consequence of the new social thinking, it came that the order of society was perceived as being based on a 'social contract', somehow concluded by men, which increasingly replaced the medieval view of a divine hierarchy of estates with its traditional structure and institutions. The ultimate goal of the social order was now derived from human nature. If the Scholastics had not denied the relevance of human instincts seeking individual advantage in social action, in the modern world view it was up to human action to design and establish a rational social order through which the behaviour of individual agents would be guided in a way that ensured a best possible result for the whole. Thus, on the one hand, there was a major step towards an individualist perspective in social thinking, which was, on the other hand, at the same time placed into the context of a collective entity – the modern absolutist state. It was the supreme goal of the state, and the duty of its regent, to pursue the realization of the 'Common Weal'.

Explicitly, the change of the *Zeitgeist* is manifest in the writings of philosophers, who presented their views on social and economic phenomena in the form of systems of natural jurisprudence, as was the case with Hugo Grotius and Samuel Pufendorf, or empiricist philosophy, as represented by Thomas Hobbes and John Locke. Except for Locke, discussion of economic issues occupies only rather small parts of their works. In this respect, their focus is on theoretical problems, such as property, price formation, money, interest, whereas specific recommendations on policy issues are few and unsystematic.

Hugo Grotius (1583–1645): *Mare liberum* 1609, *De jure belli ac pacis* 1625
Thomas Hobbes (1588–1679): *Leviathan* 1651
Veit Ludwig von Seckendorff (1626–1692): *Teutscher Fuerstenstaat* 1656
Samuel Pufendorf (1632–1694): *Elementa jurisprudentiae universalis* 1660, *De jure naturae et gentium* 1672, *De officio* 1673
John Locke (1632–1704): *Second treatise of government* 1689
Baruch/Benedict de Spinoza (1632–1677): *Tractatus theologico-politicus* 1670
Johann Joachim Becher (1635–1682): *Politischer Discurs* 1668
Philipp Wilhelm von Hoernigk (1638–1712): *Oesterreich über alles wann es nur will* 1684
Gottfried Wilhelm Leibniz (1646–1716): *Nouveaux Essais sur L'entendement humain* 1704, *Essais de Théodicée* 1710, *Principes de la nature et de la Grâce fondés en raison* 1714, *La Monadologie* 1714 (public. date 1720)

In contrast, mercantilist and cameralist authors usually show little concern about the philosophical and methodical fundamentals of their treatment of economic problems. Unlike the philosophers and theoreticians of natural jurisprudence, they were primarily interested in discussing practical issues of politics and economic policy. The main content of their books, e.g. the works of Seckendorff or Becher, consists in the discussion of concrete issues, resulting in detailed policy recommendations how to promote economic and social welfare, not least as a means to enhance the power of their state in the concert of nations at a time when nation states took shape on the European continent and in England.

But at least implicitly, their writings reflect the new voluntaristic approach in social thinking that social and economic relations and the goals pursued in human action could be thoroughly understood by the power of human reason and could therefore be shaped according to goals chosen by rational reasoning (Sommer 1920/25, 90). Another aspect in which the indebtedness of mercantilist and cameralist authors to the philosophers becomes evident is their focus on relations between states and on collectives within states (Pribram 1983, 83).

Samuel Pufendorf has always been widely recognized as eminent scholar of natural jurisprudence, political theory (*Staatstheorie*) and social philosophy. In particular, his work *De statu imperii Germanici*, originally published under the pen name Severinus de Monzambano, has left a lasting imprint on the discussion about the political structure of the German Empire, even after its dissolution.[1]

Important works in the history of economic thought emphasize the impact of Pufendorf's contribution to the development of economics towards a science of its own in its early stages. According to August Oncken's *Geschichte der Nationalökonomie* (1971, 226) judgement, Pufendorf's work became most relevant in Western Europe, whereas 'intellectual discourse in Germany had declined to a level too low to benefit from it. Both, the physiocrats and Adam Smith have drawn from him', as the new political economy of the West was a continuation of 'the new impulse which Pufendorf had given to the intellectual current of natural jurisprudence'. In his History of economic analysis (1954, 116–117), Joseph Schumpeter mentions Pufendorf as one of the main representatives of the new current of thought, together with Grotius, Hobbes and Locke. He points to his Elementa jurisprudentiae universalis as the 'work to get a general idea of the range and level of that type of social science'.

The most thorough presentation and discussion of Pufendorf's utterances on economic problems can be found in Wilhelm Roscher's *Geschichte der National-Ökonomik in Deutschland* (1874). Roscher is full of praise for Pufendorf's 'excellent' price theory, 'the best available on this fundamental field of political economy down to James Stewart'. In addition to a meticulous discussion of value and price formation, Pufendorf deserves credit for introducing the distinction between price changes originating from the side of money, or from the side of goods (Roscher 1874, 311–312). With respect to interest, Pufendorf rejects prohibition of usury, yet at the same time denounces the banking business for lending borrowed

[1] There is a rather recent republication of the original Latin and a contemporary German translation of the book in Hammerstein (1995).

money at a higher rate of interest. As advocate of the absolutist state, he approves the use of state power to promote the Common Weal. He supports Grotius' idea of *dominium eminens*, a kind of super-ownership of the state, and a rather far-reaching right to tax subjects. Various active measures of promotion of agriculture, industry and commerce, which are taken from the arsenal of mercantilist's policy tracts, are recommended. Individual pursuit of wealth should be encouraged, prohibition of luxuries should help parsimony (Roscher 1874, 314–315). At the same time, Pufendorf does not raise principal objections against such traditional institutions as craft gilds and serfdom – *Leibeigenschaft* – of peasants. Pufendorf's favourable attitude towards comprehensive state powers finds expression in his discussion of money, whose use as means of exchange is based on 'convention and imposition (by the state)'. It does not require any special natural properties, materials other than metal, such as cloth and leather, could serve for that purpose as well (Roscher 1874, 311).

Schumpeter (1954, 122) 'adverts' to the 'well-rounded presentation of the philosophers' economics' in Pufendorf's treatise. Distinguishing value in use and value in exchange (or *pretium eminens*), he lets the latter be determined by the relative scarcity or abundance of goods and money. Market price then gravitates towards the costs that must be incurred in production. On the other hand, Pufendorf's 'analysis of interest … is distinctly inferior to that of the late scholastics', the latter having anticipated the essentials of the economics of the philosophers.

Karl Pribram (1983, 90) refers to Pufendorf's application of the natural law doctrine to the theory of social contract through which citizens submit to the state, in order to protect and promote their well-being. In this context, 'Pufendorf was well aware of the logical difficulties involved in the problem of establishing a unified will by combining individual wills'.

Pufendorf's strong identification with a powerful absolutist state induced him to depart from Grotius' doctrine of *Mare liberum*. If Pufendorf supported the idea of free international trade, which promoted the interest of all nations, in his view it was legitimate that the nation state could impose restrictions on international trade 'insofar as the preservation and the independence of a nation are at stake'. For example, 'it can quite legally prohibit to bring a foreign nation its necessities of life when its subjects lack them', but it has no right to prevent export of luxuries (Demals 2016, 58).

The contributions to this volume offer an in-depth discussion of a variety of aspects of Pufendorf's work.

Arild Saether offers a concise account of Pufendorf's life and work. Thereafter, the contribution surveys the influence of Pufendorf's natural law works on scholars of European Enlightenment, e.g. Locke, Montesquieu, Rousseau, Diderot. The authors of Scottish Enlightenment Francis Hutcheson and Adam Smith were all indebted to Pufendorf. Enlightenment as such ended in the last years of the eighteenth century, and Immanuel Kant eradicated natural law. However, with the Declaration of Human Rights adopted after World War II, natural law of the Enlightenment resurrected.

F. van Holthoon asks in what way Pufendorf's natural jurisprudence influenced David Hume and Adam Smith. He had no direct influence on their work, but he provided them with a clear statement of conventional wisdom in politics and morality as represented by natural jurisprudence. Hume and Smith took natural jurisprudence as conventional wisdom and as the starting point of their innovations in economics.

Pufendorf's natural law comprises ethics, jurisprudence, society and political economy. In his second contribution, *Arild Saether* gives a comprehensive account of Pufendorf's political economy, which embraces theories of human behaviour, private property, value and money, foundation of states and council decisions and finally division of state powers and principles of taxation. His political economy was dispersed across Europe and North America. Thus, Pufendorf played an important role for the emergence of economics as a social science, through his influence on authors of the seventeenth and eighteenth centuries, e.g. Locke, the French philosophers of the Enlightenment, Rousseau and the Physiocratic model builders, Hutcheson, and, finally, on Adam Smith.

Nicolaus Tideman's contribution focuses on Samuel Pufendorf's theory of the origin of property rights in comparison with John Locke's ideas on this subject. John Locke's theory of property seems intended as a commentary on Pufendorf's theory, though Locke does not mention Pufendorf by name. The key difference between Locke and Pufendorf arises because Locke treats Pufendorf's proposition that ownership requires implicit or explicit agreement as if it was intended to be normative, so that Pufendorf would have been claiming rightful ownership requires agreement. Locke then argues that agreement is not needed for rightful ownership when natural opportunities are abundant and, implicitly, people are not in community with one another. Locke's normative argument is valid under these conditions, but not otherwise.

Hans A. Frambach elaborates on Pufendorf's contribution to the conceptual foundations of the modern state with its specific tasks and responsibilities. He remains today an example of a profound and differentiated thinker who combined intellectual acuity with recommendations for action. Especially, his insights into decision-making mechanisms are, from a contemporary point of view, still of far-reaching significance. The article sees modern fields of application of Pufendorf's thought as extending to socioeconomic problems of selfishness and the societal challenges of ever-increasing variety and heterogeneity. For this purpose, reference is made to models such as Amitai Etzioni's 'communitarian paradigm' and Ian Ayres and John Braithwaite's 'responsive regulation'.

Francesco Forte and *Sabato Vinci* apply Pufendorf's theory of justice, specifically with respect to his distinction between universal and distributive justice, to the problem of corporate governance, in particular relating to the problem of prevalence between shareholders objectives and company objectives, in case of conflict between them. The contribution shows that Pufendorf's ideas provide interesting insights for modern ethics studies and modern business economics studies, about topics such as the relationship between natural law and positive law, public goods and the relationship between private company ownership and its social responsibility.

Daniel Eissrich starts from Joseph Schumpeter's claim that scholastic scholars had a significant influence on Grotius and Pufendorf, and consequently also on Adam Smith. Even before Schumpeter, the German theologian Joseph Cardinal Höffner had referred to the dependence of the philosophers of natural law on the

Spanish late scholastics in the context of international law. He also made important contributions to the rediscovery of the economics of the late scholastics. The contribution provides an overview of Höffner's work and shows connecting lines between the scholastics and Grotius and Pufendorf.

Karl-Heinz Schmidt reports on references to Pufendorf in German works in the history of economic thought. Thereafter, he addresses the question in which relation Pufendorf's oeuvre should be seen to 'modern' history of economic thought.

Whereas in classical political economy 'economic' is what concerns the individual urge to pursue personal wealth, Pufendorf had an alternative view based on the ideas of human nature, which is the subject of the contribution of *Dirk Ehnts* and *Erik Jochem*. According to him, man is sociable. His self-interest is often applied towards this end and not an end in itself. Man, without society, is not perfect and cannot hope to strive for happiness. He needs support from society to protect himself from his fellow man and to increase the chances of realizing this drive towards sociability. Economics could be rebuilt on stronger foundations as neuroscience seems to confirm Pufendorf's view of human nature in general.

***

The chapters in this volume are the revised contributions to the 34th Heilbronn Symposion in Economics and the Social Sciences in 2019. On behalf of the entire Heilbronn group, we would like to thank the city council and the Lord Mayor of the City of Heilbronn for their continued generous support.

References

Demals, T (2016) Mercantilism and the science of trade, in: Faccarello, G and Kurz, HD (eds.) Handbook on the History of Economic Analysis, vol. II. Edward Elgar, Cheltenham, UK, pp 52–74

Faccarello, G, Kurz, HD (eds.) (2016) Handbook on the History of Economic Analysis, vol. II. Edward Elgar, Cheltenham, UK

Hammerstein, N (ed.) (1995) Staatslehre der frühen Neuzeit, vol. 16 of Bibliothek der Geschichte und Politik. Deutscher Klassiker Verlag, Frankfurt

Oncken, A (1971) Geschichte der Nationalökonomie 1. (einziger) Teil, Die Zeit vor Adam Smith, repr. of the ed. Leipzig 1902. Scientia Verlag, Aalen

Pribram, K (1983) A History of Economic Reasoning. Johns Hopkins University Press, Baltimore, London

Roscher, W (1874) Geschichte der National-Ökonomik in Deutschland. Oldenbourg Verlag, Munich

Schumpeter, JA (1954) History of Economic Analysis. Allen & Unwin, London

Sommer, L (1920/25) Die österreichischen Kameralisten in dogmengeschichtlicher Darstellung, repr. of 1st part, Vienna 1920, 2nd part, Vienna 1925. Scientia Verlag, Aalen

Pufendorf and His Importance for the European Enlightenment in General

Arild Sæther

Abstract Samuel Pufendorf was born in Saxony in 1632. He made a remarkable career. After studies at the universities of Leipzig, Jena and Leiden, he became professor of natural law at University of Heidelberg in 1660. Eight years later, he took up a similar position at University of Lund. Thereafter, he became historiographer and counsellor, first in 1677 at the court in Stockholm, and 11 years later in Berlin. He died in 1694 as a true European.

Throughout his life he produced volumes of dissertations, essays and books. The most important were his natural law works *De Jure Naturae et Gentium* in eight books from 1672, and an abridged version *De Officio Hominis et Civis* from 1673. Natural law, deduced from reason and with the dignity and equality of man as its foundation, became a university subject at many European universities. In the eighteenth century, Pufendorf was the most read European philosopher.

The first to actively use Pufendorf's natural law works was the Enlightenment scholar John Locke. The famous philosophers of the French Enlightenment, Charles-Louis Montesquieu, Jean-Jacques Burlamaqui, Jean-Jacques Rousseau and Denis Diderot, as well as three important scholars of the Scottish Enlightenment, Gershom Carmichael, Francis Hutcheson and Adam Smith, were all indebted to Pufendorf. Although it can be discussed if the Enlightenment as such ended in the last years of the eighteenth century, there can be no doubt that Immanuel Kant and his followers eradicated natural law. However, when the Declaration of Human Rights was decided after WWII, as the common standard of achievements for all people and nations, natural law of the Enlightenment resurrected. The final challenge is how Pufendorf's ideas again can be brought to the forefront.

A. Sæther (✉)
Agder Academy of Sciences and Letters, Kristiansand, Norway
e-mail: arild@saether.no

J. G. Backhaus et al. (eds.), *Samuel Pufendorf and the Emergence of Economics as a Social Science*, The European Heritage in Economics and the Social Sciences 24, https://doi.org/10.1007/978-3-030-49791-0_2

Keywords Natural law · Ethics · Jurisprudence · Political economy · Declaration of human rights · John Locke · French enlightenment · Scottish Enlightenment

JEL Codes B 11 · B 12 · B 15 · B 31 · D 40 · D 46 · D 62 · F 50 · H 20 · H 50 · K11 · K12 · K40 · N00 · N01

1 Who Was Samuel Pufendorf?

Samuel Pufendorf was born in Dorfchemnitz, Saxony in 1632. He grew up during the violence and devastation of the Thirty Years War. Although he and his family escaped direct violence, they saw and heard of horrors almost every day. His childhood experience set its imprint on his life and works.

In 1645, he qualified for admission to the humanistic Prince's School of St. Augustin in Grimma. After five mostly happy years of studies, which included grammar, logic, rhetoric, the Bible, Lutheran theology and the Greek and Roman classics, he graduated at the top of his class in the autumn of 1650. Following the wish of his father, who had passed away 2 years earlier, he moved to Leipzig, and like his older brother Esaias (1628–1689), matriculated at the University with the intention to study theology. However, already in his first semester he realised that theology, as taught by the professors, was dogmatic, and he soon developed an aversion to this pedantic orthodoxy. Schroeder (2008, 74) contends that, disenchanted with theology, he changed direction and turned first to law, thereafter he visited lectures in natural philosophy, cameral sciences and even medicine.

In 1657, he moved to the University of Jena and became the protégé of Professor Erhard Weigel (1625–1699), who introduced him to the works of Hugo Grotius (1585–1645), Thomas Hobbes (1588–1679) and the methods and philosophy of René Descartes (1596–1650).

On completion of his master's degree, Pufendorf was not able to find work close to home. However, his brother Esaias, who had joined the Swedish Foreign Service, secured for him a post as a tutor for the children of the Swedish envoy at the Court in Copenhagen.

His arrival in Copenhagen the summer of 1658 could not have been at a more inconvenient time. A war had broken out between the Nordic rivals Sweden and Denmark–Norway. The Swedish army besieged the city and Pufendorf was arrested, accused of being a spy, and thrown into a cell at Kastellet fortress.

Throughout more than 8 months of harsh captivity he reflected and meditated on his studies of natural law and especially upon what he had read in the works of Descartes, Grotius and Hobbes and not least the teaching of Weigel, and he managed to produce a manuscript on natural law. After 8 months, he was released and travelled with the Swedish envoy and his two sons to Leiden, where they matriculated at the University in March 1660.

Here Pufendorf pursued studies in classical philology, at the time the speciality of the University. He apparently did not intend to publish his manuscript, which he had started in Copenhagen, but his teachers and friends strongly urged him to do so. He followed their advice and the *Elementorum Jurisprudentiae Universalis,* EJU (Elements of universal jurisprudence), (1927 [1660])), was published in The Hague in 1660. Wehberg (1922, xi) claims that all 'the original ideas of Pufendorf' are found in it. Behme (2009, ix) adds that Pufendorf with this work inaugurated the modern natural law movement in the German-speaking world. It certainly established Pufendorf as a major figure in natural law and made the foundation for his later works that were to sweep across Europe and North America.

Pufendorf had strategically dedicated the book to Prince Elector Karl Ludwig of the Palatinate. In return, the Prince, in 1661, invited Pufendorf to the University of Heidelberg. In October 1661, he accepted an offer to become 'extraordinarius professor iuris gentium (international law) et philologiae.' Later this position was transformed into a chair in natural law and politics.

Most of his time in Heidelberg was taken up with lecturing, writings and consulting. He taught international law, natural law and philology using his own works and the writings of Grotius. He developed and extended the ideas he had presented in his book. He filled his appointment with much credit, and he drew large audiences of students to his lectures.

Pufendorf's years in Heidelberg were among the happiest of his life. An important and satisfying event took place in 1665 when he married Katharina Elisabetha (1629–1713), the widow of one of his deceased colleagues. She brought with her into the marriage one daughter and together they had two.

From his dissertations and his books, his almost 8 years in Heidelberg turned out to be very productive. In short, he read books that had not been available to him before, he researched and he wrote. In 1667, he published his historical and political work: *De Statu Imperii Germanici* (On the Constitution of the German Empire), (2007 [1667]). This book is a broadside and a merciless criticism of the disastrous condition of public law in the Roman–German Empire and the guild of constitutional jurists that defended it. The book raised 'a hue and cry' throughout Germany, and it was quickly banned from universities and condemned by the imperial censor and the Pope, the Empire's spiritual head. Nonetheless, since it expressed what many already thought, but did not dare to say, it soon became very popular. With this book, his reputation was extended to non-academic circles. He achieved both fame and criticism. At the end of his stay in Heidelberg, Pufendorf had designed and partly completed a new masterpiece that became his major work in natural law.

In 1666, a new university had been established in Lund, Scania, the former Danish province, that became Swedish in 1658. The founders had ambition to create a university with an international direction. Pufendorf, who now had become famous on a European scale, should make the new university 'illustrious'. He was therefore offered a full professorship in natural and international law with a salary substantially higher than the other professors.

Pufendorf with his family moved to Lund in 1668 to take up his new position. At the university, he did not put the expectation of his superiors to shame. Many international students were drawn to Lund because of his reputation. He tutored many students, and many of them lived in his household. His time in Lund turned out to be a new productive period in his life.

In 1672, Pufendorf published his major natural law work *De Jure Naturae et Gentium* (On the Law of Nature and Nations) (DJNG, 1933 [1672, 1688]) based on the manuscript he had brought with him from Heidelberg, and the year after an abridged version *De Officio Hominis et Civis* (The Duty of Man and Citizen) DOH, (1927 [1673,1682])..

His stay at the University of Lund was also troublesome. Shortly after the publication of his books, strong reaction came from prominent professors of theology, Professor Josua Schwartz (1632–1709) and the Bishop of Lund and Professor Peder Winstrup (1605–1679). They accused him of heresy and atheism and claimed that the book was a prescription of anarchy and godlessness. They also asserted that the author was an enemy of both religion and government, and which was offensive a seducer of youth.

When University of Lund was closed in 1677, because of new hostilities between Denmark and Sweden, Pufendorf accepted an offer of a position as Royal Swedish historian and State counsellor at the Court in Stockholm. During his stay in Stockholm, he concentrated his work on historical, political and theological studies. An enlarged revised edition of his major work was published in Frankfurt in 1684. In the years 1682–1686, he published his encyclopaedic work on European history and comparative politics in the German language. Thereafter, he produced volumes upon volumes on the history of the Swedish kings, based on archival studies. He also issued a series of polemic essays. In 1687, he published *De habitu religionis christianae* ad vitam *civilem* (On the nature of Christian religion in relation to civil life) in response to the revocation of the Edicts of Nantes in 1685, Pufendorf (2002a [1687]).. In this essay, he strongly advocated religious tolerance and the right to resist religious persecution.

In 1688, Pufendorf moved again, this time to Berlin, where he took up the position as historiographer and counsellor at the Court of Brandenburg-Prussia. He continued his historical writings and produced numerous books. A second essay on religion, *Jus feciale divinium cive des consensuset dissensu protestatium* (The divine feudal law: Or, Covenants with mankind, Pufendorf (2002b [1695]), was written but published after his death. Here, he advocated a reconciliation and union of the Lutheran and Calvinist reformed churches.

On a journey to Stockholm where he was elevated into the Swedish aristocracy, he became ill on the strenuous return journey to Berlin. He died in 1694 as a true European and is entombed in St. Nicolaikirche.

2 Pufendorf's System of Natural Law

In retrospect, Pufendorf's life can be seen as a long, but rapid, journey where he worked diligently both to make life better for himself and his family, but also through his work to improve the conditions in Europe and make it better to live in for all people. Born in a time of turmoil and violence and seeing the consequences of unscrupulous wars, his main vision was to enlighten people about the right conditions for enduring peace. The means to make this vision true were his academic writings, his teaching of students, his tutoring of prospective civil servants and his work as a political advisor to three important, and given the conditions of the time, enlightened Protestant statesmen.

2.1 *Pufendorf's Writings*

His writings can be divided into three groups, Tully (1991, xiv–xv). The first group is his attempts to construct a comprehensive political and moral philosophy based on a set of universal principles or natural laws. It is developed primarily in his three natural law texts.

However, this approach was somewhat moved aside when he moved to Stockholm and took up his work there. He did not completely give up his natural law writings, but he concentrated on historical analyses.

The second group is therefore Pufendorf's attempt to analyse the relations within and among contemporary European states, by means of a comparative and historical analysis of their interest and relative powers with a view to predictions and recommendations to state builders in general and the rulers he served. When he moved to Berlin in 1688, he continued these writings. His numerous books on historical themes belong to this group. Special attention should be drawn to his monumental introduction to the history of the principal states of Europe. This work, 'with its rigorous concept of state interest and relative powers and its comprehensive design, was republished throughout the eighteenth century' (Tully 1991, xv). Several history writers across Europe adopted his method and to some extent just copied him. One of these was the Dano–Norwegian philosopher Ludvig Holberg (1684–1754).[1]

The third group comprises Pufendorf's attempts to define the correct subordinate relations of religion to politics in Protestant states after the Peace of Augsburg, which recognised diversity within Christianity. He advocated toleration and the unification of the different Protestant creeds. His views are primarily expressed in his two essays.

The idea of an objective moral and judicial order based on human nature is as old as philosophy. Formulated as a doctrine and called natural law, it is usually connected with Stoic and Roman jurists in the antiquity, with the Schoolmen, particularly from Thomas Aquinas (c. 1225–1274) to Francois Suarez (1548–1617) in the Middle Ages, and with the sixteenth- and seventeenth-century political theorists, in particular Grotius, Hobbes and Pufendorf. Some of the terms used have survived the development through the centuries, unchanged: human reason, justice and the belief that society is created through agreements.

---

[1] When his first book *En introduksjon til historien til Europas nasjoner* (An introduction to the history of the European nations) was published in Copenhagen in 1711, he was accused of having plagiarized Pufendorf.

This order can function in two ways: it can be seen in opposition to the present political order and will therefore have in it a revolutionary content, or it can view the present order as reasonable and necessary and will therefore favour status quo (Lindberg 1976). The first interpretation can be found with the Greek Sophists (400 BC), who criticised slavery, and with the Monarchomachs, and others who fought against the absolute power of the kings in the fifteenth and sixteenth centuries, and with revolutionaries in France and North America in the late seventeenth century. The second interpretation defended the existing order, dominated by the Catholic culture in the late Middle Ages, and in the Lutheran culture in the sixteenth and seventeenth centuries.

This could imply that the philosophers belonging to the last strand, such as Pufendorf, did not contribute to the political and social upheavals and progress that occurred in Europe and America in these centuries. Nothing could, however, be more wrong.

It is true that most seventeenth-century natural law philosophers defended the rulers they served and thereby the existing order. There were at least two reasons for this fact. First, this century was characterised by upheavals, wars, destruction, extreme violence and death. To advocate radical changes in state governance or revolutions against the present rulers would probably only create more havoc and devastation. Second, they had no choice. During these years, there were limited legal protection for most people, and freedom of expression did not exist in most European countries. Consequently, there were limits to what scholars could write without losing the support of their benefactors and thereby their livelihood, or even their heads. Considering these facts, it is astounding how they in their writings dared to discuss both improvements, and alternatives to the present order. Alternatively, they left so much ambiguity in their discussions that their writings could be used by their descendants to advocate political changes.

Pufendorf's writing was also open to interpretation. He can be characterised as an eclectic who united authoritarian and liberal elements. This approach made it possible to break away parts of his doctrines and use them in new connections. He also developed his theories in connection with the political realities in existing states. He was not a radical, who wanted violent changes and he did not challenge the masters he served. Furthermore, he also needed his benefactors support in his controversies with his colleagues at the universities of Heidelberg and Lund, and most importantly in his struggle with the leaders of the Lutheran orthodoxy in many European countries. These struggles with his adversaries were fierce at the time and could have seriously threatened his position, without him having the support of his masters. However, these clashes also strengthened his position and made him a well-known scholar in the seventeenth century.

Haakonssen (1996, 43) claims that there are several ambiguities in Pufendorf's representation of his natural law, but that 'these ambiguities gave rise to a debate which lasted for a generation or more, and which was as fierce as any in the history of philosophy'. Furthermore, 'it also helped to secure to Pufendorf an influence that was European in scope and lasted well into the eighteenth century'. Therefore, when Jonathan I. Israel (2001, 802), in his study *Radical Enlightenment,* calls Pufendorf 'a German natural law theorist', he is positively wrong. Pufendorf was a true European scholar.

Pufendorf sought to mediate between Grotius and Hobbes. He wanted to unify Hobbes' natural law doctrine of self-interest with Grotius' natural law doctrine of 'man's inclination for society' and to integrate these ideas with the Cartesian and scholastic methods of the sixteenth-century thinkers. He sought to bridge the apparent antagonism between man's self-interest and man's existence as a social being. The duties of man and citizen will converge in a state where a superior has been granted the right to govern others in exchange for the security and protection that he can offer them. His writings on natural law include ethics, jurisprudence, government and political economy. These elements are integral parts of a totality.

2.2 *Pufendorf's Method*

In his *De Jure Naturae et Gentium,* Pufendorf employed an 'eclectic' method, in which he defended man's ability to understand truth and draw conclusions based on observations from the reality of life. This method involved rational analysis and argumentation. His objective remained the same and his analysis was based on systematic understanding and demonstrative certainty of his subjects, which he also developed from his study of history and contemporary events. He therefore substantiated his opinions, his arguments and the truths he claims to have discovered by numerous quotations, just as Grotius and others of his predecessors had done. These he found in the Bible, the Koran, the Roman Corpus Juris Canonici, and not least in the writings of the Ancient Greek and Roman philosophers and jurists. He has a few quotations from the philosophers of the Middle Ages, but again numerous quotations from philosophers, jurists and historians of the fifteenth and sixteenth centuries. In the *Index of Authors Cited,* in the 1688 edition, 400 names are found. These Pufendorf frequently quotes. The *Index* encompasses 43 French, 30 Italian, 10 Spanish and 5 Portuguese authors, all from Catholic countries. From predominantly Protestant countries, the *Index* contains 33 German, 24 Dutch and 14 English authors. When he discusses issues or argues for a certain opinion, he uses the views of many of these scholars in support of and to give weight to his own views. He admits that he prefers to cite the ancient authors. 'To add to them by calling in a cloud of more recent writers seemed superfluous' (DJNG Preface, vii). In particular, he has excluded the followers of what he calls the Roman sect. The reasons for their omission were their adherence to the scholastic method and juristic clericalism. Furthermore, they did not recognise the principle of human sociability as a sufficient basis for natural law. However, the content of his works proves that he was familiar with many authors belonging to the Catholic Church, for example Professor Francois Suarez from the School of Salamanca.[2] It should be noted that at the time

[2]The name was introduced by Marjorie Grice-Hutchinson (1952) in her book, *The School of Salamanca.*

it was not 'comme il faut' for Protestant writers to quote from too many Catholic writers and 'vice versa'.[3]

2.3 *Man's Social Life: the Foundation of Natural Law*

Pufendorf stresses that he has made the social life of man the foundation for his work on natural law. The reason being that he has found no other principle, which all men could accept, without violation of their natural condition. Furthermore, he claims that it is also obvious, that since the Creator made man a social being, the nature of man is the norm and foundation of that law, which must be followed in any society. This is so whether it is universal or particular. His system of natural law is valid for all human beings, with due respect to whatever belief men might hold on the matters of religion (DJNG, ix).

Pufendorf wanted to remove natural law from both civil law and moral theology.

> From the first flow the most common duties of man, particularly those which render him capable of society [sociabilis] with other man; from the second flow the duties of man as a citizen living in a particular and definite state [civitas]; from the third the duties of a Christian. (DOH, 7)

He attempts to construct his theory of natural law based on the dignity and equality of man, human reason and man's free choice:

> The dignity of man's nature, and that excellence of his in which he surpasses other creatures, required that his actions should be made to conform to a definite rule, without which there can be no recognition of order, seemliness, or beauty. And so, man has that supreme dignity, the possession of an immortal soul, furnished with the light of intellect and the faculty of judgment and choice, and most highly endowed for many an art. (DJNG II, I, 1, 148)

He starts by pointing out that man is a moral being, who has by the Great Creator been given not 'merely beauty and adaptability of body, but also the distinctive light of intelligence'. This intelligence can be used by man to understand things more accurately. The very being of man is a state from which arise certain obligations and certain rights.

Furthermore, he claims to prove that by starting from the divine destiny of man as a spiritual and social being and following the route of strictly logical deduction, we may arrive at results as safe as those in the natural sciences physics and chemistry. Man has been given the distinctive light of intelligence, which he can use to understand things more accurately. He can compare them with one another, judge the unknown with the known and he can decide how things relate to each other. Man is free from confining his actions to one mode. He can even exert, suspend or moderate his actions. Furthermore, man 'has been granted the power to invent or apply

[3] Pufendorf must have been introduced to the Salamanca School during his stay at the University of Leiden.

certain aids to each faculty, whereby it is signally assisted and directed in its functioning' (DJNG I, I, 2, 4).

2.4 Natural Law Deduced from Reason

Pufendorf contends that most men agree that the law of nature should be deduced from reason by man himself and should flow from that source. He points out that children and the uneducated distinguish right from wrong with ease. However, this ease comes from experience that goes back to their earliest days. As soon as they show some use of reason, they have seen good deeds approved and rewarded and evil ones reproved and punished. The law of nature is therefore not innate.

The dictates of sound reason are consequently true principles that are in accordance with the properly observed and examined nature of things. Furthermore, they are deduced by logical sequence from prime and true principles.

2.5 Natural Law Founded on the Condition of Man

The true basis for the law of nature is found in the conditions and dignity of man. A society cannot exist unless its members have a common feeling, basis or ideology about the proper way to conduct its affairs. This ideology he finds in the fact that man has been endowed with a free will together with the driving forces behind human actions.

Pufendorf points out that *the pursuit of self-interest is man's first human attribute*, inclination or driving force. He emphasised that pursuit of self-interest is not only the first human attribute, it is also the strongest. However, in addition to this self-interest and man's desire to preserve himself by any and all means, it can be observed in the character of man 'the greatest weakness and native helplessness' (DJNG II, iii, 14, 207). He therefore states that it is easy to find the basis of natural law *because man has an attribute, inclination or driving force in addition to self-interest, it is necessary for man to be sociable.* Every man should by his life promote and cultivate a social attitude 'so far as in him lies'.

Man has duties towards himself, but he also has duties towards other men. No one should hurt another and if someone has caused damage, he should make it good. The damage should be viewed broadly to include every injury against a man's body, reputation and virtue. In this connection, he discusses both externalities and discounted value of damage.

2.6 Natural Law the Standard of Judgement

The prime source for Pufendorf's natural law is human nature. Since human nature belongs equally to all men and since no one can live a social life with a person by whom he is not rated as at least a fellow man, it is a precept of natural law. From this, it follows that all men are accounted as naturally equal, that slavery is against natural law, that man and woman have equal rights and that marriage should be by contract between equal partners.

His doctrine of the dignity and equality of men became the foundation of his natural law, and his natural law the standard that human behaviour, private property, commercial society, foundation of states, governments and system of taxation are judged against.

Furthermore, Pufendorf claims to prove that by starting from the divine destiny of man as a spiritual and social being and following the route of strictly logical deduction, we may arrive at results as safe as those in the natural sciences, physics and chemistry. Man has been given the distinctive light of intelligence, which he can use to understand things more accurately. He can compare them with one another, judge the unknown with the known and he can decide how things relate to each other. Man is free from confining his actions to one mode. He can even exert, suspend or moderate his actions. Furthermore, man 'has been granted the power to invent or apply certain aids to each faculty, whereby it is signally assisted and directed in its functioning' (DJNG I, I, 2, 4).

2.7 Law of Nations

In his law of nations (international law), Pufendorf claimed that no acute positive law exists that arises from custom or from treaties among nations. One reason for this is that there cannot be found an authority above the states that can bind them.[4] Pufendorf rejected customs and treatises as sources for international law. With his doctrine, Pufendorf became the founder of the purely natural law conception of the law of nations. His theory is therefore considered auspicious for the development of the law of nations. The history of international law is largely characterised by whether one thinks it can be deduced from natural law or if it wholly can be seen as resulting from customs and treatises, the positivistic science of law. In his *Introduction* to the English translation of *Elementorum Jurisprudentiae Universalis*, Wehberg (1922, xiv) claimed that Grotius and Pufendorf were 'champions of the great thought that in international life one should stand for all and all for one in repelling every injustice'. Pufendorf's idea of a system of universal jurisprudence valid for all nations was 'a daring one' (Ibid, xxii).

---

[4] *Elementorum Jurisprudentiae Universalis:* Definition XIII § 24. *De Jure Naturae et Gentium:* II, 3, 23.

3 The Diffusion of Pufendorf's Natural Law

A year after he had published his major work in eight books, he published his 'student edition' *De Officio* in two small books. It is 'excerpted almost entirely' from his major work, but it does not include the long and often tedious arguments that support its conclusions.[5]

What was his motivation in publishing this popularised version? His answer is given in his *Dedication* to the first chancellor of the university, and in his *Preface* entitled 'To the benevolent reader – greetings'. In the dedication, he makes an apology for having produced such a small work but tells that it is a work for beginners, 'as it can furnish some use perhaps to those who are undertaking the first step to that study'. Its content embraces merely 'the first rudiments of moral philosophy'.

In the preface, he states that his purpose has been to 'set fourth for beginners the chief headings of natural law, briefly and I think in a clear compendium'.

Pufendorf had also another reason for his popularisation. He wanted to counter his previously mentioned detractors, who had written 'a bull of excommunication' against him. The effect of his counterattack was, at first, like throwing petrol onto a fire, but ultimately the dispute tremendously strengthened his reputation.[6]

3.1 De Officio: An International Bestseller

De Officio Hominis et Civis, when it was published in 1673, 'hit the market' at the right time. It became an international 'best seller'. It spread Pufendorf's gospel of natural law, which includes ethics, jurisprudence, government and political economy, on the European continent, the British Isles and the American colonies. New editions, with or without commentaries, appeared in most European countries. It was reprinted innumerable times, and thousands of copies were produced and sold.

Latin was the Lingua Franca of the educated classes and used as a language of instruction at all universities in the seventeenth and eighteenth centuries, but *De Officio* was also translated into all the major European languages. The first translation and publication of *De Officio* into German as *Über die Pflicht des Menschen und des Bürgers* by the German historian, jurist and professor in Giessen Immanuel Weber (1657–1726) appeared in 1691. The first English translation, as *The Whole Duty of Man, according to the Law of Nature,* by the English scholar and professor at Gresham College, Andrew Tooke (1673–1732), appeared the same year. It was reissued in 1698, 1705 and 1716.

Although the Catholic Church placed Pufendorf's natural law works on the index, these works found their way into university libraries, state libraries and

---

[5] All quotations from DOH: Dedication. iii.

[6] See, for example, Bo Lindberg (1983) who claims that the great dispute he had at Lund did not diminish his reputation.

libraries of the intellectual classes, also in the French-, Italian- and Spanish-speaking parts of Europe.

French was not only the spoken and written language in France and parts of Switzerland, it was the first foreign language across Europe, after the classical languages Greek and Latin. If readers had difficulties with a text in the classical languages, they turned to the French translations. These translations were also in many cases used as basis for translations into other foreign languages. Translation of books into French, originally written in Latin, was therefore very important for the circulation of new ideas.

3.2 *Jean Barbeyrac the Preeminent French Translator*

One person is very important in this context. It is the French jurist and philosopher Jean Barbeyrac (1674–1744). Being a Huguenot, he and his family had to escape France in 1685. After spending some time at Geneva and Frankfurt am Main, he became professor of belles-lettres at the French school of Berlin. In 1711, he was called to be professor in history and civil law, at the University of Lausanne, before finally settling as professor of public law at the University of Groningen. Barbeyrac became the preeminent eighteenth-century translator of Latin natural law works into French of the seventeenth century.

In Berlin, Barbeyrac translated with many comments *De Jure Naturae et Gentium* into French. It was published in Amsterdam in 1706.[7] The year after he translated, also with an extensive preface and many comments, the abridged *De Officio*.[8] These translations saw a large number of editions and reprints. In addition, they were also, to a great extent, used as the basis for translations into other languages.

Together with Barbeyrac's recommendation for their use, they had a tremendous effect on the circulation of Pufendorf's natural law books and the diffusion of natural law including political economy. The French public, but also people from other parts of Europe that were familiar with the French language, became acquainted with the doctrine of natural law through his translations, not only of Pufendorf's works, but also of *De Jure Belli et Pacis* by Grotius, and *De Legibus Naturae* by Richard Cumberland.

[7]The French title *Le Droit de la Nature et des Gens ou Système Général des Principes les plus importants de la Morale, de la Jurisprudence et de la Politique, Traduits du Latin de feu Mr. Le Baron de Pufendorf*, Par Jean Barbeyrac, Amsterdam, Henri Schelte, 1706 (Dedication: « A sa Majesté le Roi de Prusse »).

[8]The complete French title *Les Devoirs de l'Homme et des Citoiens, tel qu'ils lui sont prescrits par la Loi The complete French title Les Devoirs de l'Homme et des Citoiens, tel qu'ils lui sont prescrits par la Loi Naturelle, Traduits du Latin de feu Mr. Le Baron de Pufendorf, Par Jean Barbeyrac, Amsterdam, Henri Schelte, 1707. (The introduction by the translator is dated «De Berlin le 1. Mars 1707»). He based his translation upon the eleventh edition of the original, which was prepared in 1703 at Frankfurt am Main by Professor Immanuel Weber of the University of Giessen.*

Barbeyrac should therefore be given a great deal of honour with regard to the great popularity of natural law or moral philosophy as a university subject, and the use of Pufendorf's *De Offico* as a textbook. His own fame rests chiefly on the preface and annotations to his translation of Pufendorf's natural law work.

3.3 Editions and Translations of De Officio

Sieglinde Othmer (1970, 129) and Klaus Luig (1972, 539–557) have both made investigations into the diffusion of natural law by looking at the number of editions and translations of Pufendorf's natural law works. The combined major results of Luig's and Othmer's studies of *De Officio* until the 1770s is shown in Table 1.

In all, this work has been published in more than 151 editions. Of these editions, 106 are in Latin and 45 in other European languages: Danish, Dutch, English, French, German, Italian, Russian and Spanish. There are 31 editions in the local language and in addition 14 editions in French but published in another country than France: 8 in The Netherlands, 3 in Germany/Austria, 2 in Switzerland and 1 in the British Isles.

Most of the 20 editions in French can be attributed to Barbeyrac. In addition, several of the translations into other local languages are based on one of Barbeyrac's French editions, not the Latin original. His extensive commentaries are often added to other editions and translations. Luig's and Othmer's investigations are extensive but not complete. For example, a Swedish translation from 1747 has been missed.

Since many of these translations are not from the original Latin text but from Barbeyrac's French translation, Pufendorf's original meanings could easily have been distorted in such translations. Unfortunately, it is also a fact that many

Table 1 *De Officio Hominis et Civis*, editions and translations

	Latin	Local	French
The Netherlands	12	3	8
Germany/Austria	59	7	3
British Isles	10	7	1
Switzerland	5	–	2
France	–	6	–
Sweden	10	1	–
Italy	8	4	–
Denmark	–	1	–
Russia	–	2	–
Poland	2	–	–
Spain	–	1	–
Total	106	32	14

Sources: Klaus Luig (1972, 546) and Sielginde Othmer (1970, 140)

translators took a great freedom in their translations and 'adapted the text' if they did not agree with the original.

Of the professors who adopted the *De officio* as a textbook, many published their own comments, sometimes separately, but usually together with the text. It should also be noted that some professors published their own books on natural law or moral philosophy that closely shadowed Pufendorf's work. Therefore, several imitations of *De Officio* have been published. Some authors admitted that they built closely on Pufendorf, while others tried to disguise their source.

From this, it can be concluded that the popularity of Pufendorf's 'student edition' lasted well into the second half of the eighteenth Century.

3.4 *Editions and Translations of* De Jure Naturae et Gentium

The popularity of Pufendorf's 'student edition' also led to many translations and new editions of his major natural law work. The results of Othmer's study are shown in Table 2.

According to the investigation by Othmer, in all, 44 editions of this work have been published, 20 in Latin, 13 in local languages and 11 in French outside France. The editions in French are based on Barbeyrac's work. In addition to the translations into French, this work has also been translated into German, English and Italian. Of the 44 editions that were included in this study, 31 were published after 1706.

By the middle of the seventeenth century, Pufendorf's natural law works could be found in university and state libraries across Europe and North America. For more than 100 years, these books were among the most read academic books in Europe and the New World.

In Protestant Europe, these works could be found in the university libraries because they were used by the professors, and were part of the curriculum for those studying jurisprudence, philosophy or ethics. In Catholic Europe, Pufendorf's natural law books were in many cases blacklisted and, in some cases, banned. However, they were needed by scholars to be studied, so they could counteract and refute the

Table 2 *De Jure Naturae et Gentium*, editions and translations

	In Latin	In local languages	In French
The Netherlands	4	–	5
Germany	12	3	2
England	–	7	1
Switzerland	1	–	3
France	–	2	–
Sweden	3	–	–
Italy	–	1	–
Total	20	13	11

Source: Sieglinde Othmer (1970, 139)

dangerous ideas presented in these works. Therefore, Pufendorf's books could also be found in most Catholic university libraries across Europe although students in the seventeenth and eighteenth centuries were not permitted to read them. Knowledge of Pufendorf's natural law works was, according to Jan V. M. de Vet (1996, 209–35), disseminated through reviews in the learned journals in the Netherlands and elsewhere.

It should be emphasised that *De Officio* was not only read by university students and scholars. It was a book that was known and spread among the educated classes from emperors and kings to aristocrats, landowners, bureaucrats and people of the clergy, businesspeople and others who could read and write. It could therefore also be found in many large and small private libraries and book collections throughout Europe. These book collections might range from only a handful to several hundreds or thousands of volumes.

3.5 Natural Law a University Subject

In 1661, Pufendorf taught natural law together with international law and philology in Heidelberg. At Lund he taught the subject from 1668. Owing to his reputation and influence, and as a result of the popularity of *De Officio*, natural law became part of university studies in natural law or moral philosophy at most Protestant universities across Europe, and even at some Catholic universities.

After Heidelberg, in 1660–61, study programmes and chairs in Pufendorfian natural law were established at many European universities.[9] In Germany, Heidelberg was followed by Jena in 1665, Greifswald in 1666 or 1674 (it had recently been conquered by Sweden), Königsberg in 1673, Marburg in 1674, Helmstedt in 1675, Erfurt in 1676, Altdorf in 1680, Tübingen in 1684 or 1686, Kiel in 1689 (at this time in the Danish-Norwegian province Holstein), Frankfurt and der Oder in 1690, Giessen in 1692, Halle in 1694, Rostock, Wittenberg and Leipzig in 1711 and Göttingen in 1734.[10] Moreover, this listing does not claim to be complete.

In the Netherlands, natural law had been part of the curriculum at Leiden as early as the 1640s using the works of Grotius. From 1662, Pufendorf's first natural law book was used. The same year it was also used at Groningen. In Switzerland, natural law became part of the curriculum, first at Lausanne in 1711, and a few years thereafter at Geneva and Basel. Uppsala was first in the Nordic countries in 1665. It was followed by Lund in 1668, Åbo and Dorpat (Tartu in today's Estonia) in 1690, Kiel in 1665 or 1689 and Copenhagen in 1695.

[9] Natural law had been taught at universities or academies since the Middle Ages. But with Grotius' *De jure belli et pacis* from 1625 a change took place. The first chair in the subject was, according to Lindberg (1976), established at University of Uppsala in 1655.

[10] According to articles by Dufour (1986), Hammerstein (1986), Mautner (1986), Denzer (1987), Haakonssen (2012) and the book by Israel (2006).

In the United Kingdom, John Locke taught natural law at Oxford in the early 1660s. However, it was at the five universities in Scotland, first at Glasgow and Edinburgh, but soon followed by St. Andrew and at King's College and Marischaf College in Aberdeen, that moral philosophy, as natural law was called, gained a strong position in the early part of the eighteenth century.

All major libraries in Europe and North America had in the eighteenth century copies of Pufendorf's natural law works in their collection. His *De Officio* was used at almost all universities in Protestant Europe in the beginning of the eighteenth century. For more than 100 years, this book was among the most read academic books in Europe and the New World.

Although natural law did not become a university subject in the Catholic universities (with some exceptions), this does not imply that natural law, and Pufendorf's works, were not known among scholars and students.

For more than 100 years, his books were among the most read academic books. His ideas had a tremendous influence on the way of thinking in most European countries in the century between the English revolution of 1688 and the French of 1789. Walter Simons (1934, 14a) argues that the title of the 1706 French translation of *De Officio* by Jean Barbeyrac is *Les devoirs de l'homme et du citoyen* (The duties of man and citizen) which is indicative of the often truly revolutionary ideas of Pufendorf. We meet this title, with one term changed, in the heading of the French National Assembly's famous declaration of human rights from 1789. It has the title *Déclaration sur les droits de l'homme et du citoyen* (Declaration on the rights of man and the citizen).

4 An Obstetrician and a Champion of the Enlightenment

With his integrated theory of natural law and with *De Officio* becoming an international bestseller, Pufendorf became famous all over Europe and in the New World. His representation is a systematic integration of moral, legal, societal and political economy relations under the general rubric of natural law. Based on the social life of man, he constructed a natural law on the dignity and equality of man, human reason, religious toleration and man's free choice. Natural law became a fashion, and new chairs in this subject were created at many universities. From these facts, the conclusion can be drawn that thousands of students and scholars across Europe had had an introduction to and became acquainted with Pufendorf's natural law writings. It is also reasonable to conclude that many of these students and scholars would want to get a deeper insight into his topics of natural law. They would then turn to Pufendorf's advanced work *De Jure Naturae et Gentium*. Here, they would also find references to further studies.

4.1 An Obstetrician to the Enlightenment

There can be no doubt that Pufendorf with his natural law based on the dignity and equality of man, on the use of reason and belief in progress and on religious toleration was on obstetrician to the birth of the European Enlightenment.

Horst Dreitzel (1995) discusses tolerance and the freedom of opinion and expression in the German Empire between the Peace of Augsburg in 1555 and the beginning of the Enlightenment a century and a half later. Here, he describes Pufendorf's position within the context of the crisis of the confessionalism theory of the state at the end of the seventeenth century. An overview of theories of toleration and freedom of conscience leads him to the conclusion that Pufendorf's theory marks the transition to the Enlightenment. According to Dreitzel, he belongs to the founders of a modern tolerant state because he separated the political function of religion from revealed religion. This view is also supported by the three authors of a history of Lund University called *Lärdomens Lund* (Lund a place of learning). Carl Fehrman, Håkan Westling and Gøran Blomquist (2004) discuss Pufendorf's influence and conclude: 'Through his secularized view on society and the judicial system Pufendorf's achievements points forward towards the Enlightenment in the 18th century'.

4.2 A Champion of the Enlightenment

Pufendorf's natural law became part of the common knowledge to such an extent that it may partly explain why he is almost forgotten. However, today's classics of the Enlightenment John Locke, Charles Louis Montesquieu, Jean Jacques Rousseau, Francis Hutcheson and Adam Smith, to mention just a few, used him centrally in elaboration of their own ideas. With his theory of natural law, he has therefore had a significant influence on both the birth and what shaped the development of the European Enlightenment.

Pufendorf's natural law works contributed to the beginning and advance of the Enlightenment, characterised by belief in progress. His ideas become common knowledge to such an extent that this may help to explain why he today is ignored by most contemporary philosophers, historians, political scientists, economists and finally historians of economic thought.

However, there are a few that think highly of his contribution to the Enlightenment. Some of these should be mentioned. Leonard Krieger (1957) in his *The German Idea of Freedom* contends that the natural law of the Enlightenment had its great creator in Pufendorf. It was his work through the medium of Christian Thomasius that prepared the ground for the Eighteenth-Century System of Jurisprudence. The connection between theology and law was weakened in Germany by Pufendorf and was finally broken by Thomasius.

Will and Ariel Durant (1962–68, 658–59) in their monumental work *The Story of Civilization* assert that 'His writings remained for half a century the dominant work in political analysis of social relations'.

Lois Robert Derathé (1970, 16) contends that one thing is clear regarding Pufendorf himself: 'no one writing on law and morality for more than half a century after 1672 could afford to ignore him'. Moreover, he added, 'Nor, indeed, can anyone writing on this period today'.

Alfred Dufour (1986, 102–106) investigates what opinion our classicists, John Locke, Jean Jacques Rousseau, Charles Louis Montesquieu and countless more, all of whom had studied Pufendorf's natural law works, had of his natural law writings. Many of them expressed that they considered these works to be fundamental, and necessary, for the study of civil law and politics, and that they used his theories when they developed and elaborated their own. In his analysis, Dufour also points to the recognition Pufendorf had among the representatives of the belles-lettres, at both the end of the seventeenth century and the end of the eighteenth. As an example, he draws attention to Jean Le Clerc (1657–1736), who was the editor of the famous *Bibliothèque universelle et historique* from 1686 to 1693. He claims:

> The books by Hugo Grotius, The Law of War and Peace, and the one by Samuel Pufendorf, called On the Duty of Man and Citizen, are admirable when it comes to the general principles. Especially the second one, which is the shortest, establishes, with great neatness and tidiness, the grounds of Moral, of Politics and of Jurisprudence. When reading it with close attention, one will find principles allowing to solve most of the main issues raised in those Sciences.

Approximately 90 years later, the chief editor of the *Encyclopédie*, Denis Diderot (1713–1784), strongly praised Pufendorf and in his *Plan d'une Université pour le Gouvernement de Russie* (A university plan for Russia) from 1775 he recommended *De Officio* as a textbook for the students. However, not everyone had anything but praise for Pufendorf. Dufour (1986, 105–106) quotes two French administrators, Henri-Francois d'Aguesseau (1668–1751) and Francois Richer d'Aube (1686–1752). The first was Chancellor and the second 'Maitre des requetes' to Louis XV. D'Aguesseau wrote in 1716 this note of warning to his son:

> Amongst the Moderns, scholars of the North have great consideration for the big treatise De jure naturali, gentium et civil. I wish you would have more courage than I did, my son. But I have to confess, and maybe I should be ashamed, that I did not read this work through. In truth the author is deep; but it is written in the fashion of Peripatetitians, who often darken what they want to define with abstract terms and technical expressions. (Ibid)

However, his warnings did not include Pufendorf's popularised abridged edition:

> That said, I do not want to warn you any further, you should rather judge by yourself; in any case, should you be as unlucky as your father and see boredom seize you, you could still read the sole concise Barbeyrac gave us of Pufendorf's work. …
>
> … on this matter one can even get more benefits from such a concise than from a long treatise because it is good to start with setting the mind on the path, to show it [the mind] the general principles which have to lead it, before making it go in a long career which vastness could frighten it. (Ibid)

Simone Zurbuchen (1998, 413–428) in her article *Samuel Pufendorf and the Foundation of Modern Natural Law* discusses the place of his natural law works in the history of the Enlightenment. She claims that it depends to a large extent on the perspective of interpretation. 'Whereas historians of ideas who consider him as an ancestor of the moral philosophy of the Enlightenment focus on the "modern" elements of his thought, contextualist historians such as [Detlef] Döring accentuate his indebtedness to the past.'

4.3 International Law

With his doctrines, Pufendorf also became the founder of the purely natural law conception of the law of nations. His theory is therefore also considered auspicious for the development of international law. The history of international law is largely characterised by whether one thinks it can be deduced from natural law or if it wholly can result from customs and treatises, the positivistic science of law. In his law of nations (international law), Pufendorf claimed that there does not exist any acute positive law that arises from custom or from treaties among nations. One reason for this is that there cannot be found an authority above the states that can bind them.[11] For him the source of the law of nations was natural because reason defines it.

In his *Introduction* to the English translation of *Elementorum Jurisprudentiae Universalis*, Wehberg (1922, xiv) claimed that Grotius and Pufendorf were 'champions of the great thought that in international life one should stand for all and all for one in repelling every injustice'. Pufendorf's idea of a system of universal jurisprudence valid for all nations was 'a daring one' (Ibid, xxii).

4.4 Pufendorf in the Anglo-American Literature

In an article on Pufendorf in the *Cambridge History of Political Thought 1450–1700*, Dufour (1991) also discussed the use of his works in Anglo-American literature. In the English literature, he mentions William Blackstone (1723–1780), who, in his *Commentaries on the Laws of England*, published 1765–1769, makes numerous references to Pufendorf. In the American literature, he draws attention to the 'first minister', John Wise (1652–1725), who used Pufendorf as an authority in his defence of a democratic church constitution, *A vindication of the governance of the New England Churches*. Second, the politician and spiritual leader of the American Revolution, James Otis (1725–1783), used Pufendorf together with Grotius and

[11] *Elementorum Jurisprudentiae Universalis*. Definition XIII § 24. *De Jure Naturae et Gentium* II, 3, 23.

Locke as authorities to bolster his influential pamphlet, *The Rights of the British Colonies Asserted and Proved* (1764).

4.5 The US Declaration of Independence

Pufendorf's natural law works could be found in the libraries of the colleges of the American colonies. The founding fathers of the American Revolution that had studied law were familiar with his work. Thomas Jefferson, one of the founding fathers, the third president and the principal author of the US Declaration of Independence from 1776, had in his library, according to Frank Dewey (1986, 66), both the French translation by Barbeyrac of *De Jure Nature et Gentium* and the 1749 edition of the English translation by Basil Kennet in his library in 1815. He used Pufendorf's works frequently both in his practice as a lawyer and as a politician,Wills (1978).

Fritjof von Haft (1997, 81), in his *Introduction to the study of law*, argues that Pufendorf with his doctrine of the dignity and equality of humans can be considered 'the spiritual father of the American revolution'.

Finally, James R. Stoner Jr. (2011, 1) in his article about the American revolution, *Declaration of Independence*, states boldly that 'No public document gives more prominence to the idea of natural law, nor relies more crucially upon natural law as a promise, than the Declaration of Independence'.

Samuel Pufendorf's academic career, his research and literary production, his teaching of natural law in Heidelberg and Lund, and his service to three enlightened Courts, in Heidelberg, Stockholm and Berlin made him not only the obstetrician but also the champion of the Enlightenment and also definitely a true European. In the next sections, the influence of Pufenodorf's natural law writings on a selected group of Enlightenment scholars will be analysed. The first is John Locke, who is known as one of the philosophers that made the groundwork for the Enlightenment in Europe and North America, and the others are a selected group of scholars of the French and Scottish Enlightenment. These scholars have been selected because they also used Pufendorf's writings on political economy extensively in the development of their own theories of political economy and because of their contribution to the progress of political economy as a science.

5 John Locke: An Admirer of Pufendorf

The first scholar of any importance, to actively use Pufendorf's first natural law work, in the development of his own ideas, was probably John Locke (1632–1704). He matriculated in the autumn of 1652 at Christ Church College, Oxford. Here, Locke made his home for more than 30 years, though he was occasionally absent from it for long periods. He was awarded his Bachelor of Arts degree in 1656, and his Master of Arts in 1659. He became Reader in Greek in 1660 and Reader in

Rhetoric in 1662. In 1663, he was appointed Censor of Moral Philosophy. Part of his duties, in this capacity, was to deliver a series of lectures, and Locke chose the topic 'The Law of Nature'.

When Locke (1954[1662-63]) prepared these lectures, he had a copy of Pufendorf's first book *Elementorum Jurisprudentiae Universalis* in his possession. Wolfgang von Leyden (1954, 39) and Roger Woolhouse (2007, 38) claimed that he had procured this book just after it was published in 1660. Michael Zuckert (1994, 243) claimed that it was 'a book Locke admired'.

Being a friend of Antony Ashley Cooper, later the first earl of Shaftesbury (1621–1683), who supported the abortive Monmouth Rebellion,[12] Locke was twice forced into exile on the continent. There he started the writing of his major work *Two Treatises of Government*, which James McCosh (1875, 27) calls 'Lock's immortal essay', and several other essays. Locke had already in 1681 bought copies of Pufendorf's other natural law works, Von Leyden (1954a, 39).[13] Consequently, there can be little doubt that Locke consulted Pufendorf when he wrote his essays and treatises, and that he used Pufendorf's works, together with the works of others, such as Grotius and Hobbes, as a point of departure in his analysis.

When returning to England in 1689 he quickly published *Essay Concerning Human Understanding* and *Letter Concerning Toleration.* In 1690, he published anonymously his *Two Treatises* (1964 [1690]) in which he discusses the state of nature, natural rights, natural law and political economy including the social contract and problems concerned with property[14] and furthermore *Thoughts Concerning Education.*

After his return, the new government recognised his services to their cause, and he made quite a career serving on several government commissions.

John Locke was an Oxford scholar, medical researcher and physician, political operative, political economist and ideologue for a revolutionary movement, as well as being one of the great philosophers of the late seventeenth and early eighteenth centuries.

---

[12] It was called the Monmouth Rebellion after the Duke of Monmouth, who claimed the English throne, and led an unsuccessful rebellion against the Roman Catholic King James II in 1685. However, James II was forced to give up the English throne to William of Orange in 1689 and fled the country.

[13] Von Leyden (1954a, b, 39) writes 'Locke possessed two copies of the Elementa, the edition of 1672, which he had bought together with De Jure Naturae, in 1681 and the edition of 1660, which he may have acquired shortly after it was published. There can be little doubt that he consulted this book when he wrote his essays'. This is also confirmed by Woolhouse (2007, 38), who states that in October and November of 1660 Locke was in Pensford and that from his correspondence, it is clear that he was occupied with 'what was called the "law of nature"'. 'Two important books on the subject had been published during the year. One of these, De Officiis secundum Naturae Jus, was by Robert Sharrock, and, …, it is very possible that Locke had read it; the other, which he evidently did read, was Samuel Pufendorf's Elementa Jurisprudentia Universalis'.

[14] This main work of John Locke was written a couple of years before he returned to England. It has been published in numerous editions and reprinted repeatedly. And it has at least been translated into French, German, Hebrew, Hindi, Italian, Norwegian, Russian, Spanish and Swedish.

5.1 Pufendorf Locke's Important Source

Locke, like most of his contemporaries, listed very few of his sources. It is therefore very difficult to establish exactly whose ideas Locke used when he put his own thoughts into writing.

Peter Laslett (1964, 130) in his introduction to a new edition of Locke's *Two Treatises of Government,* TT, claims that Locke had a deliberate policy of making as few references as he could. In his *Two Treatises,* he mentions only six writers by their names and two others by the titles of their works.

Locke is considered one of the most influential philosophers in the history of modern thought.[15]Therefore, a great number of academic scholars have discussed his contributions and commented on whom he built his theories on, and how he used their theories and built on them. Unfortunately, only a few have carried out an investigation into his use of Pufendorf. The reason is probably that very few writers on government or political economy have read Pufendorf's natural law works and are aware of his contributions. This is particularly true of social scientists and economists. There are, however, a few scholars, who have included Pufendorf's natural law works when analysing Locke's essays and treatises.

His reliance on Pufendorf is also confirmed by von Leyden (1954a, 39), who contends that there can be little doubt that Locke when writing his *Two Treatises of Government* consulted Pufendorf's work, 'for a number for points raised in it, are discussed by him'. Moreover, he points to a few cases where Locke and Pufendorf disagree and to others where they agree. Despite this he claims that it was one of the Cambridge Platonists, Nathanael Culwerwell (1619–1651), who provided Locke with an important stimulus and who had a direct influence on the formation of Locke's mature doctrines.[16]

In his introduction to a new edition of Locke's *Two Treatises of Government,* Peter Laslett (1964, 74) finds it idle to look for the source to Locke's political thinking.

> But of the writers he consulted when engaged on his book Samuel Pufendorf was perhaps of the greatest use to him, in spite of the fact that their views of constitutional matters were in such contrast. He took advantage of Pufendorf's arguments, he reproduced his positions, and he described his major work as 'the best book of that kind', better than the great Grotius on War and Peace.

In several footnotes, Laslett tells us how Locke used and built on Pufendorf. From his discussion, it is clear that Pufendorf was Locke's primary source.

How John Locke rose to dominance, within the context of seventeenth-century Anglo-American thought, is discussed by Michael Zuckert (1994, 187–188). Many examples are given by Zuckert of how Locke makes use of Pufendorf, in what manner he was influenced by him and by what means he breaks with him. When Locke,

[15] Although Laslett (1964, x) claims that Locke did not write as a philosopher.

[16] The Cambridge Platonists believed strongly that reason is the proper judge of disagreements, and they advocated dialogue.

for example, attempts 'to justify his definition [of law] in terms of criteria essential to all law', the criteria are clearly adapted from Pufendorf's discussion of law. 'Locke identifies three or perhaps four such characteristics of law …, all taken from Pufendorf' (Ibid, 192). John Locke and his debt to Pufendorf is also discussed by Michael Crowe (1977), James Tully (1980) and Helge Hesse (2009, 436).

It is therefore reasonable to claim that Locke was probably the first important scholar who actively used Pufendorf when he did his own writings. This also strongly indicates that Locke early in his life acquired a good theoretical knowledge of natural law, which included a state-of-the-art exposition of ethics, jurisprudence, government and political economy, from Pufendorf.

5.2 *Locke and the Diffusion of Pufendorf's Natural Law*

Two scholars are central to the spread of natural law or moral philosophy as it was later called: the previously mentioned Jean Barbeyrac, who translated Pufendorf's works into French, and John Locke. For some years, these two also corresponded. They had both a tremendous respect for Pufendorf and considered him one of the greatest scholars of their time.

It is clear from the earlier treatment that Locke used Pufendorf's natural law work extensively in the development of his own theories of government and political economy. Towards the end of his life he had become a highly venerated scholar, known across the British Isles, Continental Europe and North America. Locke became, according to Udo Thiel (1999, 323), one of the first and a leading figure of the Enlightenment.

Locke's ideas had a substantial effect on both the development of the science of philosophy, psychology and educational theory, government and political economy. In addition, his work influenced the development of freedom, tolerance, democracy and governments' accountability to their constituency. John Locke was an admirer of Pufendorf. He spoke highly of him, recommended his works to others, and used his natural law works in developing his own theories. Indirectly, the spread of Locke's thoughts therefore had a tremendous effect on the diffusion of Pufendorf's ideas.

Education on all levels and in most European countries in the sixteenth and seventeenth centuries was in glaring need of reform. During his exile in the Netherlands 1683–89, Locke wrote several letters to a friend giving him practical advice on the education of his son. These letters he adapted as *Thought Concerning Education,* (1968 [1683, 1693]) an essay that could have been inspired by Pufendorf's emphasis on education in his main work. It was published 4 years after his return to England and it had a remarkable influence on education in many European countries, and in particular on university education in Scotland.[17] It became a very popular reading among educators and politician concerned with the improvement of education.

[17] All Locke's writings on education have been collected and edited by James Axtell (1968).

Locke also made proposals for what authors, and which books should be recommended reading for the education of a gentleman. Here, he points directly to Pufendorf, as an author whom he found to be extremely important, and to his natural law books *De Officio* and *De Jure Naturae*.

There can be no doubt that Locke's recommendation of Pufendorf's natural law works contributed to the use and diffusion of both *De Officio* and *De Jure Naturae* across Europe and North America. In recommending Pufendorf, Locke was linking himself to a type of natural law thought that, according to Vere Chappell (1994, 229), only had begun to develop in England, because of the influence of Grotius.

John Locke is known as one of the philosophers that made the groundwork for the Enlightenment in Europe and North America. In doing this, Pufendorf was his major source and he thereby contributed to the diffusion of his ideas.

6 Natural Law and the French Enlightenment

Many philosophers made the foundation for the French Enlightenment. The moralist Pierre Nicole (1625–1714), the legal philosopher Jean Domat (1625–1696) and the magistrate Pierre Le Pesant de Boisguilbert (1646–1714) were central. They were all familiar with the natural law works of Pufendorf, and the allusions to their use of his natural law with self-interest and sociability as the driving forces in human behaviour are apparent in their writings.

6.1 Charles-Louis Montesquieu

The great philosopher of the Enlightenment, Charles-Louis Montesquieu (1689–1755) got his first education at home. Thereafter, he studied at the famous Oratorian College de Juilly near Paris and finally at University of Bordeaux. After years in Paris in order to gain legal experience, he returned to Bordeaux. There he became counsellor and later president at the Parliament and member of the Academy. For some years, he travelled around Europe and he met many important men and interested himself in political and constitutional questions. Returning to France, he divided his time between Bordeaux and Paris.

His first book *Lettres persanes* (Persian letters), a satire that sharply criticised the absurdities of contemporary France, was published in 1721. It made him famous, but he also received hostility from conservative quarters.

What became Montesquieu's (1989 [1748]) most influential work *De l'Esprit des Lois* (The Spirit of the Laws) was first published, anonymously because of censorship, in Geneva in 1748. The work had taken almost 20 years. It is a study of the laws of different countries in the light of their constitution, history and geographical position. In France, it was met with an unfriendly reception from both supporters and opponents of the regime. He was accused of forwarding a deterministic philosophy that undermined the relation between religion and natural law. The work was violently attacked by representatives of the Catholic Church. However, it received the highest praise from the rest of Europe, especially Britain. The book was a success, and it sold 22 editions in less than 2 years. In 1751, the Catholic Church banned the book and many of Montesquieu's other works. Along was also Pufendorf's *De Officio.* They were all included in the *Index of Prohibited Books.* This happened despite Montesquieu efforts to defend himself and to turn back the accusations against him. The result of his efforts was *La défense de 'L'Esprit de Lois'* (A Defence of the Spirit of the Laws) which he published in 1752.

6.1.1 Montesquieu Stands Indebted to Pufendorf

Anne Cohler (1989, xx) in her introduction to a new edition of *The Spirit of the Law* claims that the pursuit for sources of Montesquieu's thoughts and writings is handicapped by an excess of evidence: 'He seems to have read everything.' In his *Spirit of the Laws,* he cites some 300 works and makes over 3000 references. However, hardly any references can be found to the natural law philosophers. There is no reference to Grotius, only one to Hobbes, and only a few to Pufendorf and then only to his historical works.[18]

However, this does not mean that Montesquieu was not familiar with or did not use the works of the natural law philosophers in general and Pufendorf in particular.

Robert Shackleton (1961, 72) tells us how Montesquieu used Pufendorf when he delivered *Traité des devoirs* (On duties) to the Academy in 1725. 'For a model Montesquieu seems to have had recourse to the short treatise De officio hominis of the German Pufendorf, a work which he possessed in the French translation of Barbeyrac.' The copy of this book in the library at La Brède has several annotations by Montesquieu. 'To find him already in 1725 reading, studying and using Pufendorf is of capital importance.'

Mark Waddicor (1970, x) claims that 'the time has surely come for a less prejudiced and more detailed study than hitherto has been attempted on Montesquieu's debt to the philosophy of natural law'. This is necessary if Montesquieu's contribution to the history of ideas is to be properly assessed. He then attempts to carry out such a study. His study also includes a survey of many Montesquieu bibliographies. Of the natural law writers, most references are to Pufendorf, Grotius and Locke. Furthermore, he claims that although there is no proof of Montesquieu's acquaintance with the works of Pufendorf before he made some readings to the Academy in 1725, 'it is at least possible that the young Montesquieu may have been tempted to open the works of these modern theorists of natural law' (Ibid, 15).

Furthermore, Waddicor (1970, 35) emphasises that Montesquieu, in one of his notebooks, *Pensées*, writes in eulogistic terms of his predecessors: 'I give thanks to

[18] *Histoire de Suède.* Chatelain, Amsterdam 1748 and *Introducion* à l'histoire générale et politique de l'univers. Chatelaine, Amsterdam 1743.

Messr. Grotius and Pufendorf, who have achieved what a great part of that book requested from me, with a loftiness of genius that I could not have reached myself.' Likewise, Waddicor asserts that this tribute seems to have been intended for the *Preface* to *The Esprit des Lois*, but even if this was not the case, it clearly expresses that he owed much to them.

When Montesquieu gave these thanks, Waddicor contends that he 'was not trying to flatter anyone but was expressing his sincere thanks to the fact that they had prepared the way for his inquiry. – But it was above all the more sophisticated empiricism of Pufendorf – with his unmoralistic approach to many controversial problems, and his acceptance of the fact that civil law can, indeed must, vary from country to country – which seems to foreshadow Montesquieu's aim in the Esprit des Lois' (Ibid, 195).

Robert Derathé (1970, 425) claims that Montesquieu often refers to the thoughts of Pufendorf when speaking about natural law. This is particularly the case in his *Défense* when he follows Pufendorf's formulation of 'man fallen from heavens totally abandoned to himself'.

Alan Baum (1979, 27) discusses the importance of Montesquieu's early work *Traité des devoirs* (On duties) and contends that 'It was his first wholly serious book, building on the concepts of natural Law of the German Pufendorf'. Rebecca Kingston (1996, 134) claimed that this work was 'a development of the classical reflection of Cicero and of the modern scholarship of Pufendorf on the theme of duty'.

Baum also writes that the form of Montesquieu's *De Esprit des Lois* 'bears a strong resemblance to that of the treatises of Grotius and Pufendorf: his book divisions correspond to their book or chapter divisions, and his multitudinous and oft-criticised chapter divisions, to their paragraph divisions. The most obvious difference is that his chapter headings are sometimes more witty, but less informative than theirs' (Ibid. 23).

Finally, Montesquieu's library housed over 3000 volumes including 349 important works on Jurisprudence and many treatises by Grotius, Hobbes and Pufendorf. These works were either inherited or acquired before 1732.[19]

6.1.2 Montesquieu's Followers

The conclusion in Waddicor's analysis is clear: when Montesquieu studies human customs and laws, he draws extensively on the tradition of natural law. In the *Esprit des lois,* where he attempts to reconcile the eternal law with human diversity, his greatest debt is to Grotius and Pufendorf.

Montesquieu's *Spirits of the Laws* sees numerous editions and is translated to many languages. It had an enormous influence on the work of his descendants, among them the Continental and the British philosophers and politicians, the

[19] See also Waddicor (1970) footnote 65 and 66.

founding fathers of the United States Constitution, and Alexis de Tocqueville (1805–1859) in his *Democracy in America*, published in 1835 and 1840. *The Federalist Papers* written by James Madison (1751–1836), Alexander Hamilton (1755–1804) and John Jay (1745–1829) have frequent citations from this work. Therefore, Montesquieu became an important figure in the European and American Enlightenment. He passes on his own ideas and thereby also the ideas of his predecessors on political economy to many of his descendants. Elisabeth Fox-Genovese (1976, 139) in her *The Origin of Physiocrcy*, asserts that, *even those who doubt Montesquieu's influence on Quesnay do not question his profound impact on Mirabeau.*

It is important to note that Montesquieu in the British colonies was recognised as a fighter for freedom, although not for American independence. According to a study by Donald Lutz (1984, 193), on the influence of European writers on American thought, he was the most quoted philosopher in the American colonies in the second half of the eighteenth century. This is also confirmed by Bernard Bailyn (1992, 345), who contends that his name 'recurs far more often than that of any other authority in all the vast literature of the Constitution'.

Indirectly, through his writings in which he used Pufendorf's natural law works, Montesquieu contributed to the advancement of Pufendorf's human dignity, equality, the use of reason and thereby the European Enlightenment.

6.2 Jean-Jacques Burlamaqui

Jean-Jacques Burlamaqui (1694–1748) was a Swiss legal and political theorist who greatly publicised and popularised a number of ideas propounded by other thinkers. In 1719, 25 years old, he was designated honorary professor of ethics and the law of nature at the University of Geneva. Thereafter, he made a study tour of The Netherlands and England, where he met people of political influence. After a few months' visit to Oxford in 1723, he decided to return to France. On his return journey, he met Barbeyrac at Groningen. Back at the University of Geneva, he became a full professor.

Daniel Brühlmeier (1995, 63) contends that 'with a full professorship in the subject of natural law and civil law, Burlamaqui dominated legal thought and the natural law tradition in Geneva from 1723–1740'. Burlamaqui was, according to Peter Korkman (2006, x) in his study on *Burlemaqui and Natural Law*, a well-respected and popular lecturer that drew many foreign students to Geneva. Here, he lectured until 1740 when he unfortunately was compelled to resign because of ill health. In Geneva, he was also elected a member of the Council of State and he gained as high a reputation for his practical sagacity as he had for his theoretical knowledge.

6.2.1 Burlamaqui Copied from Pufendorf

His work, *Principles of natural law*, which was based on his lecture notes was published in Geneva in 1747, (2003 [1747]). This was the only work he published himself. It was intended for his students and other beginners. His treatise of law became very popular and was translated into Danish, Dutch, English, Italian, Latin and Spanish and published in more than 60 editions. The English translation became a standard textbook at University of Cambridge and the foremost American colleges. His treatise represents a digest of the thoughts of like-minded theorists, Grotius, Cumberland, and in particular Pufendorf, who is by far the most quoted author in the book.

Korkman (2006, xi) claims that this work of Burlamaqui borrowed extensively from Barbeyrac's French translations of the main natural law treatises of his time, especially from Pufendorf's *De Officio* and *De Jure Naturae,* but also from Grotius' natural law work. Often Burlamaqui omitted to mention his sources, so the typical reaction of many of his commentators has been to call him 'an unoriginal plagiarist'.

Three years after his death, some of his colleagues edited and published in 1751 a manuscript he had written, as *Principes du droit politique* (Principles of politic law). This manuscript was also based on a series of notes from his lectures. Burlamaqui himself had entrusted the manuscript to his sister and his daughter with instructions that it should not be published (Ibid: xii). It is therefore quite clear that this manuscript was meant only for his students, as a commentary to his lectures on natural law philosophers in general and Pufendorf in particular. It is therefore too harsh a judgement to contend that he was a plagiarist. In 1754, his friends also published a manuscript of his lecture notes in Latin, which in 1773 was published in French as *Élémens du droit naturel* (Elements of natural law).

6.2.2 Burlamaqui's Influence

Burlamaqui had quite an influence on students across Europe and America. His treatise on law *Principes du droit naturel* became a very popular textbook for students of law and was translated into Danish, Dutch, English, Italian, Latin and Spanish and published in more than 60 editions. The English translation of *Principles of natural law* was done by Thomas Nugent (1700–1777) in 1748. He also translated *Principles of politic law* in 1752. The first combined two-volume *Principles of Natural Law and the Principle of Politic Law* was published in London (2006 [1763]). It became a standard textbook at the University of Cambridge and the foremost American colleges. Nugent also translated *Principles of politic law* in 1752. The Liberty Fund 2006 edition is based on Nugent's 1763 translation. It is clear from Korkman's introduction and extensive notes in this edition that Burlamaqui uses Pufendorf, with Bayberac's comments, widely in his representation.

Burlamaqui's vision of constitutionalism had a major influence on the American Founders. For example, his understanding of checks and balances is much more sophisticated and practical than that of Montesquieu, in part because Burlamaqui's theory contains the seed of judicial review. He was frequently quoted or paraphrased, sometimes with attribution and sometimes not, in political sermons during the American pre-revolutionary era. He was the first philosopher to articulate the quest for happiness as a natural human right, a principle that Thomas Jefferson later restated in the *Declaration of Independence*.

Mark Waddicor (1970, 100) and Terence Hutchison (1988, 323) claim that Burlamaqui passed on the ideas of the natural law philosophers to August Walras (1801–66) and to his son Leon Walras (1834–1910).

6.3 Jean-Jacques Rousseau

The foremost political thinker Jean-Jacques Rousseau (1712–1778) published many discourses and treatises. In 1750, he wins the prize from the Academy of Dijon for his so-called first discourse, *Discourse sur les science et les arts* (Discourse on Sciences and Arts). It was published in 1751 and made, according to Victor Gourevitch (2007, xxxiii), 'an immediate, resounding success throughout Europe'. In 1755, his most famous and most influential work the so-called second discourse, *Discours sur l'origine et les fondements de l'inégalité parmi les hommes* (Discourse on the Origin and Basis of Inequality Among Men), was published. It elaborated on the arguments in his first discourse. Here, Victor Gourevitch (2008, 137, 179) notes that Pufendorf, in company with Cumberland and Montesquieu, differs from Hobbes in his conception of human nature. In 1755, an article *Economie Politique* was featured in volume five of Diderot's Encyclopedia. In 1762, Rousseau's (2007 [1762]) main work, *Du Contrat Sociale, ou Princiipes du droit politique* (The Social Contract or Principles of political law), was published. It became one of the most influential works of political philosophy. In 1772, he wrote the *Considérations sur le government de Pologne* (Consideration on the government of Poland). Rousseau died suddenly in 1778. An autobiographical book, *Les Confessions* (Confessions), which he had completed in 1770, was published after his death in 1782.

6.3.1 Did Pufendorf Influence Rousseau?

In his works, Rousseau gives only a few references to the natural law philosophers in general and Pufendorf in particular. However, Will and Ariel Durant (1962-68, X, 10) claim that Rousseau early in his life became familiar with Pufendorf's natural law works. Already in his *Projet pour l'éducation de M. de Sainte-Marie* from 1740, he expressed his views on Pufendorf in the following way:

> Lastly, should my pupil stay long enough in my hands, I would take the risk to give him some knowledge about moral and natural law through the readings of Pufendorf and Grotius, because it is an honnête homme and a sensible man worthy to know the principles of good and evil and the grounds on which the society he belongs to are set.

Robert Wokler (1994, 382) investigates in detail Pufendorf's influence on the writings of Rousseau. Although he, in all of Rousseau's works, finds only five references to Pufendorf, he concludes as follows:

> Until a few years ago I believed the direct influence of Pufendorf upon the intellectual formation of Rousseau's ideas was slight, but I now hold that view to be false. Although his citations from Pufendorf are scanty, the themes they pursue form prominent features of both his philosophy of human nature and his theory of the foundation of the state, and I have come to see some of his principal arguments as quite centrally designed to challenge Pufendorf's natural jurisprudence, to the extent that it gave warrant to what Rousseau judged was the miserable history of human society and the despotic establishment of state power.

This view is supported by Gourevitch (2008, xii) who claims that Rousseau used the works of Pufendorf extensively when he wrote:

> In his [Rousseau's] day, the most systematic, comprehensive compendium on political philosophy was Pufendorf's Right of Nature and Nations, especially in Barbeyrac's learnedly annotated French translation, Droit de la nature et des gens. He seems to have kept its massive two tomes at his elbow whenever he undertook a major project in political philosophy.

6.3.2 Rousseau's Impact

Gourevitch (2008, xv) writes: 'The First Discourse had won the Academy's Prize, and had made him famous. The Second Discourse did not win the Prize, but it made him immortal.' In France, as in most other European countries, Rousseau's name and many of his works were known to the intellectual part of the population. He was loved by many, and they used his arguments to promote their own ideas. He was, however, hated by the classes that held the power. They thought his ideas undermined the present order and encouraged radical changes in the governing system. Ronald Grimsley (1967, 224) in his article *Jean-Jacques Rousseau* claims that his powerful influence on later generations was 'partly due to his vision of a regenerated human nature, but unlike merely utopian thinkers he seemed to promise a transfiguration of everyday existence, not the pursuit of a hopeless chimer'.

There has been some discussion about to what extent Rousseau contributed to the French revolution. Robert Wokler (2006, 25–56) could not find that Rousseau had any direct influence. However, there can be no doubt that Rousseau influenced the intellectual climate in France and thereby was instrumental in promoting change.

Like Locke in England and Scotland, Rousseau became an instrument for change in the way education was looked upon. In America, Rousseau became a familiar name, and his work was read by the elite. Thomas Jefferson, when he wrote the US Declaration of Independence, is known to have used the works of the natural law philosophers in general and Pufendorf in particular, together with Locke, Montesquieu, Burlamaqui and Rousseau.

6.4 Denis Diderot

Denis Diderot (1713–1784) was born in the eastern city of Langres. He went to school at the Lycée Louis le Grand in Paris. In 1732, he earned a master's degree in philosophy. He abandoned the idea of entering the clergy and decided instead to study law. His study of law was short-lived. Diderot decided to become a writer and, in doing so, he became a prominent figure during the Enlightenment.

Diderot was in 1749 approached by a bookseller and a printer named Andre Le Breton (1708–1779), who wanted him to take part in the translation into French and the publishing of Ephraim Chambers' *Cyclopaedia, or Universal Dictionary of Arts and Sciences.*[20] During his work, Diderot came up with the idea to expand the project from a reproduction into a major French Encyclopédie. He served as the co-founder, together with Jean le Rond d'Alembert (1717–1783), as well as the chief editor and major contributor to the *Encyclopédie.* A prospectus announced the project to the public in 1750, and the year after the first volume was published. The *Encyclopédie ou dictionnaire raisonné des sciences, des arts et des métiers* (Encyclopedia, or a rational dictionary of sciences, art and craft) had many unorthodox and forward-thinking articles by many prominent authors and experts in their respective fields. With the project, Diderot wanted to give information about all-important issues to the common people, who had the ability to read.

The work, however, was plagued by controversy from the very beginning. For a period, it was suspended by the court, and it was accused of seditious content because of its entries on religion and natural law. Diderot was also detained by the authorities for some time. With the support of important well-placed people, the work resumed, but the controversies stayed with it. The popularity and influence of the *Encyclopédie* increased, and also the number of subscribers. Nevertheless, the number of enemies also grew with its popularity. It threatened the governing aristocracy with its emphasis, in the spirit of Pufendorf, on religious tolerance and freedom of thought. In 1759, the antagonists were strong enough to formally suppress the *Encyclopédie.* The work continued, but important contributors no longer dared to support it.

Diderot was left to finish the task as best he could. He wrote several hundred articles, some very short, but many of them laborious, comprehensive and long. He damaged his eyesight correcting proofs and editing the manuscripts of less competent contributors. He was incessantly harassed by threats of police raids. It took many years before the subscribers in 1772 received the final 27-folio volumes of the *Encyclopédie.* Today, it is considered one of the great works of the Enlightenment.

---

[20] Ephraim Chambers (c. 1680–1740) was an English writer and encyclopaedist. He is primarily known for having produced the Cyclopedia. It had the full title: *Cyclopedia: or a universal dictionary of arts and sciences ... the whole intended as a course of ancient and modern learning compiled by the best authors, dictionaries, journals, memoirs, transactions, ephemerides, in several languages.* First published in London 1728.

All this work did not bring Diderot any wealth. Although his work was broad and rigorous, he could not secure for himself a decent income. He obtained none of the posts that were occasionally given to needy men of letters. When the time came for him to provide a dowry for his daughter, he saw no alternative other than to sell his library. When the Empress Catherine II (1729–1796) of Russia heard of his financial troubles, she commissioned an agent in Paris to buy the library. She then requested that the philosopher retain the books in Paris until she required them, and that he act as her librarian with a yearly salary. In 1773 and 1774, Diderot spent some months at the empress's court in Saint Petersburg. When he died in 1784, his vast library was sent to Russia, where the Empress had it deposited in the National Library of Russia.

6.4.1 Diderot an Admirer of Pufendorf

It is clear from numerous entries that when Diderot wrote for the *Encyclopédie*, he had Barbeyrac's translations into French of Pufendorf's *De Officio* and *De Jure Naturae* in his library and that he extensively consulted and used these works. Sometimes he only copied what Pufendorf had written. Other times he made critical assessments of Pufendorf's views. His admiration for Pufendorf is evident.

During his stay at the court of Catherine II in St. Petersburg, Diderot wrote *Plan d'une Université pour le gouvernement de Russie* (Plan of a University for the Government of Russia). Here, he recommends the use of Barbeyrac's translation of Pufendorf's *De Officio* together with Burlamaqui's *Traité Elements de droit Naturel* and Hobbes' *De Hominis* and *De Civis* for the first class of the second course of studies as well as a guidance for the Professor of Natural Law for the first year of studies at the Faculty of Law. Diderot's many references to the natural law philosophers in general and Pufendorf in particular contributed to the diffusion of Pufendorf's views on ethics, jurisprudence, government and political economy. It was not only Diderot that used Pufendorf and referred to him. Pufendorf and his writings on natural law were known to most contributors to the *Encyclopédie.* One contributor, the renowned French lawyer of that time, Antoine-Gaspard Boucher d'Argis (1709–1791), wrote an article in 1753 under the headword *Droit des gens* (Law of nations). Here, he describes Pufendorf's legal work and claims that *De Jure Naturae et Gentium* is much better for the understanding of natural law than Grotius's *De jure belli et pacis.*[21] In another headword, *Citoyen* (Citizen), he also makes a reference to Pufendorf, d'Argis (1753, Vol. 3, 488).

---

[21] Denis Diderot and Jean le Rond d'Alembert [Eds.] (1755, Vol. 5, 128): *Encyclopédie ou Dictionnaire raisonné des Sciences, des Arts et des Métiers.* Bibliothèque National in Paris.

7 Natural Law and the Scottish Enlightenment

It was Gershom Carmichael (1672–1729) who introduced the natural law tradition into Scotland. He graduated Master of Arts from University of Edinburgh in 1691. As a result, he became Regent at St. Andrew University. As a regent, his task as a teacher was to introduce the students to all aspects of the curriculum. In 1694, he applied and obtained, by public trial, a regentship at the University of Glasgow. Here, he introduced natural law as a subject in the curriculum for the students. In 1727, he was appointed the first Professor of Moral Philosophy.

David Murray (1927, 507) notes that Carmichael 'brought the teaching of philosophy abreast'. In his course in moral philosophy, he introduced and used Pufendorf's 'student edition' *De Officio Hominis et Civis* as a textbook and it was 'for long an exceedingly popular textbook'.

As noted by Hans Medick (1973, 300), Carmichael had a very high opinion of both Grotius and Pufendorf. He claimed that their works should be studied 'day and night'. He used Pufendorf's *De Officio* as a textbook and in 1718 he published in Glasgow an edition in Latin of the book for the use of his students. A second edition was published in Edinburgh in 1624 and a third posthumously in Leyden in 1769 (reproducing the 1624 text). This book included his own extensive commentaries, *Notes and Supplements* (also in Latin).[22] With Carmichael what had up to then been termed natural law or natural jurisprudence was from now on designated moral philosophy.

7.1 *Why Did Carmichael Select* De Officio *as a Textbook?*

It is not known precisely why Carmichael selected Pufendorf's *De Officio* as a textbook in his course. James McCosh (1875, 22) contends that the Parliament of Scotland in 1690 had appointed a *Commission for visiting the universities to implement reforms in the curricula*. Several of the committee members had read Locke's essay on education. It clearly affected the committee's proposals for reforms, including changes in curricula and later the abolishment of the regent system. A change was therefore in the air. McCosh also emphasised the strong influence John Locke had on the intellectual developments in Scotland. As outlined in a previous chapter, Locke was for long an admirer of Pufendorf, and there is no doubt that Carmichael was familiar with Locke's view when he made his choice of a textbook.

[22] John N. Lenhart compiled and Charles H. Reeves translated in 1985 Carmichael's Supplements and Appendix from the 1718 edition. Also, *The Introduction* to the 1769 Edition and the January 1927 review of Gershom Carmichel's notes to the *De Officio* in *Acta Eruditorum has* been translated by Charles H. Reeves and privately published by John N. Lenhart, Cleveland, Ohio. Furthermore, James Moore and Michael Silverthorne have edited, and Michael Silverthorne has translated Carmichael's writings in 2002. Our quotations are from this last translation.

Carmichael's use of *De Officio* as a textbook for his students was met with suspicion from theologians, but was accepted when he made it clear that he was not an uncritical follower of Pufendorf's ideas and that he disagreed fundamentally with his view that natural law must abstract from belief in the immortality of the soul and an afterlife.

7.2 Carmichael's Influence

Carmichael became a scholar of some renown. Robert Wodrow (1843, 95–96) claimed that he 'was exceedingly valued both at home and abroad, where he had considerable correspondence with learned men, such as Barbyrack, and other learned men abroad; and he brought a great many scholars to Glasgow'. William Hamilton (1872, Vol. 1, 30n) writes that Carmichael 'may be regarded, on good grounds, as the true founder of the Scottish school of philosophy'.[23]

James Moore and Michael Silverthorn (2002, xvi) claim that Carmichael's work 'contributed, very fundamentally, to shape the agenda of instruction in moral philosophy in eighteenth-century Scotland'.

It was largely due to Carmichael's efforts, William Taylor (1955, 251–255) wrote 'that speculative economic inquiry initiated by Hobbes, Grotius and Pufendorf, formally entered Scottish universities, and before very long, British political economy'.

It should be added that Carmichael became a very popular teacher who also attracted many students from England, Ireland and Wales to the University of Glasgow.

With Carmichael's use of Pufendorf's *De Officio* as a textbook in his classes, Natural Law had been transformed into Moral Philosophy. Terence Hutchison (1988, 192) claimed that Carmichael played a vital role both in the history of Scottish philosophy and in the history of economic thought. He is today considered one of the founders of the Scottish Enlightenment.

7.3 Francis Hutcheson

In 1710, an Irish student, Francis Hutcheson (1694–1746), matriculated in the University of Glasgow. According to James McCosh (1875), he enjoyed the privilege of 'sitting under the prelections' of Carmichael, who introduced him to the moral philosophy of Pufendorf.

During his 6 years at Glasgow, his original orthodox Calvinist views underwent fundamental change due to the influence of two of his professors, Carmichael and John Simson (1668–1740). They both promoted tempered and moderate views on

[23] Here quoted from McCosh (1875, 36) or Taylor (1955, 253).

Christianity. These views also brought the professors in conflict with the orthodox Presbyterian leaders. Charged with heresy, Simpson was suspended from teaching duties and Carmichael had to admit to his deviations from the 'right thoughts'.

Hutcheson left Glasgow in 1716 with a licence from the Presbyterian Church and returned to Ireland. In 1721 or 1722, he was invited to Dublin, by a group of Presbyterian clergymen, and asked to open a dissenting Academy for conformist students in the city. Under his leadership this Academy, which Michael Brown (2002, 78) in his *Francis Hutcheson in Dublin 1719–30* suggests 'contained a broadly humanist education', became an academic rival to Trinity College, which was supported by the official Church of Ireland.

In 1725, Hutcheson published several scholarly works on ethics. In all these works, he refers to Pufendorf who, because of his distinct intelligible reasoning, is recognised as 'the grand instructor in morals to all who have of late given themselves to that study', Hutcheson (1973 [1725], 103).

Due to illness, Carmichael retired from his Chair of Moral Philosophy in 1729 and died of cancer a few months later. Hutcheson was chosen to succeed him. When he took up the position in the autumn of 1730, he held his inaugural lecture *On the Social Nature of Man.*[24] In this lecture, he made it clear that he had high regards for Pufendorf, although he disagreed with his emphasis on self-love (Hutcheson 1993 [1732], 134–135).

Hutcheson brought with him several young gentlemen from his Academy in Dublin 'and his just fame drew many more both from England and Ireland'.[25] His importance as a professor, teacher and author was recognised even in his own time. It has been said that he was 'the personality most responsible for the new spirit of enlightenment in the Scottish universities'.[26] According to his biographer William Scott (1900, 69), he was among the first to lecture in English, and with eloquence. The University made him serve on numerous university committees. He carried substantial, although controversial, weight in the creation of a more liberal 'forward university policy'. He was the guardian and friend of his students and his care for 'the wild Irish teagues' among them was recognised. Hutcheson, as Carmichael before him, was an admirer as well as a critic of Pufendorf. He also, as already mentioned, had been introduced to Pufendorf's natural law works as a student at the University.

Elmer Sprague (1967, 99) claims that Hutcheson 'devoted himself in Glasgow to enriching the culture and softening the Calvinism of his fellow Presbyterians'.[27] The Presbytery of Glasgow tried him for 'false and dangerous' doctrines. However, he

[24] Francis Hutcheson *On the Social Nature of Man* (De Naturali hominum Socialitate Oratio Inaugurlis) 1730. It was reprinted during Smith's tenure at Glasgow as Hutcheson's successor, by the Foulis Press in 1756.

[25] Leechman (1754) in the Preface (xi) to Hutcheson's *A System of Moral Philosophy*.

[26] Gladys Bryson (1945, 8): *Man and Society; the Scottish Inquiry of the Eighteenth Century*. Here quoted from Hutchison (1988, 35).

[27] *The Encyclopedia of Philosophy* 1967 Volume Four.

managed to brush aside the charges of his accusers, although for a time the situation was quite serious.

Hutcheson had used Pufendorf's writings extensively in his early works in Dublin. Therefore, it was natural that Hutcheson continued Carmichael's practice and based his teaching upon *De Officio.* He used Carmichael's edition with his *Notes and Supplements*. He held Carmichael in high regard and claimed that he was 'by far the best commentator on that book [Pufendorf's De Officio]' and that his lecture notes were so good that they were 'of much more value than the text', Hutcheson (1747, i). It is therefore clear that he was greatly influenced by both Pufendorf and Carmichael. Brown (2002, 18) quotes a student in Hutcheson's class in the beginning of the 1740s: 'He teaches Mr. Carmichael's Compend on Pufendorf, and speaks with much veneration of him [Carmichael].'[28]

David Murray (1927, 508) contends that Hutcheson lectured on Pufendorf's *De Officio* until 1742. From that year, he used a compendium based on his lecture notes, *Philosophiae Moralis Institutio Compendiaria* which had been published without his authorisation. A new edition, with his consent, was published in 1745. In 1747, it was published as *A Short Introduction to Moral Philosophy.*, Hutcheson (1969 [1747]). It is clear that Hutcheson in this work built very closely on Pufendorf's natural law works and, in some sections, he just copied him. As a student textbook, it became very popular and was published in three editions in Latin and four editions in English. To sum up, Hutcheson made his students read and study Pufendorf's *De Officio*. When he lectured, first using as a textbook *De Officio* and later his own compend, he made it clear to his students where he deviates from Pufendorf. Furthermore, he urged his students to find the sources and study them carefully.

By 1734–35, Hutcheson had already begun writing a manuscript called *A System of Moral Philosophy.* It contains, according to Mautner (1999, 261), 'an attempt to give a utilitarian interpretation of the current ideas of natural law and natural rights'. It rejects Hobbes's view of man's unsocial nature. This work was, as also noted by Daniel Carey (2000, v), 'by no means identical' with his compendium.[29] However, it remained un-published during his lifetime even though an almost complete version had circulated among friends from 1737. His son, Francis Hutcheson M.D., published it posthumously in 1755, 9 years after his death.

7.3.1 Moral Philosophy Becomes Ethics, Law of Nature, Economics and Politics

With Carmichael and Hutcheson's use of Pufendorf's works on natural law in their classes, the term 'natural law' was replaced by 'moral philosophy'. Hutcheson's textbook, *A Short Introduction to Moral Philosophy*, was divided into three parts:

[28] Wodrow (1843, 191) 'About this time [i.e. 1730] Mr. Hutcheson comes to Glasgow. ... He teaches Mr. Carmichael's compend and Pufendorf and speaks with much veneration of him, which at least is an evidence of his prudence.'

[29] Hutcheson (2000 [1747]), *Introduction* by Daniel Carey.

Ethics, Law of Nature, Economics and Politics. Hutcheson's textbook was based not only on Carmichael's edition of Pufendorf's *De Officio,* as the preface candidly acknowledged, but also on *De Jure Naturae et Gentium.* Hutcheson himself had no problems admitting this fact. He had written his book claiming that each lecturer must use his own judgement, his own methods, and create the best account of the subject that he thinks will appeal to his students.

Not many authors have studied the relationship between Pufendorf, Carmichael and Hutcheson. However, a few important sources should be mentioned. Richard Teichgraber III (1986, 21) writes that the chief sources of Hutcheson's and Smith's thinking were two seventeenth-century figures who, until very recently, have not figured prominently in the history of eighteenth-century English-speaking thinkers, Grotius and Pufendorf. They both reflected in their writings 'a great debt to these highly revered natural law jurists'. Enzo Pesciarelli (1989, xviii) notes Pufendorf's influence on Hutcheson through his teacher, 'Master Carmichael', whom she calls 'a divulger in Scotland of the works and thoughts of Pufendorf'. Hutcheson's dependence on Pufendorf is also emphasised by Knud Haakonssen (1996, 65).

7.4 Hutcheson's Influence

Hutcheson was a reformer and a libertarian who believed like Pufendorf that the world could, and should, be better organised by application of reason. It was according to Edwin George West (1976, 42–43) Hutcheson and not Jeremy Bentham (1748–1832) who originated the famous phrase, 'the greatest happiness of the greatest number'.

Several authors, for example Alec Macfie (1952, 127) and Edwin West (1976, 42), write about Hutcheson's influence on Smith. Pesciarelli (1989, xix) claims that Hutcheson transmitted to Smith, Pufendorf's way of thinking, and in particular; 'a view of society represented as an enormous arena of dealers, buyers and sellers'.

Here it should, however, be mentioned that William Robert Scott (1900, 230–33) in his Hutcheson biography, compares his *Introduction to Moral Philosophy* (1747) and *System of Moral Philosophy* (1755) with Adam Smith's works. He found that the economic topics such as division of labour, theory of value, money, state and foreign trade, and maxims of taxation discussed by Hutcheson are repeated by Smith in his *Lectures on Jurisprudence* and again in *The Wealth of Nations.* Scott realised that Hutcheson's *System of Moral Philosophy* contained many reproductions of the views of Pufendorf, Grotius and Locke upon 'Politics and Economics'. However, he does not seem to be aware of how closely Hutcheson builds on Pufendorf. His argument is rather weak:

> It might, of course, be contended that Smith consulted the authorities direct; but when it is remembered that he heard these very passages read and expounded in the Glasgow classroom, and further that the System of Moral Philosophy was published a few years after his appointment to the Chair of Moral Philosophy, when he would be preparing his own lectures, it seems reasonable to trace Hutcheson's influence here. (Ibid, 231–232)

Today Hutcheson is by many seen as the forerunner of the social theories of the Scottish Enlightenment. These theories gained influence far beyond the borders of Scotland. According to many, for example Donald Winch (1978) and David Norton (1982), he influenced both Hume's *A Treatise of Human Nature* and Smith's *Wealth of Nations*. The question of who influenced Adam Smith will be discussed in the next section of this presentation.

Hutcheson's influence in America was considerable. Hutcheson's compendium, *A Short Introduction to Moral Philosophy,* was used as a textbook at several American colleges, for example College of Philadelphia, College of New Jersey (Princeton University) and Harvard College, in the second half of the eighteenth century. Norman Fiering (1981, 199) in his *Moral Philosophy at Seventeenth Century Harvard* claimed that Hutcheson was 'probably the most influential and respected moral philosopher in America in the eighteenth century'.

Several of the Founding Fathers therefore had a good knowledge of the ideas of the moral philosophers in general and in particular Pufendorf and Hutcheson. Garry Wills in his *Inventing America* from 1978 argues that the phrasing of the Declaration of Independence was due largely to Hutcheson's direct influence. A comparison of Hutcheson's favoured government with the constitution of the United States unveils also an astonishing degree of compatibility.[30]

Hutcheson, who based his teaching and writings on Pufendorf, is recognised as the first major philosopher of the Scottish Enlightenment. This Enlightenment asserted the fundamental importance of human reason.

7.5 Pufendorf as a Predecessor of Adam Smith

In 1737, Adam Smith (1723–1790) matriculated at the University of Glasgow and took up a seat in Hutcheson's moral philosophy class.

Smith completed his course for the Master of Arts degree with distinction and graduated in 1740. Being one of the best students, he won a Snell Exhibition Scholarship at Balliol College, Oxford. The scholarship was for 11 years, but Smith decided to leave after the sixth year. These years felt long and were not very happy with apparently no visits home in the interim. Later he spoke very harshly of the anti-Scot prejudice of the professors. He also mentioned that their rather boring lectures could not inspire him. Balliol College at that time was not the institution it is today. James McCosh (1875, 164) tells us in his *Scottish Philosophy*, for example, that at Oxford, when the heads of the College found Smith reading Hume's *Treatise of Human Nature,* they seized the work and reprimanded the youth.

Smith used the libraries of the University Colleges, read Greek, Roman and modern literature, studied the works of the natural law philosophers in general and

[30] The claim that there has been such a direct and distinctive influence has according to Mautner (1993, 5) been hotly disputed.

Samuel Pufendorf in particular, and expanded his language knowledge, particularly French. However, he decided after 6 years to cancel his Snell scholarship and in August 1746 he returned to Scotland as a well-educated academic.

The next 2 years he spent quietly at home, probably uncertain of what to do, but undoubtedly continuing his self-studies. In 1748, he was invited by leaders of a local philanthropic society to give a series of lectures in Edinburgh. He moved to Edinburgh and in the next couple of years, he delivered lectures on rhetoric and belles-lettres. In these lectures, Smith used his notes from the classes Hutcheson had taught. He made his final course in Edinburgh in 1751 one of jurisprudence.

In 1751, Smith accepted an offer of a Chair in Logic at the University of Glasgow. After only a year, he moved to the Chair in Moral Philosophy that Hutcheson, his former teacher, had occupied. From the beginning, Smith in his teaching used Hutcheson's compend together with his notes from his lectures in Edinburgh. However, in the next few years, he developed his own lecture notes and, based on these, published in 1759 his first book *The Theory of Moral Sentiments* TMS (1982a [1759]). This book covered the ethical part of his course. The book turned out to be a success. A second, revised edition appeared 2 years later in 1761.[31] The work was widely praised, and it gained quite an audience and it saw six editions in Smith's lifetime.

The book ends with a promise to produce a further book on jurisprudence, but unfortunately he did not keep his promise. However, in 1895 Professor Edwin Cannan (1861–1935) became aware of a manuscript, which according to the title page consisted of a 'JURIS PRUDENCE or Notes from the lectures in Justice, Police, Revenue and Arms' delivered by Adam Smith, Cannan E [Ed.](1896) and Smith (1982b [1762-63]). It has been determined that this manuscript relates to lectures that Smith held in 1763–64. In 1958, the late Professor John M. Lothian (1896–1970) discovered two sets of lecture notes made by former students of Smith. One related to Smith's lectures on rhetoric and belles-lettres as delivered in 1762–1763 and the other related to his lectures on jurisprudence delivered at the same time.[32] It should also be mentioned that another important manuscript from Smith's pen has been found. It probably dates from before 1763[33] and has been given the title *An early draft of part of the Wealth of Nations*.[34]

---

[31] The third edition appeared in 1767, the fourth edition in 1774, and the fifth in 1781. These editions differ little from edition two. Edition six, which was published in 1790, contains extensive additions and changes.

[32] Adam Smith's *Lectures on Rhetoric and Belles Lettres* has been edited by J. C. Bryce and published by Oxford University Press 1983, an exact photographic reproduction by Liberty Classics 1985. The two discovered lecture notes on jurisprudence 1762–1763 and 1763–1764 have been edited by Meek, Raphael and Stein and published as *Lectures on Jurisprudence* by Oxford University Press 1978, an exact photographic reproduction by Liberty Classics 1982.

[33] Ronald Meek and Andrew S. Skinner (1973, 1103) claim that it must have been written before 1763.

[34] Published in William R Scott (1965 [1937]): *Adam Smith as Student and Professor.* Pp. 317–356 or as an appendix to Meek, Raphael and Stein *Lectures on Jurisprudence,* pp. 560–581. According to Raphael and Macfie (1982[1976], 23), 'these documents show that Smith had gone a consider-

During the 1750s and 1760s, Smith produced some smaller dissertations and essays. The best-known being *A dissertation on the Origin of Languages* and an *Essay on the History of Astronomy*. Smith held many important positions at the university and was, for example, elected both Dean of the Faculty and Vice Rector.

In 1764, Adam Smith resigned from his Chair at the University of Glasgow and accepted a position as tutor to the young Duke of Buccleuth. Together, from 1764 until 1766, they toured France, Switzerland and Italy. The last 9 months they stayed in Paris where Smith had the opportunity to meet and discuss political economy with Francois Quesnay, Anne Robert Turgot and others belonging to the group that was later called the Physiocrats. Smith returned to his hometown in 1767. A generous pension from the Duke enabled Smith to spend most of his time in the next years writing.

This led to the publication in 1776 of his second book and major work in political economy, *An Inquiry into the Nature and Causes of the Wealth of Nations* WN, (1976 [1776,1904, 1937]). In his lifetime, Smith saw five editions of this book in English and translations into German, Danish/Norwegian and French. The book earned Smith tremendous fame and the reputation as The Father of Modern Political Economy.

7.6 Smith's Reliance on Pufendorf

In his discussion of the authors and sources that Adam Smith used in his writings, Sæther (2017a, 178–181) focused on four of his biographers, Dugald Stewart (1981 [1793]), John Rae (1965 [1895)), William R. Scott (1937) and Ian Simpson Ross (2012). They all stress that Smith was influenced by his teacher Francis Hutcheson. The first two, Stewart and Rae, do not at all look into the text that Hutcheson used.

William Scott agreed that Hutcheson was Smith's primary source. However, he acknowledged that Hutcheson, when Smith was a first-year student, still used Carmichael's Latin edition of *De Officio* as a textbook in his obligatory course in moral philosophy and that Smith in his final course at Edinburgh returned to Carmichael's treatment of Pufendorf. Smith therefore had to study *De Officio* carefully. Furthermore, when Hutcheson departed from the opinions of the esteemed author of the textbook he used, this must have stirred his interest. This might particularly have been the case when Hutcheson disagreed with Pufendorf's emphasis on self-interest. Smith must have been fascinated by Pufendorf's model that individual pursuit of self-interest, checked by man's inclination to live in society with others, would lead to the best society. Professor Hutcheson would probably also in his lectures have urged his students to go back to the original sources and explore

able way in his economic thinking by the time he left Scotland for France in 1764, and that this early material provided a sound foundation for developments which were certainly stimulated by the visit to France'.

the differences. However, this did not impress Scott to investigate a connection between Smith and Pufendorf.

Ian Ross gives a full account of Smith as a student, teacher, moral philosopher, historian, customs official and economist. He emphasises that in addition to Hutcheson's obligatory course in moral philosophy, Smith benefitted from Hutcheson's teaching of a 'private' class on the Lessons of the Law of Nature and Nations. No textbooks are mentioned but it is not unreasonable to assume that he referred to both Grotius' *De Jure Belli ac Pacis* and Pufendorf's *De Jure Naturae et Gentium.* These books Smith could study in the Glasgow University Library. Furthermore, Ross claims that Smith, in his fourth year at Oxford, choose to follow the path of a student in civil law. In this path or direction, he possibly continued the study of the works of the natural law philosophers, including Pufendorf. These authors were read at Oxford at this time. Smith and the other students could study all the natural law works of Grotius and Pufendorf in the Balliol and Bodleian libraries.

Ross also argues that Smith in his Edinburgh freelance lectures in 1750–51 taught the Grotius–Pufendorf tradition of the laws of nature and nations. He therefore had to use the works of these natural law philosophers when he prepared these lectures. Smith also had his notes from Hutcheson's class in moral philosophy, the books Hutcheson had authored and Locke's *Two Treatises of Government,* all of which were strongly influenced by Pufendorf. In addition, Ross points out that Smith in first lectures at the University of Glasgow in the early 1750s used Hutcheson's Latin *Compendium* from 1742, as his textbook together with his own Edinburgh lecture notes. It has been determined in the previous chapter that Hutcheson in this book built very closely on Pufendorf's natural law works and that he in some sections just copied him.

It is also important to point out that Smith acquired a copy of Pufendorf's major Latin work *De Jure Naturae et Gentium.* A French translation could also be found in his private library.[35] In this work, which is a jewel, not only because of its scholarship, but also because it serves as a reference for the works of the moderns, the Scholastics, the Greeks, the Romans as well as the writings in the Old and New Testament and the Koran. In this work, Smith could find both the inspiration and the first access to important references for his own works. It is therefore reasonable to assume that Smith had Pufendorf's natural law works ready at hand when he prepared his lectures and wrote his books.

All these points, one by one and together, *suggest* that Smith, early on, became familiar with Pufendorf's natural law works (including substantial tracts of political economy), and that he used them extensively when he prepared his lectures in Edinburgh and Glasgow.

It is recognised by most writers that discuss Adam Smith's sources that his two books have their point of departure in his lecture notes. Therefore, it is surprising

[35] A French translation of *De Jure Naturae et Gentium libri octo* by J. Barbeyrac (2 vol., Amsterdam 1720–1734) can be found in Smith's library, as reported in H. Mizuta's Adam Smith's Library, Cambridge 1967.

that only a few authors point to Pufendorf as one of his primary sources. Scott (1900, 231), in his Hutcheson biography, admits that Hutcheson's work 'Contains many reproductions of views of Pufendorf, Grotius and Locke upon Politics and Economics'. Furthermore, he refers to Edwin Cannan (1896) who states that 'Hutcheson's function was to collect and classify them, so they were available for Smith' (Ibid). Then Scott comes up with the remarkable statement: 'It might of course be contended that Smith consulted the authorities direct.' Yes indeed, it might. Hutcheson had urged his student to investigate the sources, and, in all probability, Smith did.

Adam Smith, as with most of the eighteenth-century authors, very reluctantly relinquished the names of the literature that he had at his disposal and used. He was definitely not a writer that overwhelmed his readers with numerous citations and references in his books. Therefore, the lack of such citations and references do not communicate anything about his use of the literature he had at his disposal in general and Pufendorf's works in particular. However, some information can be found in his library, Mizuta (1967).

Smith refers only twice to Pufendorf in *The Theory of Moral Sentiments*. He presents him first together with Mandeville as a follower of Hobbes, who claimed that man is driven to take refuge in society, not by any natural love to his own kind, 'but because without the assistance of others he is incapable of subsisting with ease or safety'.[36] Second, he presents him together with Barbeyrac and Hutcheson, in a discussion of how different authors have treated the practical rules of conduct.[37] In his *Lectures on Jurisprudence*, in which Pufendorfian natural law, including political economy, is predominant, there are five direct references to Pufendorf: first, in a discussion about a man's natural rights; second, in a discussion of how Hutcheson follows Pufendorf on rights; third, in discussion about the property of the state; fourth and fifth, in a treatment about testamentary succession. In *The Wealth of Nations*, we do not find any direct references to Pufendorf. This is in spite of the fact that strong elements of Pufendorfian natural law can also be found in this work.

The lack of recognition of his use of Pufendorf does not, however, tell us anything about Pufendorf's influence on Smith. From this investigation and discussion, it follows that there are paragraphs, sections, and other clues and allusions in all of Smith's work that point directly to both Pufendorf's *De Officio* and his major natural law work *De Jure Naturae et Gentium.* Pufendorf must therefore have had a strong influence on Smith.

At the time when Smith wrote his books, Pufendorf's natural law works had been translated into several European languages. They were also published in new editions with or without commentaries and reprinted repeatedly. His views were known not only to university academics but also to many educated people outside the closed university circles. Smith could therefore have assumed that his readers would have known his sources without him explicitly making references to them.

---

[36] TMS VII, iii, 1, 1.

[37] TMS VII, iv, 1, 1.

Ingrid Merikoski (2010) in an article entitled *Adam Smith and the Virtues of Enlightenment* claims that Adam Smith to his contemporaries of the Scottish Enlightenment was recognised for his 'profoundly original contributions to moral philosophy and natural jurisprudence'. However, she refers to a book by Charles Griswold with the same title. Griswold challenges readers to look again at Smith's the *Theory of Moral Sentiments* since this is Smith's integral text where he describes a moral vision that serves as a guarantor of civility in commercial society. The vision is based on the cultivation of virtue, the 'bettering of our condition'. The necessary tools for the cultivation of virtue include impartiality, sympathy and reason. The fact that Smith in his book built on Pufendorf's two first books of his *De Jure Naturae et Gentium* is not discussed by either Merikoski or Griswold.

8 The Resurrection of Natural Law and the New Enlightenment

Many scholars' claims that the Enlightenment ended in the last years of the eighteenth century, often choosing the French Revolution of 1789 and the subsequent Reign of Terror, or the beginning of the Napoleonic wars 1804–15, to date the end. Others contend that it is fruitless to both discuss if the Enlightenment ended and if so, what brought it to an end?

It is not the purpose of this presentation to get involved in this debate. However, although it might be discussed if the Enlightenment ended, it is definitely the case that the Natural law of the Enlightenment ended.

Pufendorf employed an eclectic method in which he defended man's ability to understand reality and to draw conclusions on the basis of observations from life. This method he used to develop his natural law theories. However, his way of reasoning was challenged.

8.1 The Elimination of Natural Law

At the end of the eighteenth century, the German philosopher, Immanuel Kant (1724–1804), from Königsberg, East Prussia, lectured, researched and wrote on philosophy. Kant is considered one of the most influential critics of the natural law philosophy of the Enlightenment. Andreas Aure (2014, 70) in his article *Hugo Grotius – Individual Rights as the Core of Natural Law* contends that Kant in his famous tract on international law, *Zum Ewigen Frieden* (Perpetual Peace) from

1795, scorned Grotius, Pufendorf and Vattel,[38] calling them miserable comforters because no state or ruler cares about their arguments.

More damaging to the natural law tradition, however, was Kant's denial of the possibility of making inferences from empirical reality or nature. Kant's major work, *Kritik der reinen Vernuft* (Critique of Pure Reason), which was first published in 1781, made him famous and he gained a tremendous influence on the development of philosophy. He claimed that 'Jeder philosophische Denker baut, sozusagen, auf den Trümmern eines anderen sein eigenes Werk' (Every philosopher built his work, so to speak, on the ruins of someone else's work).[39] Kant built on the apprehension that man does not have the faculty to comprehend reality and to draw conclusions from it. This view was in opposition to Pufendorf's, who, as mentioned, defended man's ability to understand reality and to draw conclusions on the basis of observations from the reality of life.

Unfortunately, Kant's view had a tremendous impact on the development of philosophy, on the writings on the history of philosophy and unfortunately also on the writings of the history of economic thought.

Richard Tuck (1987, 100) in his article, *The 'modern' theory of natural law,* claimed that it is a familiar observation that late eighteenth-century Europe witnessed, with the views of Kant and his followers, 'one of the greatest revolutions which have ever occurred in the writing of philosophy'. He boldly states 'that the survival of the post-Kantian history into our own time has proved a great barrier to a genuine understanding of the pre-Kantian writers'. In his opinion, the character of this revolution is best appreciated by contrasting two works on the history of philosophy: first, Johann Jacob Brucker's (1796–1870) *Historia criticae philosophiae* (Critical history of philosophy) from 1742 to 1744 (second edition in 6 volumes 1766) and, second, Johann Gottlieb Buhle's (1763–1821) *Geschichte der neuern Philosophie* (History of recent Philosophy) in six volumes from 1800 to 1805. Both authors were recognised academics; Brucker was a parish minister and a member of the Academy of Sciences at Berlin and Buhle a professor at Göttingen, Moscow and Brunswick. Their works were written to help philosophy students, but, as noted by Tuck, both found a wider European audience. The structure and content of these two works are, however, startlingly different.

Brucker's hero, according to Tuck, was Grotius, since he produced, in his *De jure belli ac pacis*, a new system of ethics and advanced 'open eclecticism'. In Brucker's story, Grotius was followed closely by John Selden, then Hobbes and, last but not least, Pufendorf. Brucker points 'to the strength of Pufendorf's genius, the clearness of his discernment, the accuracy of his judgment, and the variety and depth of his

[38] Emerich de Vattel (1714–67), a Swiss philosopher and legal expert, known for his work *Droit des gens; ou, Principes de la loi naturelle appliqués à la conduite et aux affaires des nations et des souverains* (The Law of Nations *or the Principles of Natural Law Applied to the Conduct and to the Affairs of Nations and of Sovereigns*) from 1758. He was strongly influenced by the German philosopher, Christian Wolff (1679–1754), who again was a follower of Pufendorf.

[39] Immanuel Kant (1923, 25) Gesammelte Schriften, band 9, Berlin.

erudition'.[40] He ends it with a thorough discussion of Pufendorf's *De jure naturae et gentium*.

A different story is told in Buhle's history of philosophy. He does not attempt to write a history of modern moral philosophy as a whole. The opposition of two schools, which are described as 'realists' and 'idealists', he asserts, characterised modern philosophy. According to Tuck (1987, 101), these schools are 'empiricism' and 'rationalism'. They have, in his opinion, 'bedevilled the history of philosophy ever since'. Grotius, who was fundamental to Brucker's account of the modern theory of ethics, is treated with 'dramatic contempt' by Buhle (Ibid). Pufendorf is put off with a short life history and a brief description of the content of his abridged *De officio*.

In his article, Tuck argues that it is in Buhle's account that we find all subsequent general works on the history of philosophy. Tuck continues: 'Grotius and Pufendorf have never re-emerged to take up places of honour in the history of modern philosophy. If they are mentioned, it is as late examples of scholasticism, and their modernity, which so impressed Brucker, is not taken at all seriously.' He concludes that a broader range of insights will be available to us once the post-Kantian history of morality is replaced with the pre-Kantian one. 'The moral theories of the late seventeenth- and eighteenth-century natural lawyers constituted, in many ways, the most important language of politics and ethics in Europe, influential over a huge area and in a wide variety of disciplines' (Ibid, 119).

Jerome B. Schneewind (1987, 123), in his article *Pufendorf's place in the history of ethics,* agrees with Tuck that Pufendorf was treated as a major figure in eighteenth-century writings on the history of ethics but unfortunately is 'largely forgotten by moral philosophers today'. As an example, he points first to a work by Christian Garve (1742–99), *Ubersicht der vornehmsten Principien der Sittenlehre* (Overview of the principles of moral philosophy) from 1798. Here, Grotius is seen as the first modern philosopher. Pufendorf, as his follower, is treated at a greater length. Schneewind then turns to Karl Friedrich Stäudlin (1761–1826)[41] and his *Geschichte der Moralphilosophie* (History of Moral Philosophy) from 1822, which he calls the first modern treatment of the history of ethics. Pufendorf is only given a page or two, as a follower of Grotius. Schneewind concludes, 'and that much, or less, is all that those interested in moral philosophy have gotten about him from their historians ever since'. [42] (Ibid, 151). This unfortunate situation Schneewind wants to change – Pufendorf should be rescued from oblivion because knowledge of him is necessary if we wish to understand the history of ethics.

Tim J. Hochstrasser (2000, 214) in his book, *Natural Law Theories in the Early Elightenment*, adds another writer W.G. Tennemann (1761–1819), with his *Geschichte der Philosophie* (History of Philosophy). He claims that they (Buhle and

[40] In W. Enfield (1837, 625). The English translation of Buhle (1744).

[41] Karl Friedrich Stäudlin was for 36 years professor of theology at University of Göttingen. He wrote on church history, moral theology and moral philosophy. On moral philosophy, he was a follower of Kant.

[42] Schneewind points to several writers of the history of moral philosophy that ignore Pufendorf.

Tennemann) only give extended discussions and summaries to those philosophers who have produced philosophical systems. In their works, 'there is no discussion of eclecticism for the simple reason that its very principles disqualify it. It does not conform to the epistemological system-building that these historians are looking for.' Pufendorf therefore has just a tiny place in their expositions.

The Hochstrasser view has been supplemented by Knud Haakonssen (2006a, 14). In his *The History of Eighteenth-Century Philosophy: History or Philosophy?*, he notes that 'Samuel Pufendorf and Christian Thomasius, have not only been taken seriously as philosophers but have commonly been written out of the history of philosophy altogether, a process that had already begun with the Wolffian takeover of the German universities and has continued ever since'.

The German philosopher, Georg Wilhelm Friederich Hegel (1770–1831), should also be mentioned in this context since he has had a huge impact on how the histories of philosophy have been taught. Philosophy was in his opinion the most important element in a liberal education. His lectures on the history of philosophy were delivered not to academic philosophers but to students. On this topic, he lectured students at the universities of Jena (1805–1806), Heidelberg (1816–1817) and Berlin (1819–1830).

Unfortunately, Hegel gave little attention to the philosophers who had been neglected by the Kantians. In his *Vorlesungen über die Geschichte der Philosophie* (Lectures on the History of Philosophy) published after his death, 1833–36, the natural law philosophers Grotius, Hobbes and Pufendorf are given, respectively, one, five and one page.[43]

A generation later, the German Historian Christian Ueberweg (1868, 120) published his massive multivolume opus *Grundriss der Geschichte der Philosophie* (Outline of the History of Philosophy), where he made do with merely nine lines for Pufendorf.

Here it should be mentioned that there was another, but related, explanation why the philosophy of natural law was brought into discredit and almost disappeared for more than hundred years, that is the positivists and their followers, the Marxists. In the previously mentioned *Montesquieu and the Philosophy of Natural law,* Mark Waddicor (1970, ix–x) claims that the philosophy of natural law has 'suffered a fate that could hardly have been envisaged in the seventeenth and the eighteenth century exponents of its universalities and eternity; it has become old-fashioned'. He contends that the positivists and the Marxists have been happy 'to throw eternal morality out of the window, confident that some magic temporal harmony would

[43] Georg Wilhelm Friederich Hegel: Vorlesungen über die Geschichte der Philosophie (Lectures on the History of Philosophy). Herausgeben von Gerd Irrlitz. Textredaktion von Karin Gurst.Verlag Philipp Reclam jun. Leipzig 1971. Diese Vorlesungen sind bisher vollständig nur in den Micheletschen Ausgaben erschienen. 3 Bände; 1. Auflage, 1833–36. Der Geschichte der Philosophie Dritter Teil Neure Philosophie. Zweiter Abschnitt. Periode des denkenden Verstandes. Erste Kapitel: Periode der Metaphysik. B. Zweite Abteilung 1. Locke 23 Seiten. 2. Grotius 1 Seite. 3. Hobbes 5 Seiten. 5. Pufendorf 1 Seite und 6. Newton 2 Seiten.

eventually follow Progress in by the front door'. Although their hopes may not have been fully realised, they did succeed in discrediting natural law.

In an article *Some natural confusions about Natural Law,* Philip Soper (1992, 2343) acknowledges a recent resurgence of interest in natural law, in both moral and legal theory. In legal theory, the return of natural law is a viable 'challenger' to positivism. In moral theory, however, the focus has been on natural law as 'a potential guide to fundamental questions of morality or public policy'. Natural law has been assigned the role of a challenger to the reigning orthodoxy, rather than that of a defending champion.

Again, Tuck (1987, 99) in his article argued that the revolution in the writings of the history of philosophy, caused by Kant and his followers, almost eliminated the natural law philosophers, including Pufendorf, from the history of philosophy textbooks. What is not so familiar, he continues, is that the writing of the history of philosophy which was transformed about 200 years ago 'has remained in its new form ever since'. However, there are some optimistic signs. During the last 20–30 years, it looks as though a new breed of philosophers has rediscovered the natural law writers and particularly Pufendorf. An increasing number of articles and books have been published where natural law, as it was presented by Grotius, Hobbes and Pufendorf, is given both a comprehensive and a systematic treatment. Hopefully, this will be reflected in future history of philosophy textbooks.

8.2 The Resurrection of Natural Law

Kant, Hegel and Ueberweg's elimination of Pufendorf's natural law had as a consequence that natural law as a university subject disappeared from universities across Europe in the nineteenth century.

In 1920, the League of Nations was founded as a result of the Paris Peace Conference that ended the First World War. The philosophy behind the League was to provide a forum for resolving international disputes and it represented a fundamental shift from the preceding hundred years. International law based on the works of the natural law philosophers Grotius and Pufendorf was pulled out of oblivion.

However, with the growth of Communism, Fascism and Nazism in the 1920s and 1930s, the League ultimately proved incapable of preventing aggressions and failed in its endowers. The totalitarian regimes had set aside the natural law principles of human dignity and equality, the use of reason and belief in progress and tolerance.

After the end of the Second World War, the League of Nations was replaced by the United Nations, who took lessons from the mistakes of its predecessor.

On 10 December 1948, the United Nations third General Assembly decided in Paris with 48 yes votes the Universal Declaration of Human Rights (General Assembly resolution 217 A) as a common standard of achievements for all people and all nations.

The Declaration was, when it was decided, primarily a reaction to the horrors, and especially the mass extermination of Jews, committed by the German Nazi regime from 1933 until the end of World War II in 1945. At the time when the Declaration was decided, the major crimes of other regimes were less widely known. However, it was also a reaction to the fact that these atrocities were carried out according to the laws of each nations.[44]

The Declaration is today regarded as the foundation of the work of the United Nations. The statement itself has 30 simple and clearly formulated and mostly short articles. The preface begins with these words:

> Whereas recognition of the inherent dignity and of the equal and inalienable rights of all members of the human family is the foundation of freedom, justice and peace in the world.

The first article in the Declaration has two sentences:

> All human beings are born free and equal in dignity and rights. They are endowed with reason and conscience and should act towards one another in a spirit of brotherhood.

In 2009, on the 60th anniversary of the Declaration, the professor emeritus of law and legal historian Wolf-Dietrich Uwe Wesel, from the Free University of Berlin, had an article in the German newspaper Die Zeit. He writes that in these sentences, *human dignity* emerges for the first time as a human right. Furthermore, he shows that this term was developed by and described more than 300 years ago by Samuel Pufendorf. Pufendorf's natural law came again to honour and dignity.

9 Conclusion: The Challenge

This contribution has tried to outline the contribution and influence of the natural law philosopher Samuel Pufendorf on the birth and development of the European Enlightenment. For more than 100 years, he was the most read scholar in Europe, but primarily due to the influence of Immanuel Kant, Pufendorf's natural law and law of nations was eliminated and forgotten. Although Pufendorf, according to Professor Uwe Wesel (2008), came to honour and dignity with the UN Declaration of Human Rights, he has still not achieved the recognition he deserves, Sæther (2017a and b).

Today if we are browsing the Enlightenment page or word in books or Encyclopaedias or enter the cue in search services on the Internet, like Google, we rarely or never find Pufendorf's name. Scholars and academics of different professions, who believe that Samuel Pufendorf has had a great contribution to the Enlightenment, and that natural law, which includes ethics, jurisprudence, government and political economy, again should resurrect, are faced with a formidable challenge. How can we strengthen our efforts to bring Pufendorf's ideas of natural law to the forefront?

[44]The deportation of the Norwegian Jews on 26 November 1942 was carried out according to laws decided by the Quisling Nazi regime.

References

Aure AH (2014) Hugo Grotius – Individual Rights as the Core of Natural Law. In G Fløistad [Ed.] (2014), pp. 75-94
Axtell, JL (1968) The Educational Writings of John Locke. Cambridge: Cambridge University Press
Bailyn B (1992) The Ideological Origin of the American Revolution. Cambridge MA: Belknap Press of Harvard University
Baum A (1979) Montesquieu and Social Theory. Pergamon Press Oxford, Pp. 509-605
Behme T (2009) Introduction. In S Pufendorf (1672 [1660]) Two Books of the Elements of Universal Jurisprudence
Brown M (2002) Francis Hutcheson in Dublin 1719-30. The Crucible of his Thought. Dublin: Four Courts Press LTD
Brühlmeier D (1995) Natural Law and Early Economic Thought in Barbeyrac, Burlamaqui and Vattel. Ch. 2, pp. 53–71. In JC Laursen [Ed.] (1995)
Cannan E [Ed.] (1896) Lectures on Justice, Police, Revenue and Arms, delivered in the University of Glasgow by Adam Smith. Oxford
Carey D (2000) Introduction to Hutcheson, Francis (1755)
Chappell V [Ed.] (1994) The Cambridge Companion to Locke, Cambridge: Cambridge University Press
Cohler A M (1989 [1748]) Introduction. In Montesquieu (1989) The Spirit of the Laws. Cambridge: Cambridge University Press
Crowe M B (1977) The Changing Profile of Natural Law. The Hague: Nijhoff
Denzer H (1987) Pufendorf (1632-94). In Klassiker des Politischen Denkens, Zweiter Band von Locke bis Max Weber. Eds. H Maier, H Rausch, H Denzer. Fifth edition. München: Verlag CH Beck
Derathé L R (1970) Jean-Jacques Rousseau et la Science politique de son temps. 2nd ed., Paris: VRIN
Dewey F (1986) Thomas Jefferson, Lawyer. Charlottesville VA: The University Press of Virginia
Dreitzel H (1995) Toleranz und Gewissenfreiheit im konfessionellen Zeitalter: Zur Diskussion im Reich zwischen Augsburger Religionsfrieden und Aufklärung. In D Breuer: Religion und Religiosität im Zeitalter des Barock. Wiesbaden:
Dufour A (1986) Pufendorfs Ausstrahlung im französischen und im anglo-amerikanischen Kulturraum. In Modéer, KÅ [Ed.] (1986)
Dufour A (1991) Pufendorf. In Burns JH The Cambridge History of Political Thought 1450-1700, pp. 561–588
Durant W and A (1962–68) The Story of Civilization. Vol. I-XI, New York: Simon & Schuster
Enfield W (1837) The History of Philosophy from the Earliest Periods. English translation of Johann Jacob Brucker's Historia Critica Philosophiæ, London
Fehrman C, H Westling, G Blomquist (2004) Lärdomens Lund. Lunds Universitets historia 1666-2004. Lund: Lunds universitet
Fiering N (1981) Moral Philosophy at Seventeenth Century Harvard. A discipline in transition. Chappel Hill NC: North Carolina University Press.
Fox-Genovese E (1976) The Origin of Physiocracy. Economic Revolution and Social Order in Eighteenth Century France. Ithaca and London: Cornell University Press
Gourevitch V [Ed.] (2007) Introduction. In Rousseau, The Social Contract and other later political writings.
Gourevitch V [Ed.] (2008) Introduction. In Rousseau, The Discourses and other early Political writings
Grice-Hutchinson M (1952) The School of Salamanca. London: Oxford University Press
Grimsley R (1967) Jean-Jacques Rousseau. In P Edwards [Ed.]
Haakonssen K (1996) Natural law and moral philosophy. From Grotius to the Scottish Enlightenment. Cambridge: Cambridge University Press

Haakonssen K (2006a) The History of Eighteenth-Century Philosophy: History or Philosophy? In Haakonssen, K [Ed.] p.3–25.
Haakonssen K [Ed.] (2006b) The Cambridge history of eighteenth – century philosophy. Cambridge: Cambridge University Press
Haakonssen K (2012) Naturretten, Pufendorf og Holberg – men hvilken naturrett? Hvilken Pufendorf? (Natural law, Pufendorf and Holberg – but what kind of natural law? Which Pufendorf?) InVinje E and JM Sejersted (Red.): Ludvig Holbergs naturrett. (The natural law of Ludvig Holberg), Oslo: Gyldendal Akademisk
Haft F von (1997) Einführung in das juristische Lernen. Bielefeld: Verlag E und W Gieseking
Hammerstein N (1986) Zum Fortwirken von Pufendorfs Naturrechtslehre an den Universitäten des Heiligen Römisches Reiches Deutscher Nation während des 18.Jahrhunderts. In KÅ Modéer [Ed.]
Hesse H (2009) Personenlexikon der Wirtschaftsgeschichte. Denker, Unternehmer und Politiker in 900 Porträts. 2 Auflage. Stuttgart: Schäffer-Poeschel Verlag
Hochstrasser, T J (2000) Natural Law Theories in the Early Enlightenment. Cambridge UK: Cambridge University Press
Hutcheson F (1969 [1747]) A Short Introduction to Moral Philosophy, in three books; containing the Elements of Ethicks and the Law of Nature. Collected Works Volume IV, Hildesheim: GOs Verlagsbuchhandlung
Hutcheson F (1993) Two texts on Human Nature. Reflections on our common systems of morality. On the social nature of man. Edited by T Mautner. Cambridge UK: Cambridge University Press
Hutcheson F (1973 [1725]) An Inquiry Concerning Beauty, Order, Harmony and Design. Edited with an Introduction and notes by Peter Kivy, Martinus Nijhoff. The Hague.
Hutchison T (1988) Before Adam Smith. The Emergence of Political Economy. 1662-1776. Oxford: Basil Blackwell
Israel J I (2001) Radical Enlightenment. Philosophy and the Making of Maternity 1650-1750. Oxford: Oxford University Press
Israel J I (2006) Enlightenment Contested. Philosophy, Modernity, and the Emancipation of Man 1670-1752. Oxford: Oxford University Press
Kant I (1923) Gesammelte Schriften, Berlin
Kingston R (1996) Montesquieu and the Parliament of Bordeaux. Geneva: Librairie DROZ SA
Korkman P (2006) Introduction and extensive footnotes. In J-J Burlamaqui (1763[2006])
Krieger L (1957) The German Idea of Freedom. Boston: Beacon Press
Laslett P [Ed.] (1964) Introduction and notes. In John Locke: Two Treaties of Government. Cambridge: Cambridge at the University Press
Leyden W von [Ed.] (1954a) Introduction to John Locke. Essays on the Law of Nature.
Leyden W von [Ed.] (1954b) Locke's Valedictory Speech as Censor of Moral Philosophy. In Locke J (1954 [1664])
Lindberg B (1976) Naturrätten i Uppsala 1655-1720. Stockholm: Liber Tryck
Lindberg B (1983) The Doctrine of Natural Law in 17th century Sweden. In Rättshistoriska Studier pp. 71–80
Luig K (1972) Zur Verbreitung des Naturrechts in Europa. Tijdschrift voor Rechtsgeschiedenis,
Lutz D (1984) The Relative Influence of European Writers on Late Eighteenth-Century American Political Thought. The American Political Science Review. Vol. 78. No. 1
Macfie A L (1952) Note on the growth of political economy. Glasgow: In Fortuna Domus University of Glasgow.
Mautner T (1986) Pufendorf and 18th century Scottish Philosophy. In K Modéer, Rättshistoriska Studier, Nordiska Bokhandlen, Stockholm pp. 120–131
Mautner T [Ed.] (1999) Dictionary of Philosophy. London: Penguin Books Ltd
McCosh J (1875) The Scottish Philosophy, Biographical, Expository, Critical, From Hutcheson to Hamilton. London: Macmillan and Co
Medick H (1973) Naturzustand und Naturgeschichte der bürgerlichen Gesellschaft. Göttingen:

Meek, R L and A S Skinner (1973) The Development of Adam Smith's Ideas of The Division of Labour. Economic Journal. lxxxiii
Meek R L, D D Raphael and P G Stein (1982) Introduction. In Adam Smith Lectures On Jurisprudence. It is an exact photographic reproduction of the Oxford University Press edition of 1978. Indianapolis: Liberty Press
Merikovski I A (2010) Adam Smith and the Virtues of Enlightenment. Grand Rapids MI: Acton Institute
Mizuta H (1967) Adam Smith's Library. A Supplement to Bonar's Catalogue with a Checklist of the whole Library. London: Cambridge University Press for the Royal Society
Moore J and M Silverthorn [Eds.] (2002) Natural Rights on the Threshold of the Scottish Enlightenment. The Writings of Gershom Carmichael. Indianapolis: Liberty Press
Murray D (1927) Memories of the Old College of Glasgow. Glasgow: Jackson Wylie and Co., Publisher to the University
Norton D F (1982) Common-sense Moralist, Sceptical Metaphysician. Princeton NJ: Princeton University Press
Othmer S C (1970) Berlin und die Verbreitung des Naturrechts in Europa. Berlin: Walter de Gruyter & Co
Pesciarelli E (1989) Aspects of the Influence of Francis Hutcheson on Adam Smith. History of Political Economy. Vol. 31. No. 3. Durham NC: Duke University Press
Pufendorf S (1931 [1660, 1672]) Elementorum Jurisprudentiæ Universalis Libri Duo (The Elements of Universal Jurisprudence), Photographic Reproduction of the Edition of the 1672 Cambridge edition, with a List of Errata which refers to the first edition of 1660, which was published in The Hague. The Translation of the 1672 edition by WA Oldfather. Oxford: The Clarendon Press
Pufendorf S (2007 [1667]) The Present State of Germany (De Statu Imperii Germanici).m Translated by Edmund Bohun in 1696. Edited with an Introduction by MJ Seidler. Indianapolis: Liberty Fund
Pufendorf S (1933 [1672, 1688]) De Jure Naturae et Gentium Libri Octo (On the Law of Nature and Nations in eight books), DJNG. The translation of the edition of 1688 (with references to the first edition of 1672 by CH and WA Oldfather. Reprinted 1964, New York: Oceana Publications Inc, and London: Wiley & Sons Ltd
Pufendorf S (1927 [1673, 1682]) De Officio Hominis et Civis Juxta Legem Naturalem Libri Duo (The Duty of Man and Citizen According to the Natural Law in Two Books), DOH. A Photographic Reproduction of the Edition of 1682 with a List of Errata that refers to the first edition of 1673. A Translation of the Text by FG Moore. New York: Oxford University Press
Pufendorf S (2002a [1687]) Of the Nature and Qualification of Religion in Reference to Civil Society. Translated from De habitu religionis christianae ad vitam civilem by J Crull with an introduction by S Zurbuchen. Indianapolis: Liberty Fund
Pufendorf S (2002b [1695]) The Divine Feudal Law: Or, Covenants with Mankind, Represented. Translated from Jus feciale divinium cive de consensus et dissensu protestantium by T Dorrington. Edited and with an introduction by S Zurbuchen. Indianapolis: Liberty Fund
Rae J (1965 [1895]) Life of Adam Smith. Macmillan Co. London. Reprinted with an Introduction by Jacob Viner. New York: Augustus Kelley Bookseller
Raphael DD and AL Macfie (1982[1976]) Introduction to Adam Smith's Theory of Moral Sentiments. Indianapolis: Liberty Classics
Ross IS (2012) The Life of Adam Smith. Second Edition. Oxford: Oxford University Press
Schneewind JB (1987) Pufendorf's place in the History of Ethics. Synthese 72, pp. 123–155, Berlin: D Reidel Publishing Company
Schroeder K-P (2008) Vom Sachsenspiegel Zum Grundgesetz. Eine deutsche Rechtsgeschichte in Lebensbildern. Berlin: Verlag CH Beck.
Scott W R (1965[1937]) Adam Smith as Student and Professor. Glasgow: Jackson, Son & Company
Scott W R (1900) Francis Hutcheson. His Life, Teaching and Position in the History of Philosophy. Cambridge: The University Press

Shackleton R (1961) Montesquieu, A Critical Bibliography, Oxford: Oxford University Press
Simons W (1934) Introduction to Samuel Pufendorf's De jure naturae et gentium libri octo (On the Law of Nature and Nations), Volume two The translation of the edition of 1688 (with references to the first edition of 1672), New York: Oceana Publications Inc, and London: Wiley & Sons Ltd
Smith A (1982a [1759, 1790, 1976]) The Theory of Moral Sentiments, Glasgow, sixth edition, Edited by DD Raphael and AL Macfie. Oxford: Oxford University Press, Reprinted by Liberty Press/Liberty Classics, Indianapolis:
Smith A (1982b [1762–63]) Lectures on Jurisprudence, Report of 1762-3 and Report dated1766 together with an Appendix containing the "Early Draft" of The Wealth of Nations from the 1760's. Edited by R L Meek, DD Raphael and PG Stein 1978, Oxford: Clarendon Press. Photographic reproduced and published Indianapolis: Liberty Classic
Smith A (1965 [1937/1763]) An early draft of part of the wealth of nations. In R W Scott (1965[1937]): Adam Smith as Student and Professor, pp. 317–356
Smith A (1976 [1904 /1789/1776]) An Inquiry into the Nature and Causes of the Wealth of Nations. Fifth edition, Edinburgh. Reprint of the 1904 Cannan edition with a new Preface by G J Stigler. Chicago: The University of Chicago Press
Soper P (1992) Some natural confusions about Natural Law. Michigan Law Review. Vol. 90. No.8, pp. 2343–2423
Sprague E (1967) Francis Hutcheson. In Paul Edwards The Encyclopedia of Philosophy, pp. 99–101
Stewart D (1983 [1793]): Account of the Life and Writings of Adam Smith, LLD. Edited by JS Ross. In WP Wightman and JC Bryce [Eds.]
Stoner Jr. J R (2011) Declaration of Independence. Princeton NJ: Witherspoon Institute
Sæther A (2017a) Samuel Pufendorf – The Grandfather of Modern Political Economy. Doctor Philosophy thesis. Bergen: Norwegian School of Economics
Sæther A (2017b) Natural Law and the Origin of Political Economy. Samuel Pufendorf and the History of Economics. London and New York: Routledge. Taylor & Francis Group
Taylor W L (1955) Gershom Carmichael A Neglected Figure in British Political Economy. South African Journal of Economics. Vol. 23, pp. 251–255
Teichgraeber III RF (1986) Free Trade and Moral Philosophy. Rethinking the Sources of Adam Smith's Wealth of Nations. Durham NC: Duke University Press
Thiel U (1999) Locke. In Thomas Mautner [Ed.] Dictionary of Philosophy
Tuck R (1987) The 'modern' theory of natural law. In Anthony Pagden, [Ed.]
Tully J (1980) A Discourse on Property: John Locke and His Adversaries. Cambridge: Cambridge: University Press.
Tully J (1991) Locke. In Burns JH, [Ed.]
Ueberweg F (1868) Grundriss der Geschichte der Philosophie von Thales bis auf die Gegenwart (Outline of the history of philosophy from Thales to the present) [microform]. Dritter Theil: Die Neuzeit, Berlin: Mittler
Vet de JJVM (1996) Some Periodicals of the United Provinces on Pufendorf: Reconnoitring the Reception of his Ideas in the Seventeenth and Eighteenth Centuries. In Palladini F und G Hartung [Hg.]
Waddicor MH (1970) Montesquieu and the Philosophy of Natural Law. The Hague: Niijhoff
Wehberg H (1922) Introduction to Pufendorf (1931 [1660, 1672])
West EG (1976) Adam Smith the Man and His Work. Liberty Press, Indianapolis,
Wesel von U (2008) Unantastbar. Die Zeit. Nr. 49. 27. November. Frankfurt: West EG (1976) Adam Smith the Man and His Works. Indianapolis: Liberty Press
Wills G (1978) Inventing America. Jeffersons Declaration of Independence. Vintage Books. Ann Arbor: The University of Michigan Press
Winch D (1978) Adam Smith's Politics: An Essay in Historiographic Revision. Cambridge
Wokler R (1994) Rousseau's Pufendorf: Natural law and the foundations of Commercial society. History of Political Thought. Vol. XV. No. 3, pp. 373–402
Wokler R (2006) Rousseau on Rameau and revolution. In JT Scott [Ed.]

Wodrow R (1843) Analecta: Materials for a history of remarkable providence. Mostly relatively to Scotch Ministers and Christians. Glasgow: Printed for the Maitland Club
Woolhouse R (2007) Locke. A Biography. Cambridge: Cambridge University Press
Zuckert MP (1994) Natural Rights and the New Republicanism. Princeton NY: Princeton University Press
Zurbuchen S (1998) Samuel Pufendorf and the Foundation of Modern Natural Law. An Account of the State of Research and Editions. Central European History. Vol. 31, No.4, pp. 413–428

Pufendorf, Hume and Adam Smith: A Question of Influence

F. L. van Holthoon

Abstract In what way did Pufendorf's natural jurisprudence influence David Hume and Adam Smith? He had no direct influence on their work, but he provided them with a clear statement of conventional wisdom in politics and morality as represented by natural jurisprudence. Hume and Smith took natural jurisprudence as conventional wisdom and as the starting point of their innovations in economics.

Keywords Natural law and jurisprudence · Direct and contextual influence · The character of Hume's and Smith's innovations

JEL Codes B11 · B41 · K10

1 The Obituary of Istvan Hont

Often I have asked myself what we mean by saying that A influenced B; the assumption of influence is made too easily, that is clear. When two authors launch the same idea, it does not necessarily mean that A influenced B, because he came earlier. I once dealt with the assertion in the case of Spinoza and Hume (Holthoon, 2011, XII). Both argued that passions, not reason, determine our behaviour. Hume writes a notorious sentence about this issue: 'Reason is and ought only to be the slave of the passions' (Hume, 1978, II, 3, iii, 415). This quotation has a Classical origin and Hume ads 'ought' to it which gives the notion of the dominance of the passions a different meaning from the way Spinoza used it.

There are two forms of influence to distinguish. Those who assume that Spinoza influenced Hume are thinking of a direct influence. The other form of influence is contextual. It exists when a number of authors are discussing the same subject using

F. L. van Holthoon (✉)
University of Groningen, Groningen, The Netherlands

J. G. Backhaus et al. (eds.), *Samuel Pufendorf and the Emergence of Economics as a Social Science*, The European Heritage in Economics and the Social Sciences 24, https://doi.org/10.1007/978-3-030-49791-0_3

the same presuppositions. The following essay confirms my impression that contextual influence often is a more challenging subject than direct influence.

Five years ago, John Robertson sent me his obituary of Istvan Hont. Robertson, professor in Cambridge,[1] is the director of the famous seminar on the history of political thought at the University of Cambridge, and he wrote his appreciation in honour of the scholar who started the seminar.

Robertson writes about Hont: Hont conceived of the natural law tradition as the key not only to explaining *The Wealth of Nations*, it would also provide the historical connection with the political economy of Marx (Robertson, 2013, 20–21).

Then and now, it seems problematic to me that the tradition of natural jurisprudence is the key to explaining *The Wealth of Nations* (WN), let alone helping us to understand Marx' *Kapital*, and the conference on Pufendorf in Heilbronn was a welcome opportunity to explore the question how Pufendorf's version of natural jurisprudence could have influenced Smith in writing *The Wealth of Nations*. Let me quote the conclusion of each section in this essay to highlight my scenario for dealing with a rather complicated issue.

(i) On the continent, natural jurisprudence was used in two ways: first to accommodate positive law systems and reform them and secondly to emphasize the merits of a harmonious civic order. In Great Britain, natural jurisprudence was seen as a self-evident expression of conventional wisdom. So both in Britain and on the continent, natural jurisprudence was seen as a repository of conventional wisdom, but on the continent this wisdom was an expression of the will of God, while in Great Britain moral philosophers tended to be traced to human nature long before Adam Smith (and David Hume) made this a central priority in their moral philosophy.

It is hard for us, living in an age of relativism, to appreciate the rock bottom quality of seventeenth- and eighteenth-century conventional wisdom. Pufendorf and Smith shared their belief in the rulings of natural jurisprudence as self-evident truths. That the father is head of the family was a self-evident rule. Only the madman would disagree that this should be so.

(ii) Pufendorf did not have a direct influence on Smith and Hume, but as a gatekeeper of the Enlightenment he may have made Smith and Hume attentive readers of his works. The fact that Pufendorf only had an indirect influence on Smith (and Hume) is consequential for the way we interpret his influence. Schumpeter remarked that Pufendorf added no new ideas to economic theory (Schumpeter, 1954, 117).[2] So Pufendorf had no influence on Hume's and Smith's innovations in economic theory. Furthermore, Pufendorf did not invent natural jurisprudence, but put the often age-old theories in a new form. It was

[1] In 2020, he will retire from his post.

[2] Schumpeter writes: 'he … does not seem to me to have added much to the stock of knowledge and to the analytic apparatus of the late scholastics'. I owe this quotation to Karl Heinz Schmidt who mentions Schumpeter's remark in his contribution to this volume.

his way of presenting natural jurisprudence that made him the gatekeeper of the Enlightenment (Saether, 2020).

(iii) Hume and Smith were supporters of 'established government'. They accepted the need for reform, but were adverse to revolution.

(iv) Hume called *sympathy* – that 'powerful principle in human nature' (Hume, 1978, III, 3, i, 577–578) – and *sympathy* became key to Smith's moral philosophy. Hume discarded sympathy as that powerful principle in his *Enquiry Concerning Human Understanding* and made *utility* take its place while Smith developed the introspective qualities of sympathy as a concept.

(v) Adam Smith used two models to make his moral philosophy operative. Model 1 is the *impartial spectator* who guarantees that each economic actor knows what is proper and fair. Model 2 is the *invisible hand*; it gives the economic actor the opportunity to make business transactions into a win–win situation for those involved in a transaction.

(vi) What does contextual influence mean in the case of Pufendorf, Hume and Smith? Natural jurisprudence in its practical application maintains a 'safe, respectable and happy condition of our fellow citizens'. Both Pufendorf on the one side and Hume and Smith on the other believed in a society of orders where each order had its special place. Until we understand the practical implications of their views, we cannot understand their moral philosophy.

2 Natural Law and Natural Jurisprudence: Two Perspectives

According to Robertson's obituary, Hont claimed that Pufendorf had a direct influence on Smith. Hont writes: This same model of sociability and its concomitant anthropology played a key part in Adam Smith's theory of commercial society and in his conception of the 'Age of Commerce' and the decisive fourth stage of human history (Hont, 2005, 159–160).[3]

This quotation is incorrect for two reasons. First, Pufendorf, as I have argued, was not primarily interested in commercial affairs let alone in the fourth stage of the commercial society.[4] And second, in *The Wealth of Nations* to which Hont referred with his theory of commercial society, Smith does not mention commercial society as the fourth stage.[5]

[3] The fourth stage is the age of commercial society.

[4] Hume and Smith took their concept of sociability from Hutcheson. Hutcheson wrote: 'God gave us a sense of the fitting and the beautiful; associated with this sense, as moderator of all the grosser pleasures is shame; he also gave the keen spur of praise. The effect of all these is to make life social and kindly, and to make all the duties which are honourable and beneficial to others most advantageous and at the same time most pleasant for the agent himself, and to make even the innate self-love of our nature in no way contrary to our common and benevolent affections' (F. Hutcheson 2006, 'On the Natural Sociability of Mankind').

[5] We may assume that he had the commercial society as the fourth stage in mind, when he developed his economic theory.

Before I deal with this quotation, let us have a look at the history of natural jurisprudence as it came to function in continental Europe and on the British isles.

Work on the codification of the laws of the Roman Empire began in 529 at the court of Emperor Justin. Tribonius and his commission of lawyers concentrated their work on the interpretation of texts, and they showed, so it seems, no interest in natural law as a theoretical standard, even though Cicero had used it as such in his *De Legibus*.[6]

The *Corpus Juris Civilis* had an immense influence on later generations. As 'Roman law', it came to function as a model for legislation. In Chap. 44 of his *Decline and Fall of the Roman Empire*, Edward Gibbon presented a brilliant account of the evolution of Roman jurisprudence. He gives an impressive *laudatio* to the work of Justinian's lawyers (Gibbon 1995, vol. 2, 844):

> Under his reign and by his care, the civil jurisprudence was digested in the immortal works of the CODE, the PANDECTS, and the INSTITUTES: the public reason of the Romans has been silently or studiously transfused into the domestic institutions of Europe, and the laws of Justinian still command the respect or obedience of independent nations. (Gibbon, 1995, vol. 2, 778)

In this way, Gibbon gave a graphic description of the accommodation process and its influence on Western civilization, when natural jurisprudence in the guise of Roman law started to fashion domestic law systems.

In the Middle Ages, the fusion between philosophy and jurisprudence took place and natural law became the theoretical standard of interpretation. The fusion became an important tool for the Roman Church and made it possible to graft the moral code of the Church on Roman law. Gratianus and others in service of the *Curia* made natural jurisprudence into a system of rulings which we call canon law. Harold Berman considers the law reforms, which were started during the reign of Gregory VII in the eleventh century, a revolution on a par with the French Revolution, because his lawyers built a system of law which dominated medieval and early modern Europe (Berman, 1985, 18–19). The achievement of the lawyers of canon law was that they introduced the rule of law, meaning that law prevails over power.

Divine and natural law gave authority to a new system of law which was called natural jurisprudence. The pretension of the system was clear. Natural law as expressed in natural jurisprudence represented God's will and so transcended positive law wherever that was to be found in the (Western) Christian world. Because natural law was the expression of God's will, princes and laymen had to obey the canon law and the moral teaching that was attached to it.[7] To oppose the pretensions

---

[6] Expressing doubts at the same time about the practical use of such a standard.

[7] By incorporating the Christian moral code in Canon law, the Church acquired a formidable tool for social control. Jack Goody describes how the Church forbade marriage within the extended family as well along consanguine as affine lines of in-laws. So Canon law prohibited the remarriage of a man with the sister of his deceased wife. These prohibitions – drawn out to absurd proportions – also had a political purpose. The Church wanted to break the power of feudal families. Goody writes: 'Indeed the introduction of the prohibitions was partly directed against the solidarity of such [kin], against the reinforcing of blood with marriage, and it is difficult to see that their

of the Church, princes of the Empire and later of the emerging nation states ordered their lawyers to create an alternative system taking the same source as the lawyers of the Pope used: Justinian's law book. So a secular system of natural jurisprudence came into existence.

The Protestant Reformers adapted the secular system to their needs. Their natural jurisprudence was also seen as an expression of God's will, and the Protestant lawyers were as careful as the medieval princes to subject their churches to the sovereign power of the State. Pufendorf was a late example of these lawyers. His definition of natural law reads in Barbeyrac's translation as follows:

> [E]lle signifie seulement que la droite raison conseilloit d'établir telle ou telle chose, pour l'avantage de la Société Humaine ... en général; car ce qui a été introduit pour le bien particulier d'un Etat, est purement de Droit Civil ou Positif. (Pufendorf, 1718, vol. 2, 510)

So Pufendorf tells us that natural law does not prescribe but directs the mind of those in search of justice. Natural law is a principle not a system, but it has inspired the system of natural jurisprudence. For Pufendorf and many jurists in the seventeenth century, natural law and the jurisprudence, which emerged from it, were the expression of God's will, but in the Enlightenment of the eighteenth century, natural jurisprudence becomes the conventional wisdom of politics and morality which no longer is ordained by God.[8]

If we subsequently come to the functioning of natural jurisprudence in Germany and England, we notice a marked difference between the two countries. Natural jurisprudence in the Habsburg Empire was a method of accommodating between positive law systems, and it functioned as an instrument of legal reform at the same time. Hence, natural jurisprudence was sometimes called *ius commune* in German-speaking countries, or common law. Common law in England was different, because it was a version of the *ius gentium*. After the Norman Conquest, law became an untidy assembly of Saxon and Roman elements. According to Hume, the discovery of the *Pandects* in Amalfi had a salutary influence on the functioning of common law in England. He writes:

> The ecclesiastics, who had leisure, and some inclination of study, immediately adopted with zeal this excellent system of jurisprudence, and spread the knowledge of it through every part of Europe. Besides the intrinsic merit of the performance, it was recommended to them by its original connexion with the imperial city of Rome, which being the seat of their religion, seemed to acquire a new lustrum and authority, by the diffusion of its laws over the western world. (Hume, 1983, vol. 2, 520)

---

extension in the eleventh century did anything to counter this pressure'. J. Goody, *The Development of the Family an Marriage in Europe* (Cambridge 1980: Cambridge University Press), 145.

[8]There is consensus on the rulings of conventional wisdom, among these are the following: (1) Civil society cannot exist without the authority of the State. (2) A citizen of the State has to obey the political and social conventions. (3) Ideally, that citizen has no say in the administration and defence of the nation. (4) Civil society consists of monogamous families in which the husband is head of the family. (5 Relations between the members of civil society are determined by property and status. (6) Contracts further determine these relations. (7) Justice depends on the proper administration of laws and rulings. These laws and rulings also determine the margin of freedom individuals have for acting and expressing themselves.

A famous law book of the eighteenth century is William Blackstone's *Commentaries on the Laws of England*. On the first page, he refers to natural law as an expression of the will of God (Blackstone, 1890, 1).[9] That was a reference to natural jurisprudence, but nothing more follows, because on the next page he starts to discuss 'municipal law' as 'a rule of civil conduct prescribed *by the supreme power in the state*' (Blackstone 1890, 2). The express purpose of Blackstone was to streamline common law, and as a cautious modernizer he adapted it to his time. One does not get the impression that natural jurisprudence influenced him in his efforts (Skol 2010, 91).[10] There were numerous treatises on natural law in England and Scotland, and Blackstone had undoubtedly read Richard Cumberland's *Treatise of the Law of Nature*.[11] However, if so, natural jurisprudence worked only indirectly on Blackstone and that seems the general practice particularly among English (in contrast with Scottish) lawyers.

By his practical attitude to reform, Blackstone left ample room for philosophers such as Adam Smith to develop a moral philosophy, not for the purpose of ordering laws but for designing a code of conduct for society which was witnessing rapid and momentous changes.

It is time to introduce Hume in the discussion about the influence of natural jurisprudence on both Scots. Haakonssen writes about Hume's version of jurisprudence:

> Hume was undoubtedly very much influenced by modern natural law theories in Grotius, Pufendorf and others. But his real genius was to combine the strands of his inheritance in a completely new sort of natural law theory – for, indeed he is quite willing to use that label, provided we let him fill in the contents himself. (Haakonssen, 12)[12]

Indeed, his 'natural law theory' had a different foundation from that of Grotius and Pufendorf and I wonder whether it is wise to call it a version of natural jurisprudence at all. Hume appealed to the study of human nature, to the 'science of Man' as he called it in the *Introduction* to his Treatise (Hume 1978, XV). Not God, but man was the starting point of Hume's enquiry and it ended with a vista of a society which was held together by conventions and laws, or in Hume's parlance of the *Treatise*, 'artificial virtues'.

Neither Hume nor Smith used God's will to justify their system of moral philosophy. In the *Enquiry Concerning the Principles of Morals* (EPM), Hume urged his readers to rely on their own judgement to decide moral issues. How persons reach judgement was closely linked to conventional wisdom. That conventional wisdom had a self-evident character. Since Pufendorf, Hume, Smith, and their

---

[9] The fact that Blackstone's *Commentaries* were still used as a textbook in 1890 is an indication of its enormous influence.

[10] Blackstone hated anything *Gothic*. He called his labour as that of 'a Gothic castle fitted up for modern inhabitants'.

[11] Latin edition 1684, first English translation 1727.

[12] Haakonssen (1978, p. 484); but Hume talks about the laws of nature, not about natural law.

contemporaries were unaware that they lived on the threshold of a century of tremendous changes that would eventually transform the entire world.

The push towards modernity started in the Middle Ages, and the Dutch Republic in the seventeenth century was an important stage towards the Industrial Revolution, which happened in the England of the eighteenth century. Perhaps Smith and Hume had an inkling of things to come, but if so they shut their eyes for the changes. They believed in established government whether in Britain or in France. The irony is that if we maintain that Hume and Smith slavishly adopted the natural jurisprudence of Pufendorf and particularly its foundation in natural law as the will of God, we miss the important point that in *both* cases natural jurisprudence meant the conventional wisdom in jurisprudence and morality and that there was a remarkable consensus about what this conventional wisdom was.

3 Pufendorf's Influence

If Pufendorf did not dictate the terms of natural jurisprudence to Hume and Smith, what is it that made him special among his colleagues? I think it is his style of writing and thinking. Karl-Heinz Schmidt quotes a number of modern critics who are charmed by Pufendorf's insistence that a rational discourse in public life will lead to social harmony and sensible measures taken by the State (Schmidt 2020). So Pufendorf even influenced modern economists, but I am slightly puzzled by the insistence on social harmony, because reading Pufendorf that way sounds slightly anachronistic.

Then on the way back home from the conference, my wife showed me a report in a newspaper on Habermas who had just celebrated his birthday at a ripe old age. That is it, I thought! Habermas is the true descendant of Pufendorf. Habermas' plea for a rational discourse as a necessary element in a sane public opinion resembles Pufendorf's message, if in a modern version. Habermas writes in his *Strukturwandel der Öffentlichkeit*:

> Demgegenüber [dealing with the problem of the fusion of informal and formal public opinion] kann sich unter Bedingungen sozialstaatlicher Massendemokratie der Kommunikationszusammenhang eines *Publikums* nur in der Weise herstellen, dass der förmlich kurzgeschlossene Kreislauf der ‚quasi-öffentlichen' Meinung mit dem informellen Bereich der bisher nicht-öffentlichen Meinungen durch eine in organisationsinternen Öffentlichkeiten entfachte kritische Publizität vermittelt wird. (Habermas, 1990, 359)[13]

And the interface in the case of formal and informal public opinion is a rational discourse.

Now Pufendorf did not write under the conditions of mass democracy, but the notion of a rational discourse has an enduring quality which transcends time. Pufendorf had the luck that Jean Barbeyrac translated the two works which concern

[13] At least in this book, Habermas seems to be innocent of Pufendorf's existence.

us from Latin into French, the lingua franca of the moment, namely his *De Jure Naturae et Gentium Libri Octo* (1673) and *De Officio Hominis et Civis juxta Legem Naturalem Libri Duo*.[14] Barbeyrac's text of *De Officio* was a direct hit and stayed on the reading list of the educated public till the end of the eighteenth century.

Pufendorf's *Le Droit de la Nature* was popular for another reason. Horst Denzel gives an apt description of the character of Pufendorf's works. He writes:

> Wenn deshalb Pufendorf die Frage untersucht, was dem Menschen natürlich ist und was nicht, dann setzt er erwachsene und sich der Vernunft wohl bedienende Menschen voraus. Die menschliche Natur erschöpft sich nicht in der blossen Selbsterhaltung, sondern es geht ihr auch um Selbstachtung, um das Bewusstsein der Würde des Menschen.

And:

> Menschliche Natur in ihrer breiten Entfaltungsskala von der Armseligkeit des gerade geborenen Menschen bis zur Würde des in der Gemeinschaft sittlich Handelnden umfasst eine anfängliche Kulturlosigkeit und eine natürliche Entwicklung zur Kultur. (Denzel 1972, 98)

Pufendorf's broadmindedness, politically and religiously, made his text a tract for generations to come; for Hume and Smith who started to write 70 years later, it was an ideal introduction to the problem of the enlightenment of man. Usually, John Locke is considered to be the gatekeeper of the Enlightenment. Pufendorf keeps him company. He preaches religious toleration and his advice to governments is to be mild but strict.

Hobbes' *Leviathan*, published for the first time in 1651, acted as a bombshell in the British republic of letters. Hobbes' message was that individuals compete with each other, and that without a strong government and strict rules of law they are incapable of maintaining the public peace. A famous sentence reads:

> To this warre of every man against every man, this also is consequent; that nothing can be Unjust. The notions of Right and Wrong, Justice and Injustice haved there no place. Where there is no common Power, there is no Law: where no Law, no Injustice. Force and Fraud, are in warre the two Cardinall vertues. (Hobbes, 1965, 66)[15]

So there cannot be natural law as the expression of God's will.

Hutcheson reacted to Hobbes by giving man a unique moral sense which enables him to find the first direction in moral rulings. Hume and Smith took Hutcheson's thought as a lead for their own moral theories. Hutcheson accused Pufendorf of being a Hobbist (Hutcheson, 2006, 202), because the German started his enquiry with the 'amour propre' of individuals. It was the instinct of self-preservation and self-assertion which was the beginning of the development of civil society and the state.

---

[14] I used Barbeyrac's translation of *De Jure Naturae* and Michael Silverthorne's English translation: Pufendorf 1991) *On the Duty of Man and Citizen*.

[15] It is still debatable whether Hobbes meant to say that human beings are too selfish to want to reach an agreement with their fellows or that the competitive situation in which they live makes them incapable to keep the peace without the help of the State.

Yet Pufendorf was not a Hobbist. According to Hobbes, human groups had the sense to accept a higher authority, because their stateless situation was unsafe. Pufendorf argued that natural law as the expression of God's will taught mankind how to make equitable laws in this way promoting the development of civilization. The gifts of reason made man realize that he needed laws to protect his property, his family and to keep the peace in general.

Pufendorf was not at all alarmed by Hobbes' vision on man. He took him as an authority with whom he agreed and disagreed. More important to him was Grotius who in *On the Law of War and Peace* quoted an impressive array of authorities to describe, in his case, the evolution of international law. Pufendorf was a lawyer who took the *Juristenrecht* as his lead. This meant that jurists were the prime movers in the evolution of society's rules. What may have made Pufendorf's *De Jure Naturae* attractive to Smith and Hume was that Pufendorf not only addressed authorities but also made an appeal to the reason of ordinary citizens to obey the laws of the country on a voluntary basis.

Pufendorf could not provide the foundation for Hume and Smith's economic theories, but he made the political order, in which these theories should function palatable.

4 Hume and Smith's Politics

Hume planned a treatise in five books – the last two being on the arts and on politics – and executed only three leaving out politics and the arts. Adam Smith also declared that he would publish a book on politics, but he destroyed what he had already written when he stopped writing. The absence of these books raises the speculation that not being able to combine their economic analysis with their political outlook they refrained from writing on politics. The solution of this problem, I think, is much simpler: both were quite satisfied with the political order they met in life, and as I have argued elsewhere, as philosophers they were not the revolutionaries nineteenth-century commentators assumed they were (Holthoon, 2017). Donald Winch pointed out in a beautiful essay that if we try to turn Adam Smith into a nineteenth-century liberal, we miss the point of his political message (Winch, 1978, 70). There is no straight line running from Locke via Smith to Ricardo and Stuart Mill.

Smith's politics was Hume's politics. John Ramsay McCulloch tells the story that at Balliol, Smith's superiors 'entered his apartment without his being aware, and unluckily found him engaged in reading Hume's *Treatise of Human Nature*. The objectionable work was, of course, seized; the young philosopher being at the same time severely reprimanded' (Ross 1995, 77). They did not stop Smith reading Hume. Raphael and MacFie write in their *Introduction* to Smith's *Theory of Moral Sentiments* (TMS):

> Hume had the greatest influence on the formation of Smith's ethical theory. Smith rejects or transforms Hume's ideas far more often than he follows them, but his own views would have been markedly different if he had not been stimulated to disagreement with Hume. (Smith 1976a, 10)

And indeed, it is through reading Hume's Treatise that Smith came to develop his own moral theory. Moral theories became important for developing their economic analyses. I will deal with the problem how their moral theories shaped their economics in the next section. As to their politics proper we have Hume's essays first of all on the subject. Apparently, these move in two opposite directions, but I will try to show that these two strains can be reconciled within a view that takes the reality of the Glorious Revolution as a – rather regrettable – fact of life, because it led to an unstable political state of affairs. Hume's essays are an attempt to suggest ways for minimizing the risks. The first direction represents the essays Hume wrote on parliamentary politics. About the constitutional settlement since 1688, he was in two minds. On the one hand, it had established 'if not the best system of government, at least the most entire system of liberty that ever was known amongst mankind' (Hume 1983, vol. 6, 531); on the other hand, the settlement was inherently unstable. And in the opening essay '*That Politics May Be Reduced to a Science*' (1741), he urged all parties concerned to be moderate in their aims and agitation (Hume 1987, 7).

The spirit of faction was always a spoiler in politics, but there was also a more structural element which made the system unbalanced. If power is based on property, the House of Commons, representing the largest sum of property in the country, by interfering in the affairs of the executive could always force it to follow its directives. If it would do so, monarchy would inevitably become a full-scale republic. And this would not be the end of the affair. For the spirit of faction would create chaos and turn the republic into an absolute monarchy. 'Absolute monarchy, therefore, is the easiest death, the true *Euthanasia* of the British constitution' (Hume 1987, 7). So next to the lesson of moderation, Hume's counsel to the House of Commons was not to interfere with the business of government. Hume more than Montesquieu was the advocate of the separation of powers, and Hume wanted that separation of powers to defend the *status quo*. His goal was a *euthanasia* of the spirit of faction in parliament.[16]

His second direction is demonstrated by his essay '*Idea of a Perfect Commonwealth*' (1752). Using Harrington's *Oceana* as a model, he sketches the conditions for a stable republic (Holthoon 2013, 141ff.). Many critics of Hume have been asking themselves what Hume meant by this piece. The key to it, I think, may be found in one of the essays I have already discussed. In 'Of the Independence of Parliament' (1741), he writes that the stability of government can be assured:

---

[16]Montesquieu did not invent the *trias politica*. He distinguished two sources of authority: the legislative shared by the people and the nobility and the executive which was the prerogative of the monarch. In *De la Constitution d'Angleterre*, book 11, chap. 6 of *De l'Esprit des Lois*, he remarked that those two powers could block any decision or 'elles seront forcées d'aller de concert' (Montesquieu 1964, p. 589).

> In pure republics, where the authority is distributed among several assemblies or senates, the checks and controuls are more regular in their operation; because the members of such numerous assemblies may be presumed to be always nearly equal in capacity and virtue; and it is only their number, riches or authority, which enter into consideration. (Hume 1987, 46)

And so in '*Idea of a Perfect Commonwealth*', he uses Harrington's utopian scheme to suggest a rigorous dispersion of the power of the House of Commons by relegating its legislative authority to councils of the counties.

Hume knew of course that such a utopian scheme was not feasible in the British case, but it shows how concerned he was about the power of the House of Commons as a source of instability and it also illustrates how charmed he was by the constitutional arrangement in the Dutch Republic.[17] So while developing a different strain of thought in '*Idea of a Perfect Commonwealth*', it also expresses his concern with the instability of the settlement of 1688. A decentralized legislative would never be able to make the claim to power as the House of Commons could.

Before we congratulate Hume for his liberal attitude towards the American colonists, we should note that his reaction was part of his critical attitude towards the emerging British Empire. That emergence created according to him unnecessary political and financial complications. Hume was an early example of what at the end of the nineteenth century was called 'a little islander'.

Was Hume becoming a Tory at the end of his life? His letters to William Strahan in the sixties and seventies, in which he scolded the government for lack of firmness in relation to the Wilkes' riots, may suggest this. I do not think this label makes sense. Hume's worries were part of his science of politics, not the reaction of a partisan.

Adam Smith joined Hume in being a little islander. His reaction was that if the Americans did not want to contribute to the defence of the Empire, they should indeed leave and his reaction to the French revolution in 1790, the year he died, was as adverse as that of Edmund Burke, if more moderately expressed.[18] Smith spoke for both Hume and himself when he counselled caution in revolutionary times.

The support of the established government seems evidently the best expedient for maintaining the safe, respectable and happy condition of our fellow citizens; when we see that this government actually maintains them in that situation … [But when discontent and disorder makes it unable to maintain order] In such cases, however, it often requires, perhaps, the highest effort of political wisdom to determine when a real patriot ought to support and endeavour to re-establish the authority of the old system, and when he ought to give way to the more daring, but often dangerous spirit of innovation (Smith 1976a, 231–232).

Sometimes, Hume and Smith had an intimation of the momentous change which the next century would bring, and though they were realistic enough to accept reforms under duress, they did not like what they saw.

---

[17] This was already in 1752 the wrong example. The Dutch Republic at that time was already anything but stable and its government almost collapsed on the eve of the French Revolution.

[18] In *Theory of Moral Sentiments*, he criticized 'the spirit of system', TMS,VI, ii, 2, 13, 232.

5 Hume and the Development of His Moral Philosophy

How did Hume and Smith travel the road from moral philosophy to economics? A couple of sentences from Hume's essay 'Of the Refinement in the Arts' may serve as a motto to Hume's voyage. Hume writes:

> The more these refined arts advance, the more sociable men become: nor is it possible, that, when enriched with science, and possessed of a fund of conversation, they should be contented to remain in solitude, or live with their fellow-citizens in that distant manner, which is peculiar to ignorant and barbarous nations.

And

> Thus *industry, knowledge*, and *humanity*, are linked together by an indissoluble chain, and are found, from experience as well as reason, to be peculiar to the more polished, and, what are commonly denominated, the more luxurious ages. (Hume 1987, 271)

The original title of the essay was 'Of Luxury', and in it Hume criticizes the notion that luxury always is a source of corruption. On the contrary, the activity to make nice and useful things is a source of civilization and it is an expression of the joy of working and communicating with others. Hume resolutely takes his stand against the doctrine that labour is a form of divine punishment, because Adam and Eve disobeyed God in the Garden of Eden. That work is fun is the motto which links Hume's moral philosophy to his view on the economic activities of human beings.

The *Treatise* is the chronicle of Hume's effort to develop his moral philosophy. Hume's first step is to argue that there are no fixed metaphysical principles we can rely on to find truth. Truth must come from experience and what we find in the name of truth can only be a probable and not a fixed proposition. In book two, Hume then presents a theory of passions which makes it possible to develop a moral economy by which we create a win–win situation. Central at this stage in Hume's moral philosophy is that 'very powerful principle' of sympathy that 'produces our sentiment of morals in all the artificial virtues' (Hume 1978, III, 3, I, 577–578).[19] Sympathy is an associative principle and Hume borrowed the metaphor of the mirror from Locke to indicate that when we look in a mirror we can learn from our own reaction how others would react. We experience what actions of others please us and we recognize what of our actions pleases them. So by the association of passions, we are able to build a moral economy which suits both parties (Hume 1978, II, 2, v, 365).

Yet in EPM, sympathy loses its status as a powerful associative principle. Hume replaces it with Horace's principle of *utile/dulce*: what pleases us is useful and what is useful pleases us (Holthoon, 2007, 139ff.). At first sight, the change from sympathy to utility is merely cosmetic. Hume uses utility as an agreeable quality already in his *Treatise*, and we might argue that the revision was part of Hume's effort to simplify his argument, and though this was certainly one of his objectives in rewriting the *Treatise*, for two reasons the changeover from sympathy to utility is not

[19] Artificial virtues are those we acquire by convention.

merely cosmetic (Hume 1978, III, 3, I, 591).[20] Hume's statement on moral philosophy in the *Treatise* was personal and introspective. His was a soliloquy in which he looked into his own soul and reported what he saw. In EPM he preached directly to his public. The second important shift in his moral philosophy was that he no longer had a monitoring mechanism asking what is useful and agreeable. He left that question for the market of moral economy to decide.

EPM is important for another reason. Hume now stated that the burning problem of self-love is irrelevant, because the moral economy makes it possible to transcend self- and other-regarding motives. The fact that he solved the problem of self-love in morality was a great achievement. His definition of sympathy as an associative principle and his solution of the problem of self-love were an important legacy for Adam Smith.

6 Adam Smith and His Two Models

Hume in the final version of his moral philosophy eliminated introspection as a constituent in reaching moral judgements and relied on social intercourse to reach viable and satisfactory results in human transactions. Adam Smith's trajectory of his moral philosophy pointed in the opposite direction. It is fascinating to read Smith's theory of the impartial spectator and see that he closely followed the associational patterns which Hume developed in his *Treatise*.[21] In contrast with Hume, Smith paid great weight to the impartiality of the spectator. Looking at the actions of his fellow beings, the spectator tries to establish what is fair in their transactions and what is not. In the sixth edition of TMS (1790), he goes a step further. He now writes:

> The jurisdiction of the man without, is founded altogether in the desire of actual praise, and in the aversion to actual blame. The jurisdiction of the man within, is founded altogether in the desire of praise-worthiness, and in the aversion to blame worthiness; in the desire of possessing those qualities, and performing those actions, which we love and admire in other people; and in the dread of possessing those qualities, and performing those actions, which we hate and despise in other people. (Smith 1976a, II, 2, 32, 130–131)

Impartiality was internalized. To reach impartiality, we have to consult our conscience and apply our standards first of all to ourselves, before we do so to others.

The introspective character of Smith's moral judgement is remarkable. In a note attached to the second edition of TMS (1761), he responded to Hume's criticism in a letter of 28 July 1759. Hume had written:

> I wish you had more particularly and fully prov'd, that all kinds of Sympathy are necessarily Agreeable. This is the hinge of your system … Now it would appear that there is a disagreeable Sympathy as well as an agreeable.

[20] On utility and the agreeable.

[21] See the diagrams in my introduction of part two in my translation *Traktaat over de Menselijke Natuur* (2007, 328–329).

Smith responded:

> I answer, that in the sentiment of approbation there are two things to be taken notice of; first, the sympathetic passion of the spectator; and, secondly, the emotion which arises from his observing the perfect coincidence between this sympathetic passion in himself, and the original passion in the person principally concerned. This last emotion, in which the sentiment of approbation properly consists, is always agreeable and delightful. The other may be agreeable or disagreeable, according to the nature of the original passion, whose features it must always, in some measure, retain. (Smith 1976a, I, iii, 9, 46)[22]

What does this answer mean? As I understand this convoluted text, the understanding of the passion of the other, even when it strikes us as being disagreeable in the first instance, is always agreeable, because we can understand the motives involved. Adam Smith's answer is that of a philosopher rather than a practical politician. He called Hume's use of utile as an explanatory principle an 'afterthought', but as WN shows, he needed utility as an afterthought to get practical results.

It is the great merit of Andrew Skinner's work on Adam Smith that according to him the Scot saw the importance of adopting a system of analysis – a model – that gave the most plausible explanation of how certain facts stick together, while at the same time emphasizing that it only functions *as if* it is the truth. Skinner discusses Smith's early essay on the history of astronomy in which Smith explores the psychological assumptions for adopting a model (Skinner, 1979, 17). An adequate explanation of reality satisfies the imagination. The model does not only explain, but – following Newton – it explains what it can explain. The ambition to provide the definitive explanation is a hopeless undertaking.

Smith in his explanation of social reality used two models: (1) the model of the impartial spectator and (2) the model of the invisible hand, and these two models together were Smith's explanation of how social reality works. The impartial spectator prepares the mind for a just appraisal of human conduct, and the invisible hand guarantees equilibrium as the outcome of human transactions to ensure the situation where impartial decisions can be reached. Charles Griswold in stressing the unity of TMS and WN writes:

> By subordinating political economy to natural jurisprudence – and there are numerous references in *The Wealth of Nations* to justice – the schema also indicates that the study of the nature and causes of the wealth of nations is a subset of the larger enterprise of the study of government, law, and natural justice, not a replacement for that study. (Griswold 1999, 32)

So it seems that Hont's view that natural jurisprudence is the foundation of Smith's economic theory is vindicated, but as I indicated before we must be careful in our interpretation of this conclusion. Haakonssen has studied Smith's theory of justice in detail, and this is what he writes about the consequences Smith drew for the practice of politics. He quotes from WN:

---

[22] The text of Hume's letter is given in note 2; Smith's answer appears in note b at the bottom of the page. Smith has a point in that you cannot reduce a moral judgement to a utilitarian calculus and the esteem of what is good is embedded in the soul, but I do not think that Hume would deny this; however, he would leave it to every individual in the course of his transactions to decide what is good and proper, while Smith appealed to a universal principle housed in all human beings.

> To expect, indeed, that the freedom of trade should ever be entirely restored in Great Britain, is as absurd as to expect that an Oceana or Utopia should ever be established in it. (Smith 1976b vol.1, IV, ii, 43, 471)

And Haakonssen goes on:

> Smith's attitude to utopian perfectionism is clearly reflected in his view of what ought to be the priorities of a sovereign: first, defence against foreign enemies; secondly, 'an exact administration of justice'; and thirdly, 'the duty of erecting and maintaining certain publick works and certain publick institutions, which it can never be for the interest of any individual, or small numbers of individuals to erect or maintain. (Haakonssen 1981, 93)[23]

Smith accepted a social order, not very different from what Pufendorf had in mind, a view which Hume would heartily have endorsed. In short, as to politics and public administration, Smith and Hume accepted the practical application of natural jurisprudence to their society as Pufendorf had done so 70 years earlier. However, the point of *both* TMS and WN was to explore the economic world where these rules apply only indirectly and where economic activities engender no *new* rules. In retrospect, the way they looked on economic life is shocking, and at the same time it presents an important insight in the nature of economic transactions. Eighteenth-century Britain produced no rules to protect the safety of labourers, no laws to safeguard the environment, let alone social legislation to protect children at work. Children worked under dismal conditions in mines and cotton mills, and Robert Owen, who took care of his workers, was a rare exception. Both Hume and Smith accepted the conditions that the Industrial Revolution created, as a fact of life and one can only conclude that the impartial spectator was less than impartial in these cases. On the other hand, the invisible hand was and still is the best recipe for creating balance and growth in the economy. When today we start to protest against the working of the invisible hand, it is because it works so effectively, at least on the short run.

7 Natural Law and Human Rights

So Smith accepted natural jurisprudence as the canon of political philosophy and took it for granted when he started to develop his moral philosophy and his economic theory. Natural jurisprudence was the starting point for a new and exciting exploration. Smith and Hume designed a mechanism for the idea which we today call a win–win situation. If economic actors negotiate in the proper way under the proper circumstances, all parties benefit from the transactions undertaken.

The remarkable thing is that both Pufendorf and the two Scots expected that the world socially and politically would not change dramatically, which in the case of Pufendorf is understandable, but with Hume and Smith is less so. Of all the writers of the Enlightenment, including Hume and Smith, one has the feeling that they did

[23] The quotation from WN is at vol. 2, IV, ix, 51, 687–688.

not notice that they were resting on the slope of a volcano, unaware that it might erupt at any moment. These two were witnessing the beginnings of the Industrial Revolution, but they had no idea of the social impact it would cause. Only once Hume lost his good humour and lashed out at the capitalists:

> These are men, who have no connexions with the state, who can enjoy their revenue in any part of the globe in which they chuse to reside, who will naturally bury themselves in the capital or in great cities, and who will sink into the lethargy of a stupid and pampered luxury, without spirit, ambition, or enjoyment. Adieu to all ideas of nobility, gentry, and family. (Hume 1987, 358)[24]

Hume had a quick glimpse of the social impact capitalism would have on the society of orders which he cherished and then he closed the box of Pandora. Smith made a sombre assessment of the effects of the division of labour on the individual labourer (Smith 1976b, vol. 2, V, I, f, 50, 781–782). This turned the working man into a brute and automaton, but Smith did not pursue the subject.

Hume and Smith believed in the goal of achieving economic equilibrium, and they started the school of classical economics which pursued the same goal. Economic growth was seen as an accidental benefit of an optimal circulation of goods and services, and it is remarkable that this equilibrium analysis persisted long after it had become clear that economic growth had become the force for change. There was a moment in history, from 1950 onwards, that economic growth became a recipe for social politics. The recipe was that a touch of inflation would ensure full employment. Many politicians still advocate economic growth as a social policy, because the recipe is the easiest way to satisfy their voters, but those who look further have come to regard economic growth as a threat. It is exhausting the world's resources and causes climate change. We can blame the politicians for not wanting to see this threat, we cannot blame Hume and Smith of course, but we can only conclude that they were unaware that the Industrial Revolution would destroy the world they cherished and took for granted.

Pufendorf was not watching a booming world like in eighteenth-century Britain. His world was just on its way to recovery. His illusion was a different one from that of Hume and Smith. He was one who believed in *Juristenrecht.* In the course of Western history, lawyers knew what law was. However, in the future it would be rulers and citizens who would decide what rights and duties were and how laws could be framed to suit them. In the cauldron of medieval thought, there was according to Gierke room for the notion of personal right, but those rights were still part of a corporatist vision on life (Gierke 1958, 37ff.). The Reformation changed this vision radically, because according to Luther and Calvin only a personal belief in God would bring salvation. The emphasis on the individual person appeared in the Protestant interpretation of natural law. Grotius is reputed to be the first lawyer who made the connection between natural jurisprudence and personal rights and after Pufendorf Vettel and Burlamaqui, two prominent lawyers who wrote about natural

[24]To be fair, Hume referred to stockholders, not entrepreneurs, but he was undoubtedly wise enough to see the connection between the two.

jurisprudence in the eighteenth century, made the same connection as Grotius. In fact, I think that Pufendorf was rather the exception in the protestant camp, because he stuck to a medieval conception that made natural jurisprudence the domain of lawyers.[25]

The doctrine of popular sovereignty borrowed the notion of sovereignty from Jean Bodin. The sovereign or sovereign institution is above the law and makes the final decisions on any issue. In a democracy, this means in practice that issues are settled by a majority vote. In principle, every voter is his own sovereign and that shows in the powerful notion of human rights. Unfortunately human rights have become highlighted because governments and terrorist groups are committing acts that we, the silent community, consider unjust and atrocious, but human rights as a concept also operates in a different and more interesting way. The clarion call for individual rights came with the famous sentence which Jefferson wrote down in the American *Declaration of Independence:*

> We hold these truths to be self-evident, that all men are created equal; that they are endowed by their Creator with certain unalienable rights; that among these are life liberty, and the pursuit of happiness.

According to Jefferson, we are born with certain fundamental rights, and as 'the pursuit of happiness' demonstrates these rights can be quite extensively formulated. With the rise of the popularity of the notion of human rights, the authority of natural law as a concept went down. In the best case, human rights in the public domain depend on the 'will of the people' and not on the will of God.

The main conclusion which I draw from my exercise is that when we talk of influence, we should not only study a writer at work, but take the context in which he worked and communicated into consideration. If we do so in the case of Pufendorf, Hume and Adam Smith, we should conclude that they have more in common than we have with them. Their world and their assumptions have disappeared, and if we want to understand what they were talking about we must reconstruct their past.

---

[25] Under the influence of the Idealist philosophy in nineteenth-century Germany, natural jurisprudence as a paradigm declined, but the decline was not a straightforward affair. Apart from those who stuck to the old paradigm, there were those, particularly jurists, who kept open a lifeline to natural jurisprudence. (In fact, until recently law students in the Netherlands had to take a course in Roman law during their first year.) Friedrich Carl von Savigny (1779–1867) is an interesting case in this context. His work is difficult to grasp. (Rückert1984, 119). Known as an authority on Roman law, he published the Idealist manifest *Vom Beruf unserer Zeit für Gesetzgebung und Rechtswissenschaft* (1814). In it he argued that rights and laws were not the product of an abstract doctrine, but spontaneously sprung from the *Volksgeist*. For a conservative as Savigny, this created a dilemma. Savigny was against the democracy of one man one vote. So how could he determine the proper right and the proper law? He found his answer in Roman law which according to his own admission was linked to natural law. He did not use it in the same way as Pufendorf, because he did not believe in the practical application of natural law as Pufendorf did. As a scholar, he contemplated the quality of Roman jurisprudence and derived from his study the measure of good and bad while judging modern legislation. So Savigny like Pufendorf believed in *Juristenrecht*. Jurists should be the judge of jurisprudence and legislation.

The conference at which I presented my essay was about Pufendorf, not on the two Scots. So it is only fair to conclude that in one respect Pufendorf's philosophy is still very much alive. His notion of a rational discourse transcends time and circumstance. Its functioning in a democracy is a guarantee for a healthy public life.

References

Berman H., Law and Revolution, The Formation of the Western Legal Tradition, (Cambridge Mass. 1985: Harvard University Press)
Blackstone W., The Student Blackstone: Commentaries on the Laws of England, abridged and adapted to the Present State of the Law, (London 1890: Rea & Taine), R. Ker ed.
Cumberland R. Treatise of the Law of Nature, (Latin ed. 1684, Engl. Transl. 1727)
Denzel H., Moralphilosophie und Naturrecht bei Samuel Pufendorf, (Munich 1972: Beck)
Moore J and M. Silverthorne eds, Mankind, Indianapolis 2006: Liberty Fund
Gibbon E.. The History of the Decline and Fall of the Roman Empire, London 1995: Penguin, (ed. D. Wormersley)
Gierke O., Political Theories of the Middle Age, (Boston 1958: Beacon) F.W. Maitland transl.
Griswold C. Jr., Adam Smith and the Virtues of Enlightenment, (Cambridge 1999: Cambridge University Press),
Haakonssen K., The Science of a Legislator, the Natural Jurisprudence of David Hume and Adam Smith, Cambridge 1981: Cambridge University Press
Habermas J., Strukturwandel der Öffentlichkeit, Frankfurt a.M. 1990: Suhrkamp
Hobbes Th., Leviathan, London 1965: Everyman Library
Holthoon F.L. van, 'Spinoza and Hume, Two Different Trajectories', European Journal 2000, (June 2011), XII
Holthoon F.L. van, A Dialogue on David Humeon his Revision of A Treatise of Human Nature, Thirteenth Evening 'From Sympathy to Utility', Amsterdam 2007: Boom
Holthoon F.L. van, Hume, Madison, and the Transition of Republicanism, in David Hume, a Tercentenary Tribute, St. Tweyman ed., Ann Arbor 2013: Caravan
Holthoon F.L. van, A Case for the Enlightenment, Ten Essays, Berlin 2017: Logos
Hont I., 'The Language of Sociability and Commerce: Samuel Pufendorf and the Theory of the Four Stages', Jealousy of Trade, Cambridge Mass. 2005: Belknap Press
Hume D., 'That Politics may be Reduced to a Science', Essays Moral, Political an Literary, (1741), Indianapolis 1987: LibertyClassics
Hume D., A Treatise of Human Nature, (Oxford 1978: Clarendon Press), P.H. Nidditch ed.
Hume D., The History of England, (Indianapolis 1983: LibertyClassics) 6 vols
Hutcheson F., 'On the Natural Sociability of Mankind', Logic, Metaphysics, and the Natural Sociability of Mankind, (Indianapolis 2006: Liberty Fund), J. Moore and M. Silverthorne
Montesquieu Ch. de, De l'Esprit des Lois, Paris 1964: du Seuil
Pufendorf S., Le Droit de la Nature et des Gens ou Système Général des Principes les Plus importans de la Morale, de la Jurisprudence et de la Politique, Amsterdam 1718: Pier de Coup, J. Barbeyrac transl.
Pufendorf S., On the Duty of Man and Citizen, Cambridge 1991: Cambridge University Press, J. Tully ed., M. Silverthorne transl.
Ross I.S., The Life of Adam Smith, Oxford 1995: Clarendon Press
Robertson J., 'In Memory of Istvan Hont, 1947-2012', Cambridge Humanities Review, 4, 2013, 20–21
Rückert J Idealismus, Jurisprudenz und Politik bei Friedrich Carl von Savigny, Ebelsbach 1984: Gremer

Saether A (2020) Pufendorf and his importance for the European Enlightenment in general, in this volume
Schmidt K-H (2020), How to approach Samuel Pufendorf's economic ideas, in this volume
Schumpeter J (1954) History of Economic Analysis Allen & Unwin London Boston Sidney
Skol M., 'Blackstone and Bentham on the Law of Marriage', Blackstone and his Commentaries, Biography, Law, History, Portland OR. 2010: Hart, W. Prest ed.
Skinner A., 'Science and the Role of the Imagination', A System of Social Science, Papers Relating to Adam Smith, Oxford 1979: Clarendon Press
Smith A., The Theory of Moral Sentiments (Oxford 1976a: Clarendon Press), D.D. Raphael & A.L. Macfie eds.
Smith A., An Inquiry into the Nature and Causes of the Wealth of Nations, Oxford 1976b: Clarendon, R. Campbell e.o., 2 vols.
Winch D., Adam Smith's Politics, an Essay in Historiography Revision, Cambridge 1978: Cambridge University Press

Pufendorf and His Importance for the Development of Economics as a Science

Arild Sæther

Abstract Pufendorf's natural law comprises ethics, jurisprudence, society and political economy. His political economy embraces theories of human behaviour, private property and the four stages, value and money, foundation of states and council decisions and finally division of state powers and principles of taxation. His political economy was dispersed across Europe and North America.

John Locke was the first to extensively use Pufendorf's political economy when he developed his own economic theories. The French philosophers of the Enlightenment were all in debt to Pufendorf. The magistrate Pierre De Boisguilbert, the legal and political theorist Jean-Jacques Burlamaqui, the editor Denis Diderot, the translator Jean Barbeyrac, the great philosopher Charles-Louis Montesquieu, the foremost political thinker Jean-Jacques Rousseau and the Physiocratic model builders used Pufendorf's works lengthily when they wrote and advanced their own ideas about political economy.

Gershom Carmichael introduced natural law to Scotland when he taught at the University of Glasgow in the early eighteenth century. His successor Francis Hutcheson continued his practice and used Pufendorf's works when he wrote on political economy.

As Hutcheson's student Adam Smith became familiar with Pufendorf's ideas of political economy, he used these ideas extensively when he held his lectures on jurisprudence at University of Glasgow and when he wrote *The Theory of Moral Sentiment* and *The Wealth of Nations*. Pufendorf's position in the history of economic thought should therefore be well established.

Paper presented at the 34th Heilbronn Symposium in Economics and the Social Sciences. "*After 325 Years: Samuel Pufendorf's Work Reconsidered*. June 20 – 22, 2019, Heilbronn.
This presentation builds extensively on Sæther (2017a, b)

A. Sæther (✉)
Agder Academy of Sciences and Letters, Kristiansand, Norway
e-mail: arild@saether.no

J. G. Backhaus et al. (eds.), *Samuel Pufendorf and the Emergence of Economics as a Social Science*, The European Heritage in Economics and the Social Sciences 24, https://doi.org/10.1007/978-3-030-49791-0_4

Keywords Pufendorf on political economy · Human behaviour · Private property · Value and price · Money and trade · Council decisions · Principles of taxation

JEL Codes B 10, B 13, B 31, B40, D 10, D40, D42, D46, N01, K11, K12, K40

1 Pufendorf on Political Economy

In his earliest natural law work, *Elementorum Jurisprudentiae Universalis* from 1660, Pufendorf (1931) used the reformed Euclidean Aristotelian geometrical approach he had been taught by his mentor at University of Jena, Professor Eberhard Weigel. This work is arranged with twenty-one definitions, two axioms and five observations. In his main work, *De Jure Naturae et Gentium* DJNG from 1672, Pufendorf (1933) abandoned this method and substantiated his opinions, his arguments and the truths he claims to have discovered by numerous quotations, just as Grotius and others of his predecessors had done. Four hundred authors are listed in the *Index of Authors Cited* in the 1688 edition. When he discusses particular issues, or argues for certain opinions, he frequently quotes and uses the views of famous scholars in support of and to give weight to his own views.

1.1 Economic Doctrines

Pufendorf's natural law includes ethics, jurisprudence and political economy. His doctrines of political economy embrace theories of human behaviour, private property and the four stages, value and money, foundation of states and council decisions and finally division of state powers and principles of taxation. Although these theories are integrated into a whole, we find them in distinct parts, chapters and sections, of his works. The Table 1 below shows this.

1.2 A Theory of Human Behaviour

Pufendorf asserts that man is a moral being who has been given 'the distinctive light of intelligence' (DJNG I, i, 2, 5).[1] To understand things more accurately, man can use his intelligence. The reason why it is inappropriate that man should be endowed with a lawless liberty is drawn from his revolutionary principle of the natural condition of human nature, the Dignity of Man's Nature (DJNG II, I, 5, 148). He asserts

[1] DJNG Book I, Ch. I, Section 2, Page 5.

Table 1 Political economy in Pufendorf's natural law works

Topics/books	Elementorum Juris-prudentiae Universalis	De Jure Naturae et Gentium, DJNG	De Officio Hominis et Civis
Theory of Human Behaviour	Book I. Def I, III. Book II. Obs. I, II, III, IV.	Book I, i–iv. Book II, i–iv. Book III, i–ii.	Book I. Ch. 4–7.
Theory of Property & Four-Stage Theory	Book I. Def. V.	Book IV, iii–v. Book V, v.	Book I. Ch.12 and 13.
Theory of Value and Money	Book I. Def. X.	Book V, i, iii, v, vii, viii.	Book I. Ch. 14 and 15.
Foundation of States and Councils	Book II. Obs. V.	Book VII, i–ii.	Book II. Ch. 5–10.
Division of State Powers and Taxation		Book VII, iv–v. Book VIII, iv–v. Book V, x.	Book II. Ch. 11 and 12.

Source: Sæther (2017a, 39)

that man had an internal director or mediator that could evaluate a situation and help man to make the right decision. Furthermore, the natural state of man is to live in peace, and the law of nature can be deduced from the reasoning of man himself. Man's ability to distinguish between right and wrong is not innate, contrary to what both the Catholic and the Protestant church maintained. This ability is found in the condition of man, together with the driving forces, or attributes, behind human action. Pufendorf claims that self-interest is the strongest driving force (DJNG II, iii, 14, 205–7). In addition, man is born to cooperate with other men; therefore, he has another driving force; he must be sociable. He stresses that this sociability must be cultivated. Additionally, he discusses what today are called externalities and the discounted value of an incurred damage or a gain (DJNG III, i, 3, 315–16).

1.3 Private Property and the Four Stages

Pufendorf uses the human attributes of self-interest and sociability with its dictates of reason, as the basis. Private property is developed from a stage where everything was held in common, things were not yet assigned to a person (DJNG IV, iv, 2, 533). It assumes an agreement among men, whether this agreement is just tacitly understood, or clearly expressed (DJNG IV, iv, 4, 536). The process in which private property is developed is genuinely historical, and he uses his four-stage theory. It was progressively introduced, when men under the pressure of a growing population and depleted natural resources moved from one stage of economic development to the next, a stage of gathering or hunting, a stage of herding, a stage of agriculture and finally a commercial society (DJNG IV, iv, 11, 550 – V, i, 11, 690).

1.4 Value, Money and Trade

With private ownership in a commercial society, some people had goods and services they did not need, and at the same time, they wanted to acquire goods that were in other people's possession. Goods and services therefore had to be exchanged and it gives rise to prices, the introduction of money and trade, and the growth of civilization (DJNG V, i, 1, 675). Such a society where all individuals attempt to satisfy their own needs and thereby satisfy the need of others is a cornerstone of Pufendorf's doctrines (DJNG V, i, 4, 676).

The market price is determined by what today would be called the interactions of demand and supply. Shifts in demand and supply change the price. The human motives that determine demand are discussed in some details. Pufendorf is aware of what we today call the Snob effect, the Bandwagon effect and conspicuous consumption. Furthermore, he discusses the cost of production, creation of scarcity and the paradox of value. He distinguishes between the market price, the natural price and the legal price. The natural price is the price that covers all the costs that occur in bringing the goods to the market. The legal price is assumed to agree with justice and equity. However, he issues a clear warning and states that in fixing legal price, gross ignorance can lead to corruption (DJNG V, i, 9, 687). Finally, he brings up for discussion the information issue.

In his theory of money, he discusses the origin of money, money and commerce, and the question of whether governments can decide the value of money. The introduction of money is therefore closely linked to the development of domestic commerce and international trade. Debasement of money is clearly against natural law (DJNG V, i, 11–15). It is only in the highest need that a state can change the value of money. He presents a rudimentary quantity theory of money. Furthermore, he discusses different forms of monopolies, why monopolies in special cases can be beneficial, and why it is necessary for the state to regulate monopolies that are created by clandestine frauds and conspiracies (DJNG V, v, 7, 738–40). Finally, he discusses why a lender can charge interest, DJNG (V, vii, 8–12).

1.5 Foundation of States and Council Decisions

Pufendorf's starting point for the origin of a state is the presumption that man, by nature, loves himself more than society. Man's sociability, or inclination for society, leads to the formation of the first societies; however, these societies are not synonymous with a state. He claims that man enters a state by his free will to avoid greater evils. States are therefore established to gain security and protection from the evil or wickedness of men. A perfect state is constructed by two agreements and one decree in between (DJNG VII, ii, 7, 974–5). The first agreement that men who come together to form a state agree to apply the means suitable for that end can be called one of association. Thereafter, a decree on the form of government, monarchy, aristocracy or democracy must be passed by the majority. A second agreement is necessary between the rulers, that is, the individual or body to whom the government is trusted and the subjects. In this agreement of subjection, the rulers bind themselves to the care of common security and safety, and the ruled to give them obedience.

If the power of the state is expressed through a council composed of several men, there has to be a procedure, right from the beginning, about how to reach decisions. Pufendorf discusses several voting procedures: veto rights, unanimity versus simple majority, weighted voting, qualified majorities, equality of votes and the paradox of voting. He is fully aware of the possibility that voting agendas can be manipulated (DJNG VII, ii, 15–18, 986–992).

1.6 Division of State Powers and Principles of Taxation

Pufendorf starts out claiming that a state is understood to have one will. Since it is not possible to combine the individual wills of many people into one will, a unified will in a state can only be produced by having everyone in the state submitting their will to that of one man, or of a council, in whom the supreme sovereignty has been vested. It is the duty of the supreme sovereign, the one man or the council, to make clear and prescribe for the citizens what can be done and what should be avoided. He discusses the division of the highest power of the state, the legislative power, the punitive power, the judicial power, the power to wage war and declare peace and to accept or reject treaties, that is, the constituent power, and finally the power to levy taxes (DJNG VII, iv, 1–7). He discusses both the regular and the irregular forms of states. The emphasis is on the three regular forms of states, democracy, aristocracy and monarchy. He warns against the evils of corruption, and he discusses the comparative advantages of the different forms of states (DJNG VII, v, 22, 1052).

The business of a state cannot be carried out without expenses. The duties of the Sovereign with respect to the levy of taxes and his economic responsibilities are emphasized. Pufendorf stresses budget discipline, and he gives considerable attention to how taxes or other burdens are levied and collected on the citizens. In his principles of taxation, he discusses and evaluates different taxes (DJNG VIII, v, 5–7, 1281–86); furthermore, in some details how taxes should be collected; with least possible expenses, open and publicly posted, exaction should be monitored, collectors should not be corrupt and tax evaders should be brought to justice. Furthermore, taxes should be equal and just. He favoured proportional taxes, with no tax or minimal tax for the poor and taxes on consumption but not on necessities.

2 Dispersion of Pufendorf's Natural Law and Political Economy

Pufendorf's natural law including his doctrines of political economy were dispersed across Europe and North America. His abridged *De Officio* was translated into nine European languages and became an international 'best seller'. New editions with or without commentaries, appeared in many European countries. More than 150 editions have been found. The book was reprinted innumerable times and thousands of copies were produced and sold. His popularity and fame also led to the translations of *De Jure Naturae et Gentium* into four languages. It found a place in most state and university libraries. Pufendorf had taught natural law at the universities of Heidelberg and Lund. From this start, natural law became a compulsory subject at almost all Protestant and even at some Catholic universities. His natural law contributed to the beginning of the Enlightenment, characterized by belief in progress. This progress could be achieved through the self-reliant use of reason and, by reaction, to traditionalism, obscurantism and authoritarianism.

3 John Locke the First to Use Pufendorf's Political Economy

Locke's writings on applied economics have also been investigated by Karen Vaughn (1980) in her *John Locke Economist and Social Scientist.* She claimed that Locke was a far more sophisticated economist than most historians of thought have given him credit for and that he was an early social scientist with a consistent view of social action in both his economic and political writings. Her declared objectives in her study were therefore first to provide 'a comprehensive treatment of John Locke's position in the development of economic thought', second 'to establish the influences on his thought and his relationship to his contemporaries', and last to make 'the connection between his economic theory and his theory of political society'. In her study, the second objective is only superficially treated (Ibid, x).

Although she claims that the real influence on Lock's economic thought comes primarily from 'a combination of his reading of Aristotle, the Scholastics, and his contemporaries Grotius and Pufendorf on the one hand, and his own personal observation of economic problems on the other', there are no discussions or examples of how Locke built on any of these authors (Ibid, 18).[2] Vaughn leaves it at that and makes no investigation of Locke's use of Pufendorf in his writings on political economy.[3]

---

[2] In a chapter *John Locke Social Scientist,* Vaughn (1980, 108–109) mention that Schumpeter noted Locke's contributions to the seventeenth-century theory of natural law, 'and ranked Locke along with Hobbes, Grotius and Pufendorf, among others, as philosophers who despite their Protestantism, were in the Scholastic tradition'.

[3] Karen Vaughn (1980, 141) claims that her first professor Joseph Soudek, in a personal correspondence, contended that: 'In earlier times, it was taken for granted that the reading public, which was

Neither does Vaughn in her study make any attempt to assess the influence Locke had on later economic thought. She only mentions in passing that Adam Smith referred to Locke's essay in *The Wealth of Nations*.

Writings on political economy can be found in most of Locke's works. It certainly goes back to his *The Law of Nature* based on his Oxford lectures in the early 1660s, Locke (1954 [1662–63]) His work on what can be called purer political economy goes back to 1668, when he wrote a paper, or manuscript, on the consequences of *Lessening of Interest, Locke* (1965 [1668–1674]).[4] William Letwin in his Origin of Scientific Economics contends that he had not read any of the economic tracts that were published at the time (1963, 156). Letwin is not aware of the fact that Locke was well acquainted with Pufendorf's *Elementorum*, and that he later became familiar with *De Jure Naturae et Gentium*. Pufendorf is not mentioned at all in Letwin's book.

Henry William Spiegel in his book *The Growth of Economic Thought* has a different opinion (1983, 155). He claims that it was Josiah Child with his pamphlet *Brief Observations Concerning Trade, Interest and Money* published in 1668 that was responsible for bringing Locke 'into the discussion of economic matters'. Furthermore, Spiegel writes that Locke 'may have found more food for thought in Pufendorf', but leaves it at that and does not discuss it further (Ibid, 232).

However, his writings on political economy, such as human behaviour, private property, theory of value and money, foundation of states, and division of state power and taxation can be found in *Essay Concerning Human Understanding*, and in his most important and influential work, the *Two Treaties of Government*.

3.1 Theory of Human Behaviour

In his *Essay Concerning Human Understanding*, Locke outlines his theory of knowledge and his philosophy of science. In addition, he discusses other issues such as ethics and philosophy of mind.

Locke, like Pufendorf, held the view that knowledge must be acquired. Our mental faculties and our ability to use them may be said to be innate, but it is only by using these faculties that we can acquire knowledge. At birth our mind has no innate ideas, it is blank, a *tabula rasa*.

Locke starts out in *The Second Treatise* TT discussing the State of Nature, 1964 [1698]). Like Pufendorf, he considers what state all men are natural in (TT II, ii, 4, 287). His answer is that men are in a state of perfect freedom to decide their actions 'as they think fit, within the bounds of the Law of Nature', without having to depend on other people. He continues by claiming that the state of nature has a law of nature

---

small, was well enough educated to be able to supply the source of non-original ideas. Only the really obscure writers tended to be credited for their ideas.'

[4] The full title was 'Some of the consequences that are like to follow upon lessening of interest to 4 per cent'.

to govern it. This obligates everyone to reason, which in turn means for all mankind 'that being equal and independent, no one ought to harm another in his Life, Health, Liberty or Possessions' (TT II, ii, 6, 289). Since all men are the workmanship of one wise creator and are in this world to do his business, each one must take care of his own self-interest. 'Every one as he is bound to preserve himself' (Ibid). When his own self-interest is not threatened, he ought, 'as much as he can to preserve the rest of Mankind' (Ibid). The allusion to Pufendorf's self-interest and sociability is clear.

3.2 Theory of Property

Locke uses his theory of human behaviour to develop his theory of property. This theory is also outlined in the Second Treatise. His endeavour is to show how men come to have property 'in several parts of that which God gave mankind in common, and that without any express compact of all the commoner' (TT II, ii, 25, 304).

The starting point is the same for Locke as for Pufendorf, originally all that belong to mankind were held in common; 'and nobody has originally a private Dominion, exclusive of the rest of Mankind, in any of them, as they are thus in their natural state' (TT II, ii, 26, 304). However, when Pufendorf argued, that people in a state of nature must obtain the consent of their fellow men before the fruits of the earth can be privately appropriated, Locke outlined his labour theory of property. Locke claims that most things need cultivation before they can be used. This required the use of labour. When someone labours for a productive end, the results become that person's property. It would be improper that some, who had contributed no labour, should have the same rights equal with someone that used his labour and skills in the production. Ownership is therefore created by the application of labour. Here it should be emphasized that Locke could also have got this idea from Pufendorf, who claimed that 'it was improper that a man who had contributed no labour should have right to things equal to his whose industry a thing had been raised and rendered fit for service' (DJNG IV, iv, 6, 540).

Asked when particular things became a man's property, Locke answered using an example from Pufendorf.[5] 'He that is nourished by the Acorns he pickt up under an Oak. Or the Apples he gathered from the Trees in the Wood, has certainly appropriated them to himself. No Body can deny but the nourishment is his' (TT II, v, 28, 306). Locke's claimed that it was man's labour that removed the fruits out of the common state and made them his property.

Locke claimed that property preceded government. Government can therefore not arbitrarily dispose of the estates of its subjects. How much could each person appropriate of land or other things? 'As much as any one can make use of to any advantage of life before it spoils, so much he may by his labour fix a Property in'

[5] DJNG IV, iv, 13, 554. 'An oak-tree belonged to no man, but the acorns that fell to the ground were his who have gathered them'.

(TT II, v, 31, 308). A person can also appropriate what his employee has produced. It is possible that Locke got this appropriation idea from Pufendorf, who in his discussion of the causes of private property, emphasizes that most things require cultivation and to cultivate you need the use of labour.

Nicolas Jolley (1999, 205) in his book *Locke: His Philosophical Thought* contends that Locke (TT II, v, 28, 306–307) rejects Pufendorf's theory of property as a clumsy solution, which would effectively condemn the human race to starvation. Furthermore, it is clear that Locke like Pufendorf believed that the introduction of property would contribute to the creation of peace among men.

3.3 The Theory of Value, Money and Trade

An inquiry into Pufendorf's treatment of the theory of value and money in his natural law works, and a comparison with Locke's theory shows clearly the influence of Pufendorf on Locke. Locke does not plagiarize Pufendorf, but he builds directly on him. The difference is found in Locke's emphasis on English conditions and a substantially more advanced quantity theory of money.

About value and price, Locke takes over and uses Pufendorf's theory of value or price. He must have had *De Jure Naturae* close at hand. This is recognized by Terence Hutchison (1988, 68), Locke's account in *Some Considerations* is a rudimentary demand and supply theory. He starts out using Pufendorf's treatment of the distinction between the intrinsic value and the market value of a good. Locke claims that the intrinsic worth of a thing consists in its fitness to supply the necessities or serve the conveniences of human life. The more necessary it is to our being or the more it contributes to our well-being, the greater is its worth.

Locke (1691, 16) used the terms 'quantity' and 'vent'. The 'vent' of any good 'depends on its necessity or usefulness'. An estimation of the value of a good can be done by comparing its quantity to its vent. Quantity and vent are approximately equivalent to supply and demand, which also depend on the number of buyers and sellers. 'The price of any Commodity rises or falls by the proportion of the number of Buyer and Sellers' (Ibid, 15). Fewer buyers will lower the price; fewer sellers will increase the price. The allusions to Pufendorf are remarkable. As with Pufendorf, Locke is also aware of the fact that the most useful things, such as water and air, have no price or a small price (Ibid, 21). Letwin (1965, 224) suggests that the paradox of value (the diamond–water paradox) although known 'since the time immemorial probably entered the stream of economic theory through Locke's Considerations'. However, Letwin had not studied Pufendorf's writings on value and price and his understanding of this paradox.

In his *Two treatises*, Locke changed his view on the theory of value and combined a labour theory of property with a labour theory of value (TT II, v, 40, 314). Labour is not only the origin of property but also the determinant of its value and thereby the differences in value on everything. The contradiction between Locke's demand and supply theory and his labour theory of value is discussed by Henry

William Spiegel (1983, 164–169). However, Hutchison (1988, 70) contends that Locke did not propose a labour theory of value that determined relative prices, and therefore there are 'no outright contradiction' between the two theories.

Karen Vaughn (1980, 17) starts her exposition of Locke's contribution to economics with his theory of value. She claims that his value theory forms the basis of his economic analysis and economic policy. 'It was his one tool, his one model for dealing with all economic problems' He applied this model consistently to economic problems, and his analysis mostly yielded satisfactory explanations. Vaughn claims that Locke's account of the determination of prices often has been described as an early version of supply and demand analysis, where *quantity* was his term for *supply* and *vent* his term for *demand* (Ibid, 19). However, she adds that it was a supply-and-demand analysis of a most primitive kind. Furthermore, Vaughn claims that Locke's analysis can best be described as an analysis of shifts in demand and supply (Ibid, 21). His treatment of what determines the demand of goods, vent, is rich, but his treatment of supply and quantity is scanty. It can be argued that her statement also applies to Pufendorf's theory of value.

3.4 Money and Trade

From his general theory of value, Locke goes on to develop his theory of money. As with Pufendorf, his theory can be divided into the origin of money, the requirements and functions of money and what determines its value. Locke distinguishes two functions of money, as a 'counter' to measure value, and as a 'pledge' to lay claim to goods. He believes silver and gold, as opposed to paper money, are the appropriate currency for international transactions. Silver and gold, he says, are treated to have equal value by all of humanity and can thus be treated as a pledge by anyone, while the value of paper money is only valid under the government, which issues it.

The quantity theory of money forms a special case of this general theory. His idea is based on 'money answers all things' or 'rent of money is always sufficient, or more than enough', and 'varies very little…'. As with Pufendorf, Locke (1691, 12) understood that changes in money supply had a direct influence on prices. However, he goes further and is not far from stating the quantity theory of money as it is formulated today: 'This shows the necessity of some proportion of money to trade, but what proportion that is hard to determine, because it depends not barely on the quantity of money, but the quickness of its circulation.'

A comparison of Locke's writing on the theory of value and money, in his *Some Considerations of the Consequences of Lowering Interest and Raising the Value of Money*, with Pufendorf's writings on this issue proves that he must have used his works. Locke does not plagiarize Pufendorf, but he builds directly on him. The notion that a change in money supply will lead to changes in prices he probably borrowed from Pufendorf. Another example is the idea that abundant money will lead to a fall in interest.

Locke also brings up for discussion the deteriorating state of the British coin. He participated actively in calling in all debased coinage. His claim that the authorities should not debase money because it is against the law of nature comes clearly from Pufendorf. Debased coinage would be detrimental to domestic commerce.

3.5 Foundation of States

Locke's view on the foundation of states is written in the spirit of Pufendorf. He first discusses what he calls prime societies, that is, marriages and extended families, and then asks what a political society is: 'Man being born, as has been proved, with a Title to perfect Freedom, and an uncontrouled enjoyment of all the Rights and Priviledges of the Law of Nature, equally with any other Man in the World, hath by Nature a Power, not only to preserve his Property, that is, this Life, Liberty and Estate, against the Injuries and Attempts of other Men; but to judge of and punish the breaches of that Law in others, as he is persuaded the Offence deserves, even with Death itself, in Crimes where the heinousness of the Fact, in his Opinion requires it' (TT II, vii, 87, 341–342). Men therefore have to come together in a community or commonwealth. This commonwealth is a Political or Civil Society, and it will then have the legislative and executive power to make decisions on behalf of all its members.

Locke emphasized that the only way men, who from nature are all free, equal and independent, are willing to put on the bonds of Civil Society, is by agreeing with others to unite for their own safety and peaceful living among others. Then, when any number have consented to make a Government, 'they are thereby presently incorporated, and make one Body Politik, wherein the Majority have a Right to act and conclude the rest' (TT II, viii, 95, 348).

The theory that the state exists only to guaranty security and legal protection was advocated by Pufendorf, and thereafter taken over by Locke. This view that Locke's position on the theory of contracts was similar to Pufendorf's is also held by Mark Waddicor (1970, 87–88) in his book *Montesquieu and the Philosophy of Natural Law*.

3.6 Division of State Powers, Corruption and Taxation

For Pufendorf and Locke, one form of government is more natural than any other form, and this form is decided on by the majority. However, they each had their preferences. Pufendorf, as Grotius before him, thought that absolute monarchy is usually the least unsatisfactory, but they were aware that each form, including monarchy, had certain disadvantages (DJNG VII, v, 9 and 22).

Like Pufendorf, Locke discusses in a chapter, *Of the Forms of a Common-wealth*, three forms of governments, democracy, oligarchy and different forms of monarchy.

He himself preferred moderate monarchies where legislative and executive functions are in different hands (TT II, x, 132, 372–373 and TT II, xiv, 159, 392–93).

Locke and Pufendorf consider corruption an evil we have an obligation to resist. He argues that corruption is a violation of trust. Men enter society for the preservation of their property. That is why they authorize a legislative to make laws and rules, set as guards and fences to the properties of all members of society. These laws and rules should also limit the power and moderate the dominion of every part and member of the society. If the legislators endeavour to take away the property of the people or to reduce them to slavery under arbitrary power, they put themselves into a state of war with the people (TT II, xix, 222, 430).

Locke does not have a detail theory of taxation as Pufendorf did. However, he claims that governments cannot be supported without great charge. Everyone that enjoys his share of the protection should pay out of his wealth his proportion of the maintenance of this protection. This tax must be with each person's consent, that is, the consent of the majority of all or by majority of the representatives, they have chosen.[6] Should any claim the power to 'lay and levy' taxes on the people, by his own authority and without the consent of the people, he thereby 'invades the Fundamental Law of Property, and subverts the end of Government' (TT II, xi, 140, 380). It is also clear that the Government cannot raise taxes on the property of the people without the consent of the people, given by themselves or their deputies. His overriding interest in taxation was, like Pufendorf, to clamp down on arbitrary taxation and its iniquities.

4 The French Philosophers and Political Economy

The French philosophers of the Enlightenment were all in debt to Pufendorf. The moralist Pierre Nicole (1625–1714), the legal philosopher Jean Domat (1625–96) and the magistrate Pierre Le Pesant de Boisguilbert (1646–1714) were familiar with Pufendorf's works and used them when they wrote. Their allusions to Pufendorf's self-interest and sociability as the driving forces in human behaviour are apparent in their writings.

Jean-Jacques Burlamaqui (1694–1748) was a Swiss legal and political theorist who greatly publicized and popularized several ideas, including political economy, propounded by other thinkers. By many he was called a plagiarist since his primary source was Pufendorf's works and he mostly copies him. Burlamaqui had quite an influence on students across Europe and America. His treatise *Principes du droit naturel* (The Principle of Natural Law) became a very popular textbook for students and was translated into six languages and published in more than 60 editions,

[6] The majority of the elected representatives meant the majority of those elected by the property owners.

Burlamaqui (2006 [1763]). Leon Walras (1977 [1874/1926], 203–4) refers to Burlamaqui's theory of value. A theory he had copied from Pufendorf.

Denis Diderot (1713–84), the chief editor of the *Encyclopédie*, was also an admirer of Pufendorf (Sæther 2017b, 180), and he used *De Jure Naturae et Gentium* comprehensively in his work. In many of his articles, he just copies Pufendorf. In others, he has references to the natural law philosophers in general and Pufendorf in particular. His contribution to the diffusion of Pufendorf's views on ethics, jurisprudence, government and political economy was considerable.

Jean Barbeyrac (1674–1744) translated into French, Pufendorf's main natural law work *De jure naturae* and his student edition *De officio*. In 1711, Barbeyrac was called to a Chair of history and civil law at the University of Lausanne. Finally, in 1717 he received his doctorate and moved to the University of Groningen, as professor of public and civil law. At both Lausanne and Groningen, he also taught natural law and introduced Pufendorf's work to a large audience. As early as 1702, he began a correspondence with John Locke. They both influenced each other.

There can be no doubt that he, because of his translations, his commentaries and his own writing, also became a well-known European scholar. On fundamental principles and particularly on the issues of political economy, Barbeyrac follows almost entirely Pufendorf. But there can also be found a few examples where he deviates from him. In the case of Pufendorf's remarks on the priceless character of certain goods and services, Barbeyrac rectifies him by saying there is nothing for which a price cannot be found.

4.1 Montesquieu on Political Economy

Charles-Louis Montesquieu (1689–1755) stands indebted to the natural law philosophers and he used Pufendorf's works extensively when he wrote his numerous discourses and his most influential work *De l'Esprit des lois* (The Spirit of the Laws), (2003 [1748])published in 1748, and his last work *La défense de 'L'Esprit de Lois'* (The defence of 'The Spirit of the Laws'). This is recognized by Robert Shackleton (1961, 72); Cecil Courtney (1968, 30–44); Mark Waddicor (1970, x and 35); Robert Derathe (1973, 42); Alan Baum (1979, 27); Alfred Dufour (1986, 102–104); Anne M. Cohler (1989, xx); Rebecca Kingston (1996, 134) and Sæther (2017a and b).

Montesquieu touches on political economy in almost all his writings, and Sæther (2017b, 185–190) points particularly to Pufendorf as a source. The focus here will be on his exposition in his main work *De l'Esprit des Lois* (The Spirit of the Laws) from 1748.

4.2 Human Behaviour

The first idea of man, in the state of nature, is to think of the preservation of his being, that is, of his self-interest. Montesquieu, like Pufendorf, rejects Hobbes' idea that man's first desire is to subjugate one another and that men live in a state of war. On the contrary, man would, because of his weakness and his feeling of inferiority, seek peace with his fellow men. Furthermore, Montesquieu contends that weakness and mutual fear would persuade them to approach one another. They will also be inclined to peace by the pleasure of being together. By being together, they also succeed in gaining knowledge, and this gives them another motive for uniting and a desire to live in society. The allusions to Pufendorf's self-interest and sociability are strong.

It is clear, as also Waddicor (1970, 66) has pointed out, that Montesquieu (1989 [1748], 6), like Pufendorf and Locke, did not believe in the existence of innate ideas. 'A man in the state of nature would have the faculty of knowing rather than knowledge.'

4.3 Property and the Four-Stages Theory

Montesquieu, unlike Pufendorf, has no rudimentary theory of how private property was progressively introduced as men under pressure of growing population and depleted resources moved from one stage of development to another. However, he compares the relationship of laws to the ways various people procure their subsistence. 'There must be a more extensive code of laws to people attached to commerce and the sea than for a people satisfied to cultivate their lands. There must be a greater one for the latter than for people that live by their herds. There must be a greater one for these last than for people who live by hunting.' (1989 [1748], 18, 8, 289). There is no further discussion of these stages, but he discusses the relationship of population to the way of procuring subsistence.

From this it is hard to understand, how some authors, e. g. Ronald Meek (1971, 33), Alix Cohen (2014, 763) and Margaret Schabas (2014, 739), can claim that Montesquieu was one of the first to anticipate that changes in the condition of mankind took place in different stages. It looks more like he is just summarizing Pufendorf's rudimentary four-stage theory.

4.4 Value, Money and Trade

Montesquieu (1989 [1748], 18, 15, 292) does not develop a theory of value, but he outlines a theory of money and trade. 'The cultivation of the land requires the use of money. Cultivation assumes many arts and much knowledge, and one always sees arts, knowledge, and needs keeping pace together. All this leads to the establishment of a sign of value.' When money is introduced, one is forced to have good civil laws.

Montesquieu uses Pufendorf's ideas and argues in the same manner as him. People, who have little in the way of commodities of commerce, trade by exchange. However, when they dealt in many commodities, there must necessarily be money (Ibid, 398). Money is a sign representing the value of all commodities. Some metal is chosen, so that the sign will be durable, so it will be little worn by use, and so that it can be divided many times without being destroyed (Ibid, 399).

Also, following Pufendorf, he warns against debasement of money when part of the metal is withdrawn from each piece of money.

However, Montesquieu also develops his own ideas. He gives, for example, a rather extensive description of how an Exchange determines the value of money in various countries and what influences these values. In this context, he gives a description of the system, instituted by John Law, that led to a chaotic economic collapse in France (Ibid, 405–412). He emphasizes that the establishment of commerce requires the establishment of an Exchange. Moreover, he discusses the aid the state can draw from banks; he discusses public debt and the payment of such debt.

Montesquieu (1989 [1748], 420) supports Pufendorf's view that interest should be permitted. On interest, he argued that 'To lend one's silver without interest is a very good act, but one senses that this can be only a religious counsel and not a civil law'. The interest should be small. If the interest is too high, a trader, who sees that it would cost him more in interest than he could gain in his commerce, will not trade at all. If the interest is zero, no one lends money and there will be no trade. Furthermore, he contends that when the risk is great, the rate of interest could legitimately be increased. It is hard not to see the allusions to Pufendorf.

It should be emphasized that Montesquieu has an extensive discussion of the nature and distinction of commerce. In addition, there is a lengthy argument on what influence commerce has had on many countries of the world. The development of commerce is the most effective safeguard against arbitrary and despotic government, and it would lead to peace.

4.5 Foundation of States and Council Decisions

Montesquieu claims that the desire to live in society is one of the natural laws. As soon as men enter a state of society, they lose their feeling of weakness, the equality that existed among them ceases and a state of war begins between people and between nations. These two states of war bring about the establishment of laws, respectively, laws of nations and civil law. Since the number of inhabitants on the earth is large, men have laws bearing on the relations they have with another. This is the law of nations. The allusion to Pufendorf's first pact of association is striking. Living in a society they must also have laws concerning the relation between those who govern and those who are governed, that is, the political law. It seems to correspond with Pufendorf's pact of subjection. Finally, they have laws concerning the relations citizen have with each other, that is, the civil law.

The laws men experience in a state of nature will be the laws of nature. In the state of nature, each human feels himself both weak and inferior, and such men will not seek to attack each another. Peace is therefore the first natural law. The second is the inspiration to seek nourishment. The marks of mutual fear would persuade people to approach each other and feel the pleasure of being together. This is therefore the third natural law. The desire to live in society is the fourth natural law (Ibid, 6–7).

All nations have a right of a nation. In addition, there is a political law for each one. 'A society could not continue to exist without a government.' To strengthen the expression, Montesquieu quotes the Italian man of letters, jurist Giovanni Vincenzo Gravina (1664–1718), 'The union of all individual strengths forms what is called the political state' (Ibid, 8). Like Pufendorf, he contends that the strength of the whole society may be put in the hands of one, or in the hands of many. However, individual strengths cannot be united unless all wills are united. Again, he quotes Gravina: 'The union of these wills, is what is called the civil states' (Ibid, 10). Montesquieu does not, as Pufendorf, discuss the problems of council decisions and voting procedures.

4.6 Division of State Powers and Principles of Taxation

Montesquieu (1989 [1748], 2–4) wrote that the main purpose of government is to maintain law and order, political liberty, and the property of the individual. As Pufendorf, he discusses three kinds of government: democracy, aristocracy and monarchy. Mark Waddicor (1970, 106–107) claims that Montesquieu, in his discussions on forms of government, maintains that 'the majority of evidence indicates that he believed in the superiority of monarchy'. However, it was not an absolute monarchy such as Pufendorf favoured; his was more a monarchy where the monarch had to share his power. Montesquieu thought monarchy 'to be more practical than democracy' and that it most likely would produce political freedom. This fact gave it a most important advantage over other regimes.

In the spirit of Pufendorf, Montesquieu (1989 [1748], 156–166) discusses the legislative power, the executive power and the judicial power.[7] However, he writes that the best form of government is one in which the three powers are separate and keeps each other in check to prevent any branch from becoming too powerful. If these powers are held in one hand as in an absolute monarchy it would lead to

[7]Thomas Hueglin (2008, 141) in his *Classical Debates of the 21st Century*, contends that 'Montesquieu expanded Lock's separation of legislative and executive power by adding the judiciary as an important third power in its own right, which had to be separate by all means'. Hueglin has no references to Pufendorf.

despotism. Montesquieu's view is taken over by Francis Hutcheson's view in his *A Short Introduction to Moral Philosophy* from 1747.

In the matter of political liberty, Waddicor (1970, 135) claims that Montesquieu's superiority over his predecessors is clear. Although they refer to a contract as a means of guaranteeing liberty, he goes further and describes the separation of powers as a more practical safeguard. This is not found in the works of Grotius or Pufendorf, although it is found in somewhat similar terms in Locke (Ibid, 135). As Pufendorf, Montesquieu (1989 [1748], 8) warns against corruption regardless of government.

In his discussion of revenue and taxation, Montesquieu brings up the same themes as Pufendorf. Whatever government is chosen for a society; revenue is necessary for the government to be able to carry out the duties of the state. To determine the revenues both the necessities of the state and the necessities of its citizens must be considered. To collect its revenue, the state must levy taxes on its citizens.

Montesquieu discusses different forms of taxes in different countries and under different governments. In a state, where all individuals are citizens, taxes can be of three categories: they can be placed on people, or on land, or on commodities, or on all of these (Ibid, 215). A tax on people can be such that they have to give up part of their income to the state. The income can be in money, as well as in produce. In the assessment of lands, registers are made for the various classes of land, but it will be very difficult to establish these differences. Duties on commodities are least felt by the people. This is particularly the case when the seller collects the tax. He will know that he is not paying it himself and the buyer, who ultimately pays it, confounds it with the price. Montesquieu concludes: 'An impost [tax] by head is more natural to servitude; the tax on commodities; more natural to liberty because it relates less directly to the person' (Ibid, 222).

A tax on people will be an unjust tax if it is levied in strict proportion to income, Montesquieu claimed. Contrary to Pufendorf, he supported a progressive income tax. However, like Pufendorf, he claimed that taxes should be clearly established and be so easy to collect that they could not be changed by the tax collectors. In the spirit of Pufendorf, he ends his treatment of taxation, with a warning about tax collectors.

Terence Hutchison (1988, 224) claims that Montesquieu's views on taxation have much in common with the four maxims subsequently enunciated by Adam Smith. However, it is surprising that Hutchison does not see the link between Pufendorf and Montesquieu, and furthermore between Pufendorf and Smith.

4.7 Jean-Jaques Rousseau on Political Economy

Rousseau's allusions to Pufendorf's works are particularly strong when Rousseau discusses issues regarding political economy (Sæther 2017b, 193–200).

4.8 Human Behaviour

Rousseau was convinced that man's original nature was good, but that it had been corrupted by the development of society. His *Discourse on the Arts and Sciences*, Rousseau (2008 [1750]) which was a response to the prize essay question: Has the restoration of the sciences and the arts helped to purify morals? Here he argued that it had not. It led to the decline of virtue. This he pursued in his *Discourse on Inequality*. In the *Preface*, Rousseau (2008 [1755], 124) starts out with the following statement: 'The most useful and the least advanced of all human knowledge seems to me to be that of man and I dare say that the inscription on the Temple of Delphi alone contained a more important and more difficult Precept than all the big Books of the Moralists.' It is clear, Victor Gourevitch (2008, 352) contends, that he has had Pufendorf's reference to the inscription in the temple 'Know thyself' at hand (DJNG II, iv, 5, 238).

Rousseau (2008 [1755], 127) sees two principles (before reason and independent of sociability): man's interests in his self-preservation and man's pity for other people, that is, the spontaneous, natural, disinclination to hurt or harm others. He believed that as reason improved, when society moved forward, it weakened the natural sentiment of pity. In nature, man was independent but as society advanced, he became dependent on other people.

From his book, *Emile*, it is also clear that Rousseau (2014 [1762], 21) along with Pufendorf, does not believe in innate ideas, for example, that man from birth knew what was right and wrong; he had to be taught.

4.9 Theory of Property

Man's first sentiment was that of his existence, his first care was that of his preservation. The Earth's products provided the nascent man with all necessary support. However, soon some difficulties presented themselves, like the height of the trees, or competition from ferocious animals. Man learned to overcome these and other obstacles. As humankind increased and spread, difficulties multiplied. Differences in terrain and climate led to differences in living. People invented tools for hunting and fishing, discovered fire, and improved their dwellings. Dealings with other people lead to the invention of language. This initial process finally enabled man to make more rapid progress and the more the mind became enlightened the more industry was perfected, that is, better tools and better dwellings were constructed. In the third discourse or an *Essay on the Origin of Languages*, Rousseau (2008 [1750], 18, 271) writes 'Human industry expands with the needs that give rise to it. Of the three ways of life available to man, hunting, herding and agriculture, the first develops strength, skill, speed of body, courage and cunning of soul, it hardens man and makes him ferocious.' He sums it up: 'The preceding division correspond to the three states of man considered in relation to society. The savage is the hunter, the barbarian a herdsman, civil man a tiller of the soil' (Ibid, 19, 272).

When agriculture was gradually introduced, it followed from the cultivation of land that its division was necessary 'and from property, once recognized the first rules of justice, necessarily followed; for in order to render to each his own, each must be able to have something; moreover, as men began to extend their views to the future and all saw that they had some goods to lose, there was no one who did not have to fear reprisals against himself for the wrongs he might do to another' (Ibid., 16, 169).

The origin of property, Rousseau claims in the Second Discourse Part II. 'Since labour alone gives the cultivator the right to the produce of the land he has tilled, in consequently also gives him a right to the land ..., is easily transformed into property', is all the more natural as it is impossible to conceive the idea of property emerging in any way other than in terms of manual labour (Ibid). The allusion to Locke's labour theory of property, which he could have got from Pufendorf, is clear. The first effect of property, as claimed by Rousseau, was negative. Men with property became knavish, and with some people imperious, and harsh with others. The division of land and labour transformed the natural inequality in the natural stage into inequality of rank.

4.10 Value, Money and Trade

Rousseau develops neither a theory of value nor a theory of money or trade. In his *Discourse on Inequality*, the *Social Contract* and his essay on *Political Economy*, he sees the introduction of money, at best, as a necessary evil. For Rousseau, the worst kind of modern society is that in which money is the only measure of value.

4.11 Foundation of States and Council Decisions

In the *Social Contract*, Rousseau (2007 [1762] claims that there comes a point in the state of nature where the conflicts between people are so great that the primitive life in the state of nature can no longer subsist,[8] 'humankind would perish if it did not change in its way of being' (2007 [1762], 49). A society must be formed in order for humankind to survive.

Since men cannot come up with new forces, but only unite and direct the ones that exist, men have no means of self-preservation other than to form, by aggregation, a sum of forces that will be strong enough to overrule the conflicts and make

[8] How Rousseau tackles this problem and a comparison between his views and the views expressed by Pufendorf can be found in Melissa Schwartzberg's article from 2008 *Voting the General Will: Rousseau on Decision Rules.*

them act in concert. The sum of men's forces can only arise from the cooperation of many: 'but since each man's force and freedom are his primary instruments of self-preservation, how can he commit them without harming himself, and without neglecting the cares he owes himself?' (Ibid). This difficulty Rousseau states in the following terms: 'To find a form of association that will defend and protect the person and goods of each associate with the full common force and by means of which each, uniting with all, nevertheless obey only himself and remain as free as before' (Ibid). This is the fundamental problem to which the social contract provides a solution. This contract can be reduced to the following terms: 'Each of us puts his person and his full power in common under supreme direction of the general will; and in a body we receive each member as an indivisible part of the whole' (Ibid, 50). The public person thus formed by the union of others is called a state when it is passive, Sovereign when active.

It is important to note that when a man joins the contract, he loses the freedom to act on his own personal appetite, but he gains liberty via the limitation of reason and the general will placed on his behaviour. Rousseau's social contract is close to Pufendorf's agreement of association.

Rousseau contends that the political aspect of society ought to be divided into two parts, the Sovereign and the Government. The Sovereign consist of all, and it represents the general will. It is also the legislative power. The Government carries out the laws and decisions made on the authority of the sovereign. If it oversteps its boundaries, it can be removed. The relations between the Government and the Sovereign correspond roughly with Pufendorf's agreement of subjection.

In book IV, chapter two, *Of Suffrage*, Rousseau (Ibid., 123) held that 'the way in which general business is conducted provides a fairly reliable indication of the current state of morals and the health of the body politics'. Furthermore, like Pufendorf, he claims that there is only one law, which by its nature requires unanimous consent. That is *The Social Pact*. When the state has been constructed, consent must be reached. Residents in the state are to submit to the sovereignty and obey (Ibid, 124). Rousseau argues that 'except for this primitive contract, the vote of the majority always obligates the rest; this is a consequence of the contract'. As with Pufendorf, the obligation to abide by a majority decision requires a prior unanimous decision. He also discusses the proportional number of votes needed to declare the general will, that is, the question of supermajorities (Ibid, 125). In his *Social Contract*, Rousseau likewise has a brief discussion on voting by secret ballot or by voice (Ibid, 135). Furthermore, he discusses the case when an assembly consists of tribes. In each tribe, most votes determine the vote of that tribe, a majority of votes of the tribes determines the vote of the people.

Rousseau (Ibid., 217–218) also discusses the question of supermajorities in his *Consideration of the Government of Poland*. The veto should only be applied to fundamental laws. For administrative decisions, a simple majority should prevail. In between, depending on the importance of the matter under consideration, any proportion of a supermajority could be possible. Rousseau claims that one might require a three quarters majority in legislation, a two-thirds majority in matters of State and a simple majority in administration and daily business. There can be no doubt that Rousseau had Pufendorf's *De Jure Naturae* close at hand when he wrote these decision rules.[9]

4.12 Division of State Powers and Principles of Taxation

In the *Social Contract*, Rousseau (Ibid., 82) discusses the legislative and the executive power. The legislative power belongs to the people and can belong only to it. The legitimate exercise of the executive power is the Government or supreme administration. The Government is an intermediate body established between subjects and the Sovereign 'so that they might conform to one another, and charged with the execution of laws and the maintenance of freedom both civil and political' (Ibid, 83).

In the *Social Contract*, Rousseau discusses, like Pufendorf, three major forms of government: democracy, aristocracy and monarchy. He stresses that not every form is suited to every country. Democracy and absolute monarchy, he rejects but settles for an elective aristocracy. 'It is Aristocracy properly so called' (Ibid, 93).

Carl Friederich (2002, 19) asserts in his *Corruption Concepts in Historical Perspective* that Rousseau was deeply concerned with what he believed to be the corruption of his age and he looked upon himself as the wise man who must raise a warning voice. Rousseau (2008 [1750], 20–22) therefore touches upon the evils of corruption in several of his writings. In his first discourse, he holds the view that the necessary consequence of luxury is the dissolution of morals, which in turns leads to the corruption of taste. Furthermore, that a senseless education adorns our mind and corrupt our judgment (Ibid, 22). In his *Discourse on Inequality*, corruption is closely related to the process of human development. His view is rather pessimistic, when human reason develops man is corrupted and declines from the state of nature. In his *Social Contract*, he discusses, as Pufendorf, corruption in democracies, aristocracies and monarchies (2007 [1762] III, 6, 91–97). He warns against corruption of the lawgiver in a democracy and he claims that luxury corrupts. In a monarchy, the lack of continuous successions may create situations where, 'intrigue and corruption will play their part'.

Rousseau's principles of taxation are laid down in his *Discourse on Political Economy* from 1755 and in his *Considerations* from 1772. His principles are very close to Pufendorf's principles in *De Jure Naturae.* Taxes levied on the people are, he claims, of two kinds: ones that are levied on things, that is, property, and ones that are personal, which are paid by the head (2007 [1772], 231–232). In his *Considerations*, he changed his mind and makes it clear that although the most convenient and least costly is without question a per capita tax, it is also the most forced, the most arbitrary, the most unjust and unreasonable. 'Taxes on property is always preferable to a tax on persons.' The best tax that will not be subject to fraud

[9] See also footnote 93, page 93.

is therefore a proportional tax on land, and on all land without exception, for all what produces ought to pay. With 'all land', he also meant land owned by the Kings, the Nobles, the Church, and land held in common. A general land registry is necessary, but the expense can be avoided, to good advantage, by assessing the tax not directly on the land but on its produce.

Rousseau discusses, in the manner of Pufendorf, three factors that should be considered when deciding on how much tax people should pay. First is the question of proportionality. A person with only the bare necessities for life should not pay anything in tax. However, if a person consumes many luxuries he should, if need be, pay a tax 'up to the full amount that exceeds his necessities'. A third factor is the utility that each person derives from social alliances. This is never considered, and it favours the rich, the privileged and the powerful. Rousseau (2008 [1755], 32) claims that all advantages and benefits of society, the lucrative posts, all exceptions, all exemption etc. are reserved for the rich. Another, no less important point to note is that the losses of the poor are far more difficult to make up for than those of the rich, and that the difficulty of acquiring always grows in proportion to need.

Duties on imports, that is, customs can, also in the manner of Pufendorf, be set on foreign goods, craved by the population, but not needed by the country. Furthermore, customs can be set on the export of domestic goods of which the country has no excess, and which foreigners cannot do without. It is not hard to understand why the privileged classes in France reacted so hatefully towards Rousseau after having read his principles of taxation.

4.13 The Foundation of Physiocratic Economic Thoughts

What did the physiocrats themselves understand with political economy and what was the foundation for their doctrines? Elizabeth Fox-Genovese (1976, 10) refers to a letter du Pont de Nemours sent to Jean-Baptiste Say in 1815.[10] Du Pont asserts that for all the physiocrats, political economy was 'the science of natural law applied, as it should be, to civilized societies', and of 'enlightened justice in all social relations – internal and external'. The underlying philosophy for the development of their economic ideas was that of Pufendorf's natural law.

The Physiocrats asked themselves whether the nature of things did not tend towards a science of political economy. Under the leadership of Francois Quesnay (1694–1774), the Physiocrats devoted their efforts to the discovery of the principles of this science and the disassociation of political economy from the general body of natural law.

In his writings on political economy, Quesnay claimed that wealth came entirely from the land, that nature was fertile and that man could tie together its reproductive forces. Agriculture was therefore the industry that created wealth. Hard labour and

[10] A letter dated 22.04.1815.

investments in agriculture would create surplus that would circulate to other sectors of the economy. His *Tableau économiqué* from 1758 is the first presentation of a circular flow between the different sectors of the economy in the history of economic thought. Today's historians of economic thought generally agree that this *Tableau* had in it the origin of modern ideas of the circulation of wealth and the nature of interrelationship in the economy.

This investigation will concentrate on the Physiocrats view on the themes of political economy, where they could have been influenced directly by Pufendorf or indirectly through his French followers.

4.14 Human Behaviour and Private Property

The Physiocrats saw both political and economic theory as integral parts of a single science grounded on private property. Fox-Genovese (1976, 48) contends that private property, in Physiocratic thought, constitutes man's first natural right. Man arrives in the world with a fundamental obligation to keep himself alive, and his survival depends upon his right to property. The original obligation to live can only be fulfilled by eating. To eat with moral sanctions, 'man must have a natural right to the fruits of the earth'. The Physiocrats defended that right in order to refute Hobbes' contention that society rests on struggle. The first man simply collected the fruits freely offered by nature. Later men turned into active cultivation of the earth, which required the use of labour. However, as everyone can recognize from his own experience, or in Quesnay's chosen phrase, no one in his right mind willingly undertakes hard labour without being assured of the absolute fruits of that labour. Quesnay's theory of property has elements of both Pufendorf's theory of right and Locke's labour theory of property.

The Physiocrats claimed that society must approve human action, efforts and tools, and must positively sanction property as a social good. In their defence of individual's right to property, in contrast to the traditional notions of the community's right to preserve social harmony, lies the heart of the Physiocratic ideology, which they summed up in the words: Property, Liberty, and Security. Spiegel (1983, 186) claims that it was in this connection that the phrase *laissez faire, laissez passer* was coined, 'a maxim that to this day has served as an affirmation of economic individualism'. The Physiocrats made a distinction between natural and positive order.

> Only in the natural order, the ideal, would harmonious individualism reach its full flowering. In the positive order of the world of reality the free play of individual forces might well be frustrated, with disadvantages that result in economic conflict rather that harmony. (Ibid)

The allusion to Pufendorf is not easily avoided. Furthermore, society must recognize individual self-interest as most respectable motive for social action. However, it was not an egoistic self-interest. Mirabeau states, according to Fox-Genovese (1976, 206), that our intellect enables us to channel our unbridled passions into the socially acceptable paths of enlightened self-interest. Her description of the

Physiocratic view of self-interest is very close to Pufendorf's self-interest and sociability.

She also claims that Quesnay had learned from Locke to mistrust the notion of innate ideas, but she is not aware of that Locke found this idea in Pufendorf's writings (Ibid, 85).

From the extract 'Rural Philosophy'[11] it becomes clear, according to Meek (1976b, 57–64), that Quesnay was familiar with the development in stages, although the order was different. When the fruits of the earth had been used and population increased, men had to cultivate the land, 'whence arose agricultural nations' (Ibid, 60). Men also had to herd together and rear domestic animals, which was the origin of herdsman. Furthermore, men had to hunt and set trap for wild animals and do the same for fish, which was the origin of hunters and fishermen. Using examples from the Genesis, he explains how these societies developed. From the interrelationships of these societies, there 'is born a new kind of secondary and artificial societies that is commercial societies'. These societies are 'less secure so far as its basis and duration are concerned, less capable of extension, and unable to form a great empire, but nevertheless free, wealthy, and powerful within its narrow boundaries' (Ibid, 62). The distinction between 'thine and mine' was here established in relation to the land.

4.15 Theory of Value

Quesnay's *bon prix* forms, according to Spiegel (1983, 193), part of his value theory. His theory is not fully developed but it has several interesting features. The *bon prix* stands in a certain relationship to the 'prix fondamental', which is the cost of production. Market price will normally be above the cost of production. If it falls below it, it will create losses for the producers. However, on the other hand, if the market price is excessively high, it will constitute a 'burden'. The bon prix is located between these extremes. It yields a profit and is therefore an incentive to maintain or expand production. The allusion to Pufendorf's discussion of natural price and market price is there.

4.16 The Foundation of States and Council Decisions

The Physiocrats maintained that natural law governed the economy. Individual rights, and the justification of private property based on these rights, was part of this natural law. The laissez-faire principle was the basis for the harmony-of-interest doctrine in which individual pursuit of an enlightened self-interest by each member

[11] *Philosophic Rurale* first appeared in 1763.

of society would lead to the maximum social good. The allusion to Pufendorf is easily seen.

Society must approve human action, effects and tools, and must positively sanction private property as a social good. The Physiocrats claim, according to Fox-Geneovese (1976, 49), that without security, property would be a theoretical right constantly violated in practice. The need for security of private property therefore justifies government. The principal duty of the government is therefore to guarantee private property.

Mirabeau in his investigation of the origin of society explained it this way: 'All social organization rests upon the desire to harvest the fruits of one's labour. That desire, illuminated by reason, affords the basis for the recognition that union offers the best means of implementing individual desires. The union itself is what we call society' (Ibid, 206).

4.17 Division of State Powers and Principles of Taxation

The physiocratic views concerning the nature of the state and the best form of government are not easy to grasp. The Physiocrats invented, for example, the name 'legal despotism' to describe the government they favoured. It included a sovereign assisted by administrators and a group of magistrates to serve as custodians of the fundamental laws of the realm. Although the views of the Physiocrats generally were relatively homogeneous, their views on the state and government were not constant but evolved over time. Being a group connected to the court, they were also in an awkward position. The Physiocrats saw both their political and economic theories as integral parts of a science founded on private property, personal liberty and individual self-interest, although an enlightened one, as the driving force in the economy. Personal security is also very important as a foundation for society. These concepts are closely related to Pufendorf's natural law philosophy.

In 1760, Mirabeau published his *Théorie de l'impô (Theory of taxation)*. It outlined the Physiocratic theory of taxation, criticizing the present system in general and the abuse of the tax-farmers (tax collectors). It shocked public opinion. The author was imprisoned, but because of important connections got out after 8 days. However, exiled to the countryside for 2 months. Mirabeau proposed that the tax farmers should be replaced with a system of a single direct tax on landed property *l'impôt unique*. His critic of the present system has allusions to Pufendorf's criticism of the tax collection abuses.

Despite his criticism of the present tax system, Mirabeau was not a revolutionary. He defended noble privilege and tax exemptions (Ibid, 143). The prince, with his absolute power, enjoys the undisputed right to demand subsidies from his subjects, who on their side had no right to refuse. If the prince requires financial assistance for the upkeep of the public domain, his purposes serve the interest of all. If a prince misuses the funds he receives, then he abuses his powers (Ibid, 215).

The Physiocrats like most other writers in the eighteenth century did not overwhelm us with quotations. There are scarcely any references to the sources of their ideas in the articles and books that comprise what can be termed the Physiocratic library. However, several historians of economic thought, for example, Fox-Genovese (1976), Eklund and Hébert (1990), Rima (1991) and Landreth and Colander (1994), point to natural law as an important source for the Physiocrats. But only one (Sæther 2017b, 204–207) has been found that points to Pufendorf's writings.

5 Pufendorf as a Predecessor of Adam Smith

Gershom Carmichael (1672–1729) introduced Pufendorf's *De Officio* as a textbook in his class in moral philosophy at the University of Glasgow. In 1716, he edited and published a new edition of the book with extensive commentaries. He also claimed that self-interest was not a prime driving force and that men did not become sociable from insecurity in order to be safe, as Pufendorf asserted (DOH I, iii, 13, 19).

In addition, Carmichael could not accept Pufendorf's opinion that 'no one would practice works of pity or friendship without having the assurance of fame or emolument' (Ibid, 26). In his supplements, he argues, as Peter Stein (1982, 669) has noted, that 'man's ability to live with others in society depends on natural feeling of sympathy for others, which men could never have invented themselves and which must have been implemented in them by the Supreme Being'.

On how things become property, Carmichael argued, as Locke and Barbeyrac did, that the right of property had its origin in labour, Moore and Silverthorne (2002, 94). They found this more satisfactory than Pufendorf's account, which made it dependent on consent.

Carmichael makes only a few remarks on Pufendorf's chapter on value but discusses the contracts it is built on in some detail. Neri Naldi (1993: 457) investigates Carmichael's ten notes on quasi contracts and claims that 'we can recognize an attempt to transform Pufendorf's list of causes influencing price determination into a compact and significantly original scheme'.

The manner in which Pufendorf proposed that men unite in society and under government by mutual agreement and consent was, as pointed out by Moore and Silverthorne (1984, 1–12), attractive to Carmichael and other supporters of the Revolution Settlement, since it excluded the claim of hereditary rights for the monarch.[12] However, they could not accept his theory that the duty of sociability recognizes that the sovereigns should enjoy absolute power over their subjects. This could not be reconciled with the rights that British subjects had won by the Glorious

[12] The Revolutionary Settlement was a series of acts passed by the English Parliament in the years 1689–71. It limited not only the power of the King but also the authority of the Parliament.

Revolution.[13] Carmichael sought to revise the absolutist implication of Pufendorf's theory by restating their obligations to be sociable in terms of a duty to respect the natural rights of others.

5.1 Francis Hutcheson Built on Pufendorf

When Carmichael died, his former student, Francis Hutcheson (1694–1746), was called to take over his position as professor of moral philosophy. He continued Carmichael's practice and used *De Officio* as a textbook in his philosophy class. With the use of Pufendorf's works on natural law by these scholars, in their classes, the term 'natural law' was replaced by 'moral philosophy'. The transformation of natural law into moral philosophy, which also included political economy, was complete. Hutcheson's textbook, *A Short Introduction to Moral Philosophy*, (1969a [1747]) builts closely on Pufendorf. It was divided into three parts: Ethics and the Law of Nature, Economics and Politics. Although the topics under each heading do not fully coincide with what would have been the division today, this division was important for the development of political economy as a science.

Few economists or historians of economic thought today seem to be aware of it, or are unwilling to acknowledge it, Hutcheson's writings are, as pointed out above, directly influenced by Pufendorf's natural law works. This influence is also clearly indicated by William Taylor (1965) and Mautner (1986). The influence from Pufendorf is particularly noticeable when Hutcheson discusses issues of political economy. The Table 2 below shows where the topics of political economy can be found in Pufendorf's *De Officio* and Hutcheson's texts *A Short Introduction to Moral Philosophy* and *A System of Moral Philosophy* (1969b [1755]).

Table 2 A comparison of political economy in *De Officio* with Hutcheson's two books *A Short Introduction to Moral Philosophy* and *A System of Moral Philosophy.*

Topic of political economy/books	De Officio Hominis et Civis	A Short Introduction to Moral Philosophy	A System of Moral Philosophy
Theory of Human Behaviour	Book I. Ch. 4–7	BI. Ch. I–VI, BII. Ch. V.	BI. Ch. 2, 3, 4, 5, 9, 10, 11
Theory of Property and the Four-Stage Theory	Book I. Ch.12, 13	BII. Ch. V, VI	BII. Ch. 7, 8
Theory of Value and Money	Book I. Ch. 14, 15	BII. Ch. XII, XIII	BII. Ch.12, 13
Foundation of States and Councils	Book II. Ch. 5–10	BIII. Ch. IV–VIII	BIII. CH. 4–9
Division of State Powers and Taxation	Book II. Ch. 11, 12	BIII. Ch. VII, VIII	BII. Ch. 3 BIII. Ch. 9

Sæther (2017a, 171)

[13] It is also called the Revolution of 1688 where King James II was overthrown and William III and his wife

Mary II became jointly King and Queen of England.

Although Hutcheson mostly followed Pufendorf, this inquiry will acknowledge some important issues where their views departed, and he developed his own theories.

5.2 Theory of Human Behaviour

Hutcheson departed from Pufendorf when he developed his theory of human behaviour. He could not agree with his emphasis on self-interest as a driving force in human behaviour. Mautner (1986, 129) and Ian Simson Ross (2010, 49) have examined Hutcheson's inaugural lecture *On man's natural sociality*.[14] Hutcheson made it clear that he wished to continue the tradition of his former teacher, Carmichael. The staple of his courses would be the classical Stoic tradition on the analysis of the social nature of man. This tradition had been revived in the seventeenth century by Grotius and Pufendorf. Hutcheson argues that there are in the human frame altruistic tendencies, which cannot be reduced to or derived from motives of self-interest. In this lecture, he therefore publicly expressed criticism of Pufendorf. This was probably necessary since, among the clergy of different denominations, there was a lot of scepticism towards Pufendorf's ethical views. Hutcheson therefore put his emphasis on man's passion towards altruism and co-operation, which he argued are the major sources of society and of the capacity of human beings to live together amicably and constructively.

He also maintained, in opposition to Pufendorf, that human motivation and man's conception of right and wrong are innate and not acquired.

5.3 Theory of Property

Hutcheson (1969a [1747], 150) also departed from Pufendorf, in his theory of property, and followed Carmichael, who built on Locke's labour theory. A stadial theory of development can neither be found in Hutcheson's work, but it is of interest to note that he, in *A System of Moral Philosophy*, discusses the advantages of the division of labour (Ibid, II, iv). This he could not have found in Pufendorf, who only stresses the importance of cooperation among men in a commercial society.

[14] Hutcheson (1730, 10–11): *De naturali hominum socialitate oratio in auguralis.*

5.4 *Theory of Value, Money and Trade*

Hutcheson (Ibid., II, xii) also outlines his theory of value and money in *A Short Introduction to Moral Philosophy*. With small adjustments, taken from Carmichael's *Commentary,* it is more or less a free translation of Pufendorf's *De Officio* (DOH I, Ch.14).[15] Like Pufendorf, he is aware of the 'Paradox of value' and he also warns against debasement of money (1747, II, xii, 14, 212).

5.5 *The Foundation of States and Council*

Pufendorf's theory of the foundation of states had a rather pessimistic starting point (DOH II, v, 7). This was changed by Hutcheson (1747, III, iv, 280) to a more positive view: 'Tis highly probable therefore that not only the dread of injuries, but eminent virtues, and our natural high approbation of them have engaged men at first to form civil societies.' Thereafter, he follows Pufendorf closely in his belief that two contracts, and a decree in between the two, are necessary (Ibid, III, v, 286). Furthermore, he claims, as Pufendorf in his *De Officio* (II, vi, 12, 108), that when power is committed to a council, the will of the state is determined by the majority unless a supermajority is required. He also touches on the problem when a question of three or more parts are put to the vote (1747 III, vi, 292). In his *System*, which built on his lecture notes from 1734–35, he has some more illustrative descriptions, probably derived from Pufendorf's *De Jure Naturae* (VII, ii, 16–18, 990–993). It is always understood that if there are no special limitation in the constitution 'the majority of the council have the right of determining the matters proposed' (1747, III, vi, 1, 240–241). The will of the council is that 'which has the plurality of votes'. However, he recommends that a certain number of the council members should be present to make the council the proper representation: 'otherwise different small cabals at different times may make the most contrary decrees'. It is also highly prudent that, when decisions are going to be made in affairs of great importance, more than a bare majority should be requisite, 'such as two-thirds, or three-fifths; particularly in altering any of the ancient laws, or in condemning any person impeached'. He also stresses that precautions should be taken against an obvious fallacy if there are three propositions to be voted on.

[15]This view has also been noted by Luigi Cossa (1893, 251) *An Introduction to the Study of Political Economy*. London. Here taken from Raymond de Roover (1974, 303).

5.6 Division of State Powers and Principles of Taxation

The powers that are requisite for governing a people are the power of making laws, the power of exacting revenues, the executive power and the power of making treaties (Ibid, 288–289).

Like Pufendorf Hutcheson (1947 III, v, 298) discusses monarchy, aristocracy and democracy, although he subdivides them differently. There are also different kinds of democracies.

Hutcheson expresses a preference for a mixed form of government, with both an assembly elected by popular vote, and a senate of a few, whose members should have approved their abilities and fidelity. This senate should be entrusted 'with the sole right of deliberating, debating and proposing business to the popular assembly' (Ibid. 300).

When a state has been established with its proper government, Hutcheson follows Pufendorf and claims that it had the right to exact tributes from its subjects by law. However, this right is not unconditional. What is exacted should not be more than what is requisite for a prudent administration of public affairs.

In his *System of Moral Philosophy*, Hutcheson outlines his principles of taxation. He follows Pufendorf's theories in *De Jure Naturae*. In a short and concise sentence, he explains that taxes should preferably be levied on luxuries rather than on necessities, on imports rather than exports (1755 III, 7, 340). He stresses that duties on imports are often necessary to encourage industry at home. Unmarried people should pay higher taxes than married.

Taxes, as also emphasized by Pufendorf, should be economical in the sense that they should be, 'easily raised without many expensive offices for collecting them', and they should be just (Ibid). To obtain a just tax system, it will be necessary with a census.

Today Hutcheson by many is seen as a forerunner of the social theories, which included political economy, of the Scottish Enlightenment. His compendium was also used as a textbook at several American universities.

5.7 Pufendorf and Smith on Political Economy

Adam Smith (1723–1790) took a place in Professor Hutcheson's class in moral philosophy in 1737. In 1740, he graduated with a master's degree and won a scholarship to Balliol College, Oxford. Six years later, he returned to Scotland as a well-educated academic. From 1748 to 1751, he gave lectures in Edinburgh on rhetoric, belles-lettres and jurisprudence. In 1751, he accepted an offer of a Chair in logic at University of Glasgow. The year after he moved to the Chair in moral philosophy. Based on his lecture notes, Smith (1982a [1759]) published in 1759 his *The Theory of Moral Sentiment.* Smith also gave lectures on jurisprudence, and notes from these 1762–63 lectures were discovered and published in 1900 as his *Lectures on Jurisprudence* (1982b [1762–63]. In 1764, Smith left the university and accepted the position as tutor to a young duke. For almost 3 years, they travelled Europe.

There Smith discussed economic problems with members of the Physiocratic group. In 1767, he retired with a pension from the duke and concentrated on his writings. This resulted in the publishing of his *The Wealth of Nations* in 1776, (1976 [1776].

Considering the evidence that biographers of Smith and the editors of his works have revealed of his ties to Pufendorf, it is surprising that none of them discuss him as an important source (Sæther 2017a, 178–185). His links can be summed up in six points. First, as a first-year student in Glasgow, Smith had, in Hutcheson's class, to study Pufendorf's *De Officio* (Scott 1965, 112). Second, as a third-year student, he benefitted from Hutcheson teaching a private class on the *Lessons of the Law of Nature and Nations* (Ross 2010, 51). Third, in his fourth years at Oxford he chooses to follow the path of civil law, where he possibly continued the study of natural law (Ross 2010, 55). Fourth, Smith acquired Pufendorf's *De Jure Naturae et Gentium* both in Latin and in a French translation (Mizuta 1967).[16] Fifth, in his freelance lectures in Edinburgh, Smith taught the Grotius-Pufendorf tradition of natural law (Ross 2010, 67). Sixth, when Smith lectured on jurisprudence at Glasgow, he used Hutcheson's compendium, which built on Pufendorf, together with his Edinburgh notes (Meek 1976b, 454). All these points, one by one and together, strongly *suggest* that Adam Smith, early on, became familiar with Pufendorf's natural law works (including substantial tracts of political economy), and that he used them extensively when he prepared his lectures in Edinburgh and Glasgow.

It is recognized by most writers who discuss Smith's sources that his books have their point of departure in his lecture notes. Therefore, it is surprising that only a few authors point to Pufendorf as one of his primary sources. Scott (1900, 231) in his Hutcheson biography admits that Hutcheson's work: 'Contains many reproductions of views of Pufendorf, Grotius and Locke upon Politics and Economics.' Furthermore, he refers to Cannan (1896) who states that: 'Hutcheson's function was to collect and classify them, so they were available for Smith' (Ibid). Then Scott comes up with a remarkable statement: 'It might of course be contended that Smith consulted the authorities direct' (Ibid). Yes indeed, it might. Hutcheson had urged his student to investigate the sources, and Smith probably did.

Adam Smith was not an author that revealed his sources and he rarely refers to Pufendorf. However, his lack of recognition does not tell us anything about his use of Pufendorf. From our discussion in the next sections it follows that Pufendorf had a strong influence on Smith and that there is enough evidence to claim that he was his major source.

The Table 3 below shows where the topics of political economy can be found in Pufendorf's natural law works and in Smith's *Lectures on Jurisprudence* LOJ, and *The Wealth of Nations* WN.

A comparison of Pufendorf's and Smith's doctrines of political economy are outlined in the next sections.

[16] Sæther (2017b, 186)

Table 3 Political economy in Pufendorf's and Smith's works

Topics	De Jure Naturae et Gentium	De Officio Hominis et Civis	Lectures on Jurisprudence	The Wealth of Nations
Theory of Human Behaviour	Book I. i–iv. Book II i–iv. Book III i–ii.	Book I. Ch. 4–7.	A: iii. 1–147. B: Pt. II, 203–209, 326–333.	Book I. i–ii.
Theory of Property Four-Stage Theory	Book IV. iii–v. Book V. v.	Book I. Ch.12–13.	A: i. 16–167, iv. 23–40, 113–179. B: Pt. I. 19–75, 149–175	Book I. x–xi. Book V. i. 2.
Theory of Value and Money	Book V. i, iii, v, vii–viii.	Book I. Ch. 14–15.	A: vi. 1–171 B: Pt. II. 203–306	Book I. i–vii, ix–x. Book II. ii.
Foundation of States & Councils	Book VII. i–ii.	Book II. Ch. 5–10.	A: i. 66, iv. 1–122, v. 1–149. B: Pt. I. 12–99.	
Division of State Powers & Taxes	Book VII. iv–v. Book VIII. iv–v. Book V. x.	Book II. Ch. 11–12.	A: iv. 1–179, v.100–139, vi. 84–86. B:Pt.I. 18–99, Pt.II.310–321	Book IV. ix. Book V. i. Pt. i–iv. V. ii. Pt. i–ii.

Source: Sæther (2017a 187).
Notes: In the column on the *Lectures on Jurisprudence* 'A' relates to his lectures from 1762–63 and 'B' relates to his lectures from 1763–64 (The 1766 report).

5.8 Theory of Human Behaviour

The Theory of Moral Sentiments TMS is not included in the table above. However, it is in this book that Smith's theory of human behaviour primarily can be found. There can be no doubt that when Smith wrote this book, he used the first three books of Pufendorf's major work *De Jure Naturae* and chapter four to seven of his 'student edition' *De Officio*.

Smith agreed with Hutcheson and Pufendorf that man has an ability to reach correct moral decisions. However, he disagreed with Hutcheson's views that man, at birth, was fully equipped to make correct decisions. Man's moral decisions are not informed by any higher principle, but by his common feeling of sympathy for others. This principle of sympathy enables man to adjust his actions to a level that is socially acceptable. Again, Smith's views are more congruent with Pufendorf's view that our sociability with others will tell us how to make the right decisions. Smith's *Wealth of Nations* contains evidence that he used Pufendorf's theory of the self-interested social man (who, by satisfying his own needs also satisfies the needs of others) to construct his own theory of economic growth in a commercial society. Hont (1986) claims that 'Smith's contemporaries recognised that the famous passage on the benevolence of the butcher, the brewer and the baker was a direct comment on the central issues of natural law'.[17] With his *Theory of Moral Sentiments* and *Wealth of Nations*, Smith made self-interest an acceptable drive for modern man. Pufendorf started this development.

Smith's *The Theory of Moral Sentiments* was an inquiry into the origin of moral approbation and disapproval that is moral judgement. It is clear that he must have had *De Jure Naturae et Gentium,* particularly Book II, ready at hand when he wrote the book. It is from the outset clear that he does not follow Hutcheson. If anyone should be in doubt, Smith discusses recent and ancient philosophy in the final part from 1790 of the sixth edition of this book.[18] Here Smith claims that the late Dr. Hutcheson was 'undoubtedly, beyond all comparison the most acute, the most distinct, the most philosophical, and what is of the greatest consequence of all, the soberest and most judicious' supporter of a system, which makes virtue consist in benevolence or love the sole principle of action, and which also directed the exertion of all other attributes (TMS VII, ii, 3, 301). Hutcheson was not willing to allow self-interest, in any case, to be a motive of virtuous actions. He went so far as claiming that 'even a regard to the pleasure of self-approbation, to the comfortable applause of our own consciences, diminished the merit of a benevolent action'. This was also a selfish motive (Ibid, 303). Smith ends his account of 'this amiable system' claiming that it has a peculiar tendency to nourish and support 'in the human heart', the noblest and the most agreeable of all affections with the consequence that it not only checks the injustice of self-love but in some measure also discourages the principle altogether by representing it as what would never reflect any honour upon those who were influenced by it (Ibid, 303–304).

However, Smith was not discouraged, and he is clearly influenced by Pufendorf (DJNG II, iv, 14–15), when he at the outset asks the fundamental question regarding how man, who is basically a creature that tries to pursue his own self-love or self-interest, can form moral judgements in which self-interest seems to be checked or transmuted to a higher plane? His answer is clear:

> How selfish soever man may be supposed, there are evidently some principles in his nature, which interest him in the fortune of others, and render their happiness necessary to him, though he derives nothing from it except the pleasure of feeling it. (TMS I, I, 1, 9)

This feeling for others, which he called sympathy, is to be found in all men. 'The greatest ruffian, the most hardened violator of the law of society, is not altogether without it' (Ibid). The term sympathy is clarified in the following way:

> Pity and compassion are words appropriated to signify our fellow-feeling with the sorrow of others. Sympathy, though its meaning was, perhaps, originally the same, may now, however, without much impropriety, be made use of to denote our fellow-feeling with any passion whatever. (Ibid, 10)

[17] Hont (1986) mentions, as an example, Governor Pownall (1978), who wrote an open letter with comments to Smith after the publication of *The Wealth of Nations*. This letter is included in the Danish-Norwegian edition and translation of *The Wealth of Nations* from 1779–80.

[18] This part was added in edition 6 from 1790. See DD Raphael and AL Macfie (1976) *Introduction* to Adam Smith's *The Theory of Moral Sentiments*. All references are to this edition.

Smith claims, like Pufendorf (DJNG II. iii. 14), that self-interest is a primary drive in all human beings.

> Every man is, no doubt, by nature, first and principally recommended to his own care; and as he is fitter to take care of himself than of any other person, it is fit and right that it should be so. Every man therefore, is much more deeply interested in whatever immediately concerns himself, than in what concerns any other man; and to hear, perhaps, of the death of another person, with whom we have no particular connexion, will give us less concern, will spoil our stomach, or break our rest much less than a very insignificant disaster which has befallen ourselves. (TMS II, I, I, 2, 82–83)

Every man may be the whole world to himself but to the rest of humankind he is a most insignificant part of it. His own happiness may be of more importance to him than that of the rest of the world. However, it may be true that every individual in his own breast naturally prefers himself to all humankind, 'yet he dares not look mankind in the face, and avow that he acts according to this principle' (Ibid). Self-interest is therefore not the only human drive. Furthermore, it is not incompatible with sympathy or benevolence. These basic motives live side by side and each has its part to play at the appropriate time. This view is in sharp contrast to Hobbes, Mandeville and Hume, who argued that all our sentiments can be deduced from certain refinements of self-love. However, it is in accordance with Pufendorf's views on self-interest and sociability: 'By a sociable attitude we mean an attitude of each man towards every other man, by which each is understood to be bound to the other by kindness, peace, and love and therefore by a mutual obligation' (DJNG II, iii, 15, 208).

Smith agreed with Hutcheson that man has an ability to reach correct moral decisions. However, he disagreed with his view that man at birth was fully equipped to make correct decisions. Man's moral decisions are not reached by any higher principle but by his common feeling of sympathy for others. This principle of sympathy enables man to adjust his actions to a level that is socially acceptable. Again, Smith's views are more congruent with Pufendorf's view that our sociability with others will tell us how to make the right decisions.

To explain how individual self-love is checked and brought down to something that can be accepted by all men in society, Smith introduces the concept of a supposed well informed or 'impartial spectator' within each individual who would judge, approve or disapprove his actions along with the concept of 'fair play' that governs the interactions between all men in society. The allusions to Pufendorf (DJNG I, iv, 1), who introduced an 'internal moderator' or 'internal director' of a man's action that would make it possible for him to choose what would seem most suitable to him, are clear.[19] The impartial spectator of Smith's may then enter into the principles of man's conduct, 'which is what of all things he has the greatest desire to do, he must, upon this, as upon all other occasions, humble the arrogance

[19] Pufendorf uses *'internal moderator'* in his *Elementorum Jurisprudentae Universalis* (2009 [1660. 1672]), BII,

Obs. II, 1, 306) and *'internal director'* in his *De Jure Naturae et Gentium* (1934 [1688, 1672] I, iv, 1).

of his self-love, and bring it down to something which other men can go along with' (TMS II, ii, 2, 1, 83).

How this can be understood in business life, he explains in the following way: 'In the race for wealth, and honours, and preferments, he may run as hard as he can, and strain every nerve and every muscle, in order to outstrip all his competitors. But if he should justle, or throw down any of them, the indulgence of the spectators is entirely at an end. It is a violation of fair play, which they cannot admit of' (Ibid).

Like Pufendorf (DJNG II, I, 5–6, 15), Smith contends that men are social beings, and social beings are dependent on each other: 'It is thus that man, who can subsist only in society, was fitted by nature to that situation for which he was made. All members of human society stand in need for each other's assistance, and are likewise exposed to mutual injuries' (TMS II, ii, 3, 1, 85).

It is not possible for man to grow up to manhood 'in some solitary place'. When he is brought into society, he is able not only to view his own passions, guided by the 'impartial spectator', but also to adjust and moderate these passions in accordance with the other members of society:

> Bring him into society, and all his own passions will immediately become the causes of new passions. He will observe that mankind approves of some of them and are disgusted by others. He will be elevated in the one case and cast down in the other; his desires and aversions, his joy and sorrows, will now often become the cause of new desires and new aversions, new joys and new sorrows. They will now, therefore, interest him deeply, and often call upon his most attentive consideration. (TMS III, 1, 3, 111)

From this, it is also clear that man, according to Smith, is not endowed by nature with an innate moral sense. Man has to be educated, that is, brought into society with others. This is in opposition to Hutcheson but in accordance with Pufendorf (DJNG II, iii, 13).

Smith also discusses in what order individuals are recommended by Nature to our care and attention.

> Every man, as the Stoic used to say, is first and principally recommended to his own care; and every man is certainly, in every respect, fitter and abler to take care of himself than of any other person. Every man feels his own pleasure and his own pains more sensibly than those of other people. The former are the original sensations; the latter the reflected or sympathetic images of those sensations. The former may be said to be the substance; the latter the shadow. (TMS VI, ii, 1, 1, 219)

After him come the members of his own family: his parents, his children, his brothers and sisters, his earliest friendships, the children of brothers and sisters and so on.

> After the persons who are recommended to our beneficence, either by their connection to ourselves, by their personal qualities, or by their past service, come those who are pointed out, not indeed to what is called, true friendship, but to our benevolent attention and good offices; those who are distinguished by their extraordinary situation; the greatly fortunate and the greatly unfortunate, the rich and the powerful, the poor and the wretched. (TMS VI, ii, 1, 19, 225)

The question concerning what motivates human actions is also discussed in Smith's *Lectures on Jurisprudence*, delivered and written in the early 1760s but not published as mentioned before 1895. In these lectures, self-interest is also looked upon as a general universal principle. He discusses human motives whenever commerce is introduced into a country. These motives can be reduced to self-interest, 'that general principle which regulates the actions of every man, and which leads men to act in a certain manner from views of advantage'. The drive of self-interest is deeply implanted in 'an Englishman as a Dutchman" (LOJ Pt, II, 327).

In The Wealth of Nations, Smith (1976 [1776]) discusses the principle which gives occasion to the division of labour.[20] The allusion to Pufendorf (DJNG II, iii, 14, 207), who emphasized the importance of cooperation among men, is there when Smith stresses that men at all times and contrary to animals, who in their natural state have no occasion for the assistance of other living creatures, is 'in need of co-operation and assistance of great multitudes' (WN I, ii, 18).

Smith starts out claiming that the division of labour is not originally the effect of any human wisdom. 'It is the necessary, though very slow and gradual, consequence of a certain propensity in human nature which has in view no such extensive utility; the propensity to truck, barter, and exchange one thing for another' (Ibid, 17). This propensity is self-interest and it is common to all men. However, man has almost constant occasion for the help of his fellow man and he cannot expect this help from their benevolence only. 'He will be more likely to prevail if he can interest their self-love in his favour, and show them that it is for their own advantage to do for him what he requires of them' (Ibid, 18). When someone offers another a bargain, this is what takes place. If you give me what I want, I will give you what you want. Then he comes up with one of his most famous statements: 'It is not from the benevolence of the butcher, the brewer, or the baker that we expect our dinner, but from their regard to their own interest. We address ourselves, not to their humanity but to their self-love, and never talk to them of our own necessities but of their advantages' (Ibid).

With the *Theory of Moral Sentiments* and *The Wealth of Nations*, Smith made self-interest an acceptable drive for modern man. Pufendorf started this development. Smith's *Wealth of Nations* contains evidence that Smith used Pufendorf's theory of human behaviour, that is, his theory of the self-interested social man, who by satisfying his own needs also satisfies the needs of others, in a commercial society, to construct his own theory of economic growth in such a society. Hont (2005, 162) claims that 'Smith's contemporaries recognised that the famous passage on the benevolence of the butcher, the brewer and the baker was a direct comment on the central issues of natural law'.[21]

[20] This chapter, Book 1, Ch. II, is almost identical to the 'Early Draft of part of The Wealth of Nations' from 1759 in *Lectures on Jurisprudence* pp. 562–581.

[21] Hont (2005, 162) mentions, as an example, Governor Pownall (1776), who wrote an open letter with comments to Smith after the publication of *The Wealth of Nations*. In the Danish-Norwegian edition and translation of *The Wealth of Nations* from 1779–80, this letter is included.

5.9 Theory of Property

In his *Lectures on Jurisprudence* Adam Smith (1982a [1762, 7]) develops his theory of property. He starts out claiming the following: 'The first and chief design of all civil governments, is, as I observed, to preserve justice amongst the members of the state and to prevent all encroachments on the individuals in it, from others of the same society.' That is to maintain everyone in his perfect rights. In the first place, he considers those rights that belong to a man as a man, 'as they are generally most simple and easily understood, and generally can be considered without respect to any other condition' (Ibid, 8). He contends that these rights correspond to what Pufendorf (DJNG IV, iii, 1–6) calls natural rights. Furthermore, he observes the distinction, 'which Mr. Hutcheson, after Baron Puffendorf, has made of rights', and he discusses these (Ibid, 9).

One of these rights is the full right of property. By this right, a man has the sole claim to a subject 'exclusive of all others', but he himself can use it as he pleases. He can, if he has lost a subject claim it from any possessor, and even if the possessor might have come justly by it, he cannot claim any restitution but must restore it to the owner. Property is considered an exclusive right by which we can prevent any other person from using it. (Ibid, 10).

How did the right to property originate? Smith asserts the following: 'The only case where the origin of natural rights is not altogether plain, is in that of property.' He continues in the spirit of Pufendorf (DJNG IV, iii, 1): 'It does not at first appear evident that, e.g. any thing which may suit another as well or perhaps better than it does me, should belong to me exclusively of all others barely because I have got it into my power' (Ibid, 13). As an example, he uses an apple. Why should it be altogether appropriated to me and all others excluded merely because I had pulled it from the tree?[22]

Property may, according to Smith, have its occasion in five sources. First by occupation, we get a thing in our power that was not the property of another before. Second by tradition, property is voluntarily transferred from one to another. Third by accession, a man has, e. g., the right to the horse's shoes along with the horse. Fourth by prescription, a right to a thing that belonged to another, arising from long and uninterrupted possession. Fifth by succession, the nearest in kin or the testamentary heir gets the property left to him by the testator.

---

[22] Pufendorf used as an example acorn (DJNG IV, iv, 13, 554). Locke took over this example but extended it to acorns and apples (TT II, 28, 306).

5.10 The Four-Stage Theory

Before considering these causes of how property is acquired, Smith like Pufendorf asserts that it is proper to observe that the regulations concerning them vary according to the state or age society is in at that time. What Smith had in mind was an inductive historical investigation, which could explain the fact that, while property was everywhere seen as an exclusive right, those goods men have allowed to be property varied considerably 'according to the state or age society is in at that time' (Ibid, 14). He claims, like Pufendorf (DJNG IV, iv, 11–13 and V, v, 11), in his rudimentary theory that there are four distinct stages that human kind has passed through: '1st, the Age of Hunters: 2ndy, the Age of Shepherds; 3rd, the Age of Agriculture; and 4th, the Age of Commerce' (Ibid).

With strong allusions to Pufendorf, Smith then explains in more detail each of these ages or stages and how property developed in each.[23] 'It is easy to see that in these several ages of society, the laws and regulations with regard to property must be very different' (Ibid, 16). Few laws and regulations are required in the age of hunters and shepherds, but in the age of agriculture and commerce many more laws and regulations are necessary. When flocks and herds come to be reared, property is introduced together with many more laws and regulations. They are necessary to prevent thefts and robberies since they are being easily committed in such an age. In the age of agriculture, they are perhaps not so easily exposed to thefts and robbery, but new ways are added whereby property might be disrupted. The laws might not be so rigorous, but they will be of a far greater number than among a nation of shepherds. In the age of commerce, the subjects of property are greatly increased, and the laws must be proportionally multiplied. 'The more improved any society is and the greater length the several means of supporting the inhabitants are carried, the greater will be the number of their laws and regulations necessary to maintain justice, and prevent infringements of the right of property' (Ibid).

5.11 Property as an Exclusive Right

Smith, like Pufendorf (DJNG IV, iv, 6), asks how occupation, that is, the bare possession of a subject, comes to give us an exclusive right to the subject so acquired. How can a man by pulling down an apple have a right to that apple and a power of

[23] Ronald L. Meek (1976b, 31–35) in his *Social Science and the Ignoble Savage* claims that the immediate source of Smith's 'four stages' probably was Montesquieu's *Spirit of the Laws* book xviii. See also Ian Simpson Ross (2010, 121). This author disagrees with both Meek and Ross, since these stages are more developed in Pufendorf's *De Jure Naturae et Gentium*. In addition, Pufendorf was also Montesquieu's source. Another Scot that built on Pufendorf's Four-Stage theory was Lord Kames (1696–1782), who had studied law at Edinburgh. In his *Historical law tracts* from 1774 and in his *Sketches of the History of Man* he described human history as having four stages.

excluding all others from it, 'and that an injury should be conceived to be done when such a subject is taken from the possessor' (Ibid, 17)?

Here again, Smith makes use of the impartial spectator. If someone has acquired a subject by occupation and if some others try to take it from him, the impartial spectator would support him in defending his property 'and even in avenging himself when injured' (Ibid, 17).

After having explained the foundation on which occupation gives the property to the occupant, he considers and discusses in some detail at what time property is conceived to begin by occupation. Thereafter he discusses in what circumstances property continues and at what time it is supposed to be at an end (Ibid, 18).

5.12 Property Based on a Common Consent or Agreement

Adam Smith does not directly use Pufendorf's tacit pact or agreement (DJNG IV, iv, 4–9) as a foundation of his theory of property. However, there are allusions and clues that indicate that he comes close to it. He introduced the notion of common consent.

Among hunters, the notion of property seems at first to have been confined to one's person, his clothes and the tools that he needed. Their occupation led them to be continually changing their place of habitat. The introduction of shepherds made habitation more fixed but still very uncertain. By the consent of the tribe, their huts have been allowed to be the property of the builder. 'The introduction of the property of houses must have therefore been by the common consent of the severall members of some tribe or society' (Ibid, 21). However, property would still not be extended to land or pasture.

Even after the introduction of agriculture, it took some time before the land was divided into individual properties. In the beginning, the land was cultivated in common and the produce distributed according to the size of families and the rank of individuals. The inclination of a single individual would not be sufficient to give him ownership of a piece of land. The rest of the community would protest against him who tried to make common land private.

The first origin of private property would probably happen when men started to live in cities, 'which would probably be the case in every improved society' (Ibid, 22). In time, property would be extended to almost every subject. Yet Smith, like Pufendorf (DJNG IV, v, 2), claims that there are still some things that must continue to be held in common. Smith discusses wild beasts, the air, running water, a fountain by the wayside, the waters of rivers and sailing on the sea (Ibid, 23).

In his 1763–64 lectures, Smith also treats the introduction of property. The nature of rights he divides into natural and acquired. The latter are divided into real and personal. Property is a real right. He continues as he did in his 1762–63 lectures. Among savage people, hunters and gatherers, property begins and ends with possessions, which are things close to their own bodies. Among shepherds, the idea of property is extended not only to what they carry with them but also to what they have deposited in their hovels, including their cattle. When people started to cultivate the earth, there was initially no private property. However, when proper agriculture was introduced, land was divided, and property begins when 'a division be made from common agreement' (Ibid, 460). The allusions to Pufendorf, who claimed that 'dominion presupposes absolutely an act of man and an agreement, whether tacit or express', are very strong (DJNG IV, iv, 4, 536). Smith ends this discussion contending that property would, in time, be extended to almost every subject.

5.13 A Labour Theory of Property

In *The Wealth of Nations*, Smith (1976 [1776] I, x, 136) has one sentence concerned with property. 'The property which every man has in his own labour, as it is the original foundation of all other property, so it is the most sacred and inviolable.' This has by some authors been interpreted as an adherence to Locke's labour theory of property – a theory that Smith took over from Hutcheson and Hutcheson took over from Locke. Knud Haakonssen (1989, 106–107) has investigated this belief and contends that Smith does not subscribe to this theory. Furthermore, he posits that Smith was obviously very strongly indebted to the continental natural law tradition of Grotius, Pufendorf, and others, and especially to the form, which this tradition has been given him by his teacher Hutcheson. Pufendorf claims that cultivation, which requires the use of labour, is important for the establishment of private property (DJNG IV, iv, 6).

5.14 Theories of Value, Money and Trade

Smith treats the theory of value and money in both his *Lectures on Jurisprudence* and in *The Wealth of Nations*. Smith made good use of Pufendorf's natural law works. Istvan Hont (2005, 51) points out that Smith's two books, *The Theory of Moral Sentiments* and *The Wealth of Nations*, 'together provide a complete analysis of market behaviour'. He adds that in these works 'Smith merged and reworked insights that were first adumbrated by Pufendorf, Nicole and other French moralists'. In her *Studies in the History of Economic Theory before 1870*, Marian Bowley (1973, 129) asserts that Smith was the conscious or unconscious heir in the direct line to the schoolmen with respect to the concept of the price mechanism and the natural prices of commodities. 'Indeed, since Hutcheson, his teacher, made him familiar with Pufendorf's work, which set out the views of the Schoolmen, the line of affiliation of thought seems obvious.'

5.15 Value in Lectures on Jurisprudence

In his *Lectures on Jurisprudence*, Smith (1982a, b [1762], 353) treats opulence. He first considers the rule of exchange, or what it is that regulates the price of commodities. Next, he notes that money can be considered the measure by which we compute the value of commodities (as a measure of value) or the common instrument of commerce or exchange. There can be no doubt that Smith must have had Pufendorf's main natural law work *The Jure Naturae et Gentium* (V. i) accessible when he prepared his lectures. The obvious reason being that he went further than Pufendorf's abridged *De Officio* and Hutcheson's *Introduction to Moral Philosophy*. The latter built, as discussed earlier, very closely on Pufendorf's works.

5.16 Theory of Price, the Natural Price and the Market Price

As an introduction Smith gives an account of the nature of wealth and the things in which the riches of the state might consist. He notes the need for cooperation in a commercial society, which was stressed by Pufendorf. But Smith also assert that a division of labour and an ample size of the market are crucial for economic development.

For every type of commodity Smith claims, as did Pufendorf (DJNG V, i, 8–9), that 'there are two separate prices to be considered, the natural and the market price' (Ibid, 356). The first is the price that is necessary to induce someone to enter a business. This price includes the cost of production and the associated risk of going into production. The market price, which might differ considerably from the natural price, 'is regulated by other circumstances' (Ibid, 357). The other circumstances that determine the price are '1st, the demand or need for it; 2dly, the abundance of it in proportion to demand; and 3dly, the wealth of the demand, or demanders' (Ibid, 358). Smith then discusses, in the same manner as Pufendorf (DJNG V, i, 10), how changes in these circumstances will influence the market price.

If a thing is of no use, such as a lump of clay, but is brought into the market, it will have no price, as no one demands it. If it should have some use, the price will be determined by the demand and the availability of supply. Something like diamonds, which is hardly of any use but still has a demand, will have a high price since the quantity is limited. On the other hand, water is a necessity but will have no price because of its abundance (Ibid, 333). This description of what has become the 'paradox of value' cannot have been taken from Hutcheson, but there are strong clues to Pufendorf's treatment (DJNG V, i, 6). The market price and the natural price of commodities coincide with each other. If the market price of a commodity is below the natural price, the suppliers cannot pay the cost of labour. This will have many effects but one being that the supply of the commodity is reduced, and the price will increase. If the market price was above the natural price the effect will be the opposite.

Smith, like Pufendorf (DJNG V, i, 6), claims that all monopolies limit the supply and raise the price of commodities and therefore are detrimental to the opulence of a nation. As an example, Smith mentions the Hudson Bay Company. In his view, all such companies are detrimental to the opulence of nations because they prevent free competition. Free competition would have brought down the price to its natural level, a level consistent with production costs and the risk the company runs. All such companies are a public nuisance (Ibid, 363).

5.17 *Theory of Money*

Smith (1982b [1762], 368) uses the same arguments as Pufendorf (DJNG IV, i, 12–14) when he claims that money serves two purposes. 'It is first the measure of value.' However, 'it is also the instrument of commerce, or medium of exchange and permutation'.

As it was for Pufendorf, it was also clear to Smith that money facilitated exchange and promoted commerce.

> They therefore took upon them to coin money of gold and silver and put a stamp on it, which tho it neither added to nor diminish'd the value gave every one who saw it the public faith that it was of such weight and such a fine(ne)ss. The first thing in all probability which would be ascertained by coinage would be the fine(ne)ss, which was most difficult to be discovered before the art of milling or stamping the edges was invented, and that of fitting the stamp precisely to the size of the metal. (Ibid, 371)

It was necessary that the government of a country should carry the trouble and expense of coinage. The stamp given by the government 'gives no additional value, it merely ascertains the value' (Ibid, 373). The motive is that money facilitates taxes and promotes commerce, which will enrich the people and thereby also benefit the government. Shrinking in the measure of value has often been caused by either the necessities or frauds of government.

5.18 *Debasement of Money*

Smith therefore brings up for discussion the effects of debasement of money in general and in particular its effects on the payments of debts and commerce. 'And here civil law of all countries and natural justice and equity are quite contrary' (Ibid, 100). Consequently, it is clear that Smith, as Pufendorf (DJNG V, I, 14–15 and V, vii, 6), held debasement of money to be against natural law and that one should restore the same value as one has received, without regard to the nominal value of money. 'Justice and equity plainly require that one should restore the same value as he received without regard to the nominal value of money, and therefore he is to restore as much in the old coins or an equal value in the new as he received' (Ibid, 101). Smith adds: 'But the civil government in all countries have constituted the exact contrary of this' (Ibid). The reason for such conduct is that governments have had difficulties in raising money. He stresses and shows, like Pufendorf (DJNG V, I, 14), that such steps are very detrimental.

Debasement of money will be detrimental to commerce. 'The effects of this operation is very prejudiciall to commerce. The great benefit of money is to give a plain, clear, and ready measure of value and medium of exchange for all commodities; but this is considerably disturbed by this means' (Ibid, 374). When an alteration is made in the value one does not readily know whether the new coin 'is equal to a certain value; this necessarily embarrasses commerce' (Ibid, 375). He claims that it is necessary that all debts should be paid by the value of the old money.

5.19 Money and Trade

Smith claims, as did Pufendorf (DJNG V, I, 11–12) before him, that money is extremely necessary as an instrument for trade. 'The intention of money as an instrument of commerce is to circulate goods nec(e)ssary for men, and food, cloths and lodging' (Ibid, 377). He stresses that it is not the money, 'which makes the opulence of a nations, but the plenty of food, cloaths and lodging which is circulated' (Ibid, 378). He attacks the theory that placed the wealth of a nation on its amount of coin and money. Trade increases the wealth of a nation. The prohibition of exportation of coin and bullion is therefore one of these hurtful regulations that has been practised by many countries.

5.20 Money in the Wealth of Nations

In *The Wealth of Nations*, Smith (1976 [1776]) discusses in Book I both the origin and use of money and the theory of value. This treatment is, as stated above, based on his *Lectures on Jurisprudence*. He contends that when the division of labour has been thoroughly established, only a small part of what a man wants is the produce of what his own labour can supply. He will then exchange a part of his produce with what other people can supply. 'Every man thus lives by exchanging, or becomes in some measure a merchant, and the society itself grows to what is properly a commercial society' (Ibid, 26). Different societies have used different commodities as a method of exchange; the most practical is money coined from gold and silver. Smith, like Pufendorf, warns also here against debasement of money, which is favourable to the debtor, and ruinous to the creditor.

In all civilized nations, money has become the universal instrument of commerce, in which goods of all kinds are bought and sold, or exchanged for one another. The rules of exchange determine what may be called the relative or exchangeable value of goods.

> The word VALUE, it is to be observed, has two different meanings, and sometimes expresses the utility of some particular object, and sometimes the power of purchasing other goods which the possession of that object conveys. The one may be called 'value in use;' the other, 'value in exchange', The things which have the greatest value in use have frequently little or no value in exchange; and on the contrary, those which have the greatest value in exchange have frequently little or no value in use. (Ibid, 32–33)

He then follows Pufendorf and presents, as in his *Lectures on Jurisprudence,* the 'paradox of value'. 'Nothing is more useful than water, but it will purchase scarce any thing; scarce any thing can be had in exchange for it. A diamond, on the contrary, has scarce any value in use: but a very great quantity of other goods may frequently be had in exchange for it' (Ibid, 33).

5.21 A Labour Theory of Value

However, Smith changes his mind and like Locke introduces a rudimentary labour theory of value. 'If among a nation of hunters, for example, it usually costs twice the labour to kill a beaver which it does to kill a deer, one beaver should naturally exchange for or be worth two deer. It is natural that what is usually the produce of 2 days or 2 hours labour, should be worth double of what is usually the produce of 1 day's or 1 hour's labour' (Ibid, 53). Since labour is not the same in all production, he modifies this view 'the produce of 1 hour's labour in the one way may frequently exchange for that of 2 hours labour in the other' (Ibid).[24]

5.22 The Natural and the Market Price

Smith starts out claiming that in every society there is an ordinary or average rate for wages, profit and rent in every different employment of labour, stock and land. 'These ordinary or average rates may be called the natural rates of wages, profit and rent, at the time and place in which they commonly prevail' (Ibid, 62). He then, more or less in the same way as Pufendorf (DJNG V, I, 8), defined the natural price. 'When the price of any commodity is neither more nor less than what is sufficient to pay the rent of the land, the wages of labour and the profits of the stock employed in raising preparing and bringing it to market, according to their natural rates, the commodity is then sold for what may be called its natural price' (Ibid). The commodity is then sold precisely for what it is worth, or for what it really costs the person, who brings it to the market. This cost does not comprehend the profit to the person who is to sell it again. If he sells it at a price, which does not allow him the ordinary rate of profit in this society, he is evidently a loser by the trade. The price

[24] Pownall (1776, 341ff) in his letter to Adam Smith was the first to criticize his labour theory of value.

that includes the ordinary rate of profit is the lowest at which he is likely to sell for any considerable time. He adds, 'at least where there is perfect liberty' (Ibid, 63). Smith claims, like Pufendorf (DJNG V, I, 9), that the actual price at which any commodity is commonly sold is called its market price. It may either be above, or below, or the same as its natural price. 'The market price of every particular commodity is regulated by the proportion between the quantity which is actually brought to market, and the demand of those who are willing to pay the natural price of the commodity, or the whole value of the rent, labour, and profit, which must be paid in order to bring it thither' (Ibid, 63). Smith calls such people the effectual demanders and their demand the effectual demand.

Changes in the factors that determine the demand will change the market price. 'The natural price, therefore, is as it were the central price, to which the prices of all commodities are continually gravitating' (Ibid, 65). Sometimes the market price will be a little above and sometimes a little below, but the price will gravitate towards the natural price.

Smith then goes on to discuss what determines the wages of labour, the wages and profit in the different employments of labour, stock and the rent of land.

5.23 Origin of Money and Debasement of Money

Smith's treatment of the origin of money follows his account in the *Lectures on Jurisprudence*, which built closely on Pufendorf's exposition. Money was introduced to facilitate exchange in a commercial society. 'It is in this manner that money has become in all civilized nations the universal instrument of commerce, by the intervention of which goods of all kinds are bought and sold or exchanged for one another' (Ibid, 32). Smith takes a strong stand against the debasement of money. Furthermore, he believes that such an operation can have detrimental effects. 'Such operations, therefore, have always proved favourable to the debtor, and ruinous to the creditor, and have sometimes produced a greater and more universal revolution in the fortunes of private persons, that could have been occasioned by a very great public calamity' (Ibid).

Smith makes it clear that the popular notion that wealth consists of money (or gold and silver) naturally arise from the double function of money, as an instrument of commerce and as the measure of value. However, it is not for its own sake that men desire money, but for the sake of what they can purchase with it.

5.24 Foundation of States and Councils

Smith (1982a, b [1762], 7) claimed in his *Lectures on Jurisprudence* that the first and chief design of a state or civil government was to preserve justice amongst the members of the state and to prevent all encroachments on the individuals in it from others in the same society. He stresses that justice is violated whenever a man is deprived of what he had a right to and could justly demand from others. Then he discusses how many ways justice may be violated, that is, in how many respects a man may be injured. He may be injured as a man, as a member of a family and as a citizen or member of a state. The allusion to Pufendorf (DJNG VII, i, 7), who claimed that states were established to gain security and protection from the evil or wickedness of men, is strong.

Smith came close to asserting, like Pufendorf, that private property arose from consent and agreement. However, he contended that the origin of government arose 'not as some writers imagine from any consent or agreement of a number of persons to submit themselves to such or such regulations, but from the natural progress which the men make in society' (Ibid, 207). From this starting point, he explains how a state and its different forms of government develops using the historical account of the four-stage theory of development, which he had inherited from Pufendorf. Numerous examples are described how different nations at various times have developed their governments and the powers of government, depending on what stage these nations have found themselves in.

There are two principles that explain why men enter into a civil society, a principle of authority and a principle of common or general interest.[25] With regard to the first principle, Smith claims that 'every one naturally has a disposition to respect an established authority and superiority of others, whatever they be' (Ibid, 318). Regarding the second principle, he claims that everyone sees that the magistrates not only support the government in general but the security and independence of each individual, and they see that this security cannot be attained without a regular government. 'Every one therefore thinks it most advisable to submit to the established government' (Ibid). In a monarchy, the principle of authority chiefly prevails. In a democracy, the principle of common or general interest is the most important. However, the principle of authority has some influence. In an aristocracy, the principle of authority is the leading one, but the other also has some effect. Smith stresses that all have a duty of allegiance to the sovereign: 'and yet no one has any conception of a previous contract either tacit or express' (Ibid, 321). He uses several lectures to argue against authors, such as Pufendorf, who believed in contracts.

In his 1763–64 lectures, Smith (1982a, b [1762], 402) repeats this view: 'It has been a common doctrine in this country that contract is the foundation of allegiance to the civil magistrate.' Then he starts out arguing that this is not the case and gives several reasons for this. He concludes: 'Contract is not therefore the principle of obedience to civil government, but the principle of authority and utility formerly explained' (Ibid, 404).

[25] In his 1766 lectures, he calls the second principle one of utility (Ibid, 401).

5.25 Voting Rules

Smith brings up for discussion in one of his 1762–63 lectures the question of what determines the voice of the people in a republic, that is, an aristocracy or a democracy. It is clear that he used both Hutcheson and Pufendorf in the preparation of this lecture. He follows Hutcheson in his *A System of Moral Philosophy*,[26] and Pufendorf in *De Jure Naturae et Gentium*[27]: 'It is a general rule that in every society the minority must submit to the majority' (Ibid, 290). However, it may often happen that the majority is not so easily determined. He uses the same numerical example as Hutcheson. There are three candidates A, B and C. A gets thirty-four votes out of hundred and B and C thirty-three each. A is chosen, although to sixty-six voters he might be the most obnoxious of all. Smith adds that this happens often in elections and that 'it is a very great grievance'. The solution when there are three candidates is to have a previous vote by which one candidate is excluded.

If this way of counting votes is used in a trial, it can have a grave result. Suppose someone is tried for murder and thirty-four out of a hundred find him guilty, thirty-three of manslaughter and thirty-three of chance-medley only. Although sixty-six absolve him from murder, he will be condemned if the questions are not made bipartite. First guilty of murder or not, the result will be acquittal. Next guilty of manslaughter or not, he will then be found guilty with sixty-seven votes.

If there is a draw when a council is voting, Smith claims, like Pufendorf (DJNG VII, ii, 15), that no decision should be made. The question of supermajority, which is discussed by Pufendorf and Hutcheson, is not discussed by Smith.

In *The Wealth of Nations*, Smith (1976 [1776], 213) discusses the duties of the sovereign and how sovereignty has developed. The first duty is that of defending the society from the violence and injustice of other states. The second duty is that of protecting, as far as possible, every member of society from the injustice or oppression of every other member in it (Ibid, 231). The third and last duty is that of erecting and maintaining those public institutions and those public works, which may be in the highest degree advantageous to a great society (Ibid, 244). Civil government supposes a certain subordination. The necessity of civil government gradually grows with the acquisition of valuable property. Some men will gain superiority or sovereignty over the greater part of their brethren. The leaders will have some or all of the four following characteristics: first, superiority of personal qualifications, of strength, beauty and agility of body; of wisdom; and virtue, of prudence, justice, fortitude and moderation of mind; second the superiority of age; third the superiority of fortune; fourth, the superiority of birth. Smith's discussion of the duties of the sovereign and subordination of the people gives allusions to Pufendorf's pact or agreement of association (DJNG VII, ii, 7).

---

[26] Book III, 6, 241.

[27] DJNG VII, ii, 15, 987.

5.26 Division of Responsibility and Principles of Taxation

In his 1762–63 *Lectures on Jurisprudence*, Smith gives numerous examples of how different nations at different times have developed their governments and the powers of government, depending on what stage these nations have been in (1982a, b [1762]). Like Pufendorf (DJNG VII, iv, 2–11), treats the development of the executive power, the legislative power, the power of the magistrate and officers and the judicial power. He discusses the duties the subjects owe the sovereign power of whatever nature, 'the monarch in monarchy, the nobles in an aristocracy and the body of people in a democracy' (Ibid, 291). At length, he outlines the different forms of crimes that subjects might commit against the sovereign power. However, the subjects not only have duties, they also have rights. He then discusses the duties that the sovereign owes to his people and he considers 'the crimes which the sovereign may be guilty of against the subjects' (Ibid:304). The allusions to Pufendorf (DJNG VII, v, 3–9) are everywhere to be found.

5.27 On Taxation

In his 1763–64 *Lectures on Jurisprudence*, Smith starts out explaining why governments need revenue and he discusses the proper means of levying revenue, 'which must come from the people by taxes, duties etc.' (Ibid, 398). The allusions to Pufendorf (DJNG VIII, V, 3–4) are numerous.

Smith's starting point is that revenue or taxes are one of the reasons 'that the progress of opulence has been so slow' (Ibid, 529). However, he continues and gives an account of how in the beginning there no government revenue and no taxes was, but when society developed 'magazines must be provided, ships built, palaces and other public buildings erected and kept up, and consequently a public revenue levied' (Ibid, 530).

There are many expenses necessary in a civilized country: 'Armies, fleets, fortified places and public buildings, judges and officers of the revenue must be supported, and if they be neglected disorder will ensue' (Ibid, 531). A land rent to serve all these purposes would be the most improper thing in the world.

Smith then claims that all taxes may be considered in two divisions: taxes upon possessions (land, stock, and money) and taxes upon consumption. Subjects, therefore, can contribute to the support of the government through a land tax and/or a tax on commodities. In Britain, except for the land tax, most taxes are upon commodities. He discusses the advantages and disadvantages of these forms of taxation. It is easy to levy a tax upon land, but it is very difficult to lay a tax on stock and money 'without very arbitrary proceedings' (Ibid, 532). The land tax has the advantage that it is levied without great expense and tends not to raise the price of commodities, as it is raised in proportion to rent. Taxes upon possessions are naturally equal, but those upon consumption are naturally unequal. The advantage of taxes on consumption is that they are not felt, since they are 'being paid imperceptibly' (Ibid, 533).

The fifth book of Smith's *The Wealth of Nations* (1976 [1776], 341–440) is devoted to public finance. It includes a review of considerable length of fiscal practices of England and other countries. In it, he offered, according to Herold Groves (1974, 18), 'a great deal of advice on these matters, advice which was taken seriously by ministers and parliament'. In this exposition, he expands his treatment of taxation in his *Lectures on Jurisprudence*, for which Pufendorf (DJNG VII, ix, 10 and VIII, v, 3–7) was his major source.

Smith has both an extensive treatment of the sources of general revenue of the society and his principles of taxation. A society needs revenue for defence, for supporting the magistrates and for all other necessary expenses of government, for which the constitution of the state has not provided any particular revenue. The revenue, which must defray all the expenses of government, is the cost of defending the society and supporting the dignity of the chief magistrate and all other necessary expenses. The revenue that will cover these expenses comes from one of two sources. Either it comes from some funds, which belong to the sovereign, or commonwealth, and which are independent of the revenue of the people or it comes from the revenue of the people.

He then goes on to treat the funds, or sources of revenue, which belong to the sovereign or commonwealth. Next, he asserts that the private revenue of individuals arises from three sources: rent, profit and wages, and those taxes must be paid from some or all of these sources. He then endeavours to give an account of the taxes that will fall on each of these sources and those taxes, which will fall indifferently upon all these sources of private revenue.

Before Smith sets out to examine specific taxes, he informs his readers that many taxes are not ultimately paid from the sources of revenue, which they were originally intended. The reason, of course, is that market forces are at work.

As an introduction, he finds it necessary to put forward four maxims that apply to taxes in general. These maxims are very close to Pufendorf's principles of taxation expressed as the duties of the Supreme Sovereign (DJNG VII, ix, 10). First, taxes should be 'equal and equitable'. They should fall on individuals 'like the expense of management to the joint tenants of a great estate, who are obliged to contribute in proportion to their respective interests in the estate'. Further, 'the subjects of every state ought to contribute to the support of the government, as nearly as possible in proportion to their respective abilities; that is in proportion to the revenues which they respectively enjoy under the protection of the state' (Ibid, 350). Smith, like Pufendorf, was a firm believer in proportionality in taxation and like Pufendorf (DJNG VIII, v, 10) he supported a no tax or a minimal tax for poor people.

Second, taxes ought to be certain and not arbitrary. The time of payment, the manner of payment, and the quantity to be paid ought all 'to be clear and plain to contributor and every other person'. Otherwise, the taxpayer may be subject to extortionate administration. Smith claimed that the certainty of what each individual ought to pay is in taxation a matter of so great importance 'that a very considerable degree of inequality, it appears, I believe, from the experience of all nations, is not near so great an evil as a very small degree of uncertainty' (Ibid, 351).

Third, taxes ought to be levied at the time or in the way it is most likely to be convenient for the contributor to pay it. Taxes on land or houses should be payable when rents normally are paid. Taxes on consumable goods and on luxury items are finally paid by the consumer, when he has occasion to buy the goods (Ibid).

Fourth, taxes should be economical to collect so that they take out of the pockets of the people, 'as little as possible, over and above what it brings into the public treasury of the state'. There are four reasons why taxes might be contrary to this principle. First, the levying of taxes may require a great number of officers, which have to be paid. Second, the taxes may obstruct the industry of the people. Third, the forfeitures and other penalties that tax evaders should have paid are not, in fact, paid since it ruined them, and hence no tax revenue is generated. Fourth, subjecting taxpayers to frequent visits and odious examinations by the tax collectors has a dampening effect on people's spirits and energy. Although this is not, strictly speaking, an expense, it is certainly equivalent to the expense (Ibid, 351).

The clues and allusions to Pufendorf's treatment of taxation in his *De Jure Naturae et Gentium* are strong. Smith uses his four maxims on taxation and starts a comprehensive examination and evaluation of particular taxes, with examples from various political systems and different countries also using an historical context. His thoroughness in this exposition is impressive.

6 Conclusion

With his natural law works, which also included ethics, jurisprudence and political economy Pufendorf became famous all over Europe and North America. For more than one hundred years, he was the most well-known philosopher and scholar.

This exposition claims that John Locke, Charles-Louis Montesquieu, Jean-Jaques Rousseau and the Physiocrats built extensively on Pufendorf's works when they wrote and developed their own ideas of political economy.

Gershom Carmichael introduced Pufendorf's *De Officio* when he taught at the University of Glasgow. His successor Francis Hutcheson continued his practice and furthermore used Pufendorf's works when he wrote on political economy.

As a student at Glasgow and Oxford, Adam Smith became familiar with Pufendorf's ideas of political economy. He used these ideas extensively when he held his lectures on jurisprudence at University of Glasgow and when he wrote *The Theory of Moral Sentiment* and *The Wealth of Nations*. Pufendorf's position in the history of economic thought should therefore be well established.

References

Baum Al (1979) Montesquieu and Social Theory, pp 509-605, Oxford: Pergamon Press

Bowley M (1973) Studies in the History of Economic Theory before 1870. London: The Macmillan Press Ltd.

Cannan E [Ed.] (1896) Lectures on Justice, Police, Revenue and Arms delivered in the University of Glasgow by Adam Smith. Oxford:

Cohen A (2014) 31. Philosophy and History: The Paradoxes of History. In Garret (2014), pp. 754-772

Cohler AM (1989 [1748]) Introduction. In Montesquieu (1989) The Spirit of the Laws, Cambridge: Cambridge University Press.

Courtney CP (1968) Montesquieu, In J Cruickshank [Ed.] French Literature and its Background, Vol. III, The Eighteenth Century, pp. 30-44, Oxford: Oxford University Press

de Roover R (1974) Business, Banking, and Economic Thought in Late Medieval and Early Modern Europe, Chicago and London: The University of Chicago Press

Dufour A (1991) Pufendorf. In J H Burns (1991): The Cambridge History of Political Thought 1450-1700, pp. 561-588.

Ekelund Jr. RB & Hébert R F (1990) A History of Economic Theory and Method, New York: McGraw-Hill, Inc.

Fox-Genovese E (1976) The Origins of Physiocracy. Economic Revolution and Social Order in Eighteenth Century France, Ithaca and London: Cornell University Press

Friedrich C J (2002) Corruption Concepts in Historical Perspective. In Heidenheimer AJ and Johnston M [Eds.] (2002), pp. 15-23

Garret A [Ed.] (2014) The Routledge Companion to Eighteenth Century Philosophy, London and New York: Routledge Taylor & Francis Group

Groves H (1974) Tax Philosophers: Two hundred years of thought in Great Britain and the United States. University of Wisconsin Press, Madison, Wisconsin.

Gourevitch V [Ed.] (2007) Introduction. In Rousseau, The Social Contract and other later political writings

Gourevitch V [Ed.] (2008) Introduction. In Rousseau, The Discourses and other early political writings

Haakonssen K (1989) The Science of a Legislator. The Natural Jurisprudence of David Hume & Adam Smith, Cambridge: Cambridge University Press

Hont I (1986) The Language of sociability and commerce: Samuel Pufendorf and thetheoretical foundations of the 'Four-Stages Theory'. In Pagden [Ed.] (1987) The Languages of Political Economy in Early-Modern Europe, Cambridge: Cambridge University Press. Or the first chapter in Hont (2005)

Hont I (2005) Jealousy of Trade. International Competition and the Nation-State in Historical Perspective, Cambridge, Massachusetts and London: The Belknap Press of Harvard University Press

Hueglin TD (2008) Classical Debates of the 21st Century: Rethinking Political Thought, Petersborough: Broadview Press

Hutcheson F (1969a [1747]) A Short Introduction to Moral Philosophy, in three books; containing the Elements of Ethicks and the Law of Nature. Collected Works Volume IV, Hildesheim: Georg Olms Verlagsbuchhandlung

Hutcheson F (1969b [1755]) A System of Moral Philosophy. Collected Works Volume V and VI, Hildesheim: Georg Olms Verlagsbuchhandlung

Hutchison T (1988) Before Adam Smith. The Emergence of Political Economy, 1662-1776, Oxford: Basil Blackwell

Jolley N (1999) Locke his philosophical thought, Oxford: Oxford University Press

Kingston R (1996) Montesquieu and the Parliament of Bordeaux, Geneva: Librairie DROZ S.A

Landreth H & Colander DC (1994) History of Economic Thought. Third Edition, Boston: Houghton Mifflin Company

Letwin W (1963) The Origins of Scientific Economics, London,Methuen & Co. Ltd. Hertford and Harlow

Locke J (1954 [1662-63]) Essays on the Law of Nature. The Latin text with a translation, introduction and notes. Edited and first published by W. von Leyden (1954), Oxford: Oxford at the Clarendon Press.

Locke J (1965 [1668-74]) Locke's Early Manuscript on Interest. Appendix 5 in Letwin, W (1965) The Origins of Scientific Economics.

Locke J (1964 [1690]) Two Treaties of Government. Editor P Laslett. Reprinted 1989, Cambridge: Cambridge at the University Press

Locke J (1691) Some Consideration of the Consequences of the Lowering of Interest, and Raising the Value of Money. In a letter sent a Member of Parliament. Printed for Awnssham and John Churchill, at the Black Swan in Pater-Noster-Row. http://socserv.socsci.mcmaster.ca/oldecon/ugcm/3113/locke/consid.txt

Locke J (1968 [1683-93]) The Educational Writings of John Locke. Edited by J Axtell, Cambridge:

Mautner T (1986) Pufendorf and 18th century Scottish Philosophy. In K Modéer (1986), Rättshistoriska Studier, pp.120-131

Meek R L (1971) Smith, Turgot and the "Four Stages" Theory. History of Political Economy. 3 (1), pp. 9-27

Meek RL (1976b) Social Sciences and the Ignoble Savage. Cambridge UK: Cambridge University Press.

Mizuta H (1967) Adam Smith's Library. A Supplement to Bonar's Catalogue with a Checklist of the whole Library. London: Cambridge University Press for the Royal Society

Montesquieu C-L (1989 [1748]) The Spirit of the Law. Translated and edited by A M Cohler BC Miller and HS Stone. Cambridge: Cambridge University Press

Montesquieu C-L (2003 [1748]) The Spirit of the Law. Translated into English by T Nugent (1752) revised by J V Prichard. The electronic edition. Copyright 2003 and 2005, Lonang Institute

Moore J and M Silverthorn (1984) Natural Sociability and Natural Rights in the moral Philosophy of Gershom Carmichael. In V Hope (1984): Philosophers of the Scottish Enlightenment, pp. 1-12. Edinburgh: Edinburgh at the University Press

Moore J and M Silverthorn [Eds.] (2002) Natural Rights on the Threshold of the Scottish Enlightenment. The Writings of Gershom Carmichael. Indianapolis: Liberty Fund

Naldi N (1993) Gershom Carmichael on 'Demand' and 'Difficulty of Acquiring': Some evidence from the first edition of Carmichael's commentary to Pufendorf's De Officio. Scottish Economic Society. Oxford UK and Cambridge MA: Blackwell Publishers

Pownall T (1776) A letter to Adam Smith. In Mossner and Ross [Eds.] (1987), Appendix A, pp. 337-376

Pufendorf S (1931 [1660, 1672]) Elementorum Jurisprudentiæ Universalis Libri Duo (The Elements of Universal Jurisprudence), Photographic Reproduction of the Edition of the 1672 Cambridge edition, with a List of Errata, which refers to the first edition of 1660, which was published in The Hague. The Translation of the 1672 edition by W A Oldfather. Oxford: The Clarendon Press

Pufendorf S (1933 [1672, 1688]) *De Jure Naturae et Gentium Libri Octo* (On the Law of Nature and Nations in eight books), DJNG. The translation of 1688 edition (with references to the first edition of 1672 by CH and WA Oldfather, Reprinted 1964, New York: Oceana Publications Inc, and London: Wiley & Sons Ltd.

Pufendorf S (1927 [1673, 1682]) De Officio Hominis et Civis Juxta Legem Naturalem Libri duo (The Duty of Man and Citizen According to the Natural Law in Two Books), DOH.A Photographic Reproduction of the Edition of 1682 with a List of Errata that refers to the first edition of 1673. A Translation of the Text by F Gardner Moore. New York: Oxford University Press.

Raphael DD and AL Macfie (1976) Introduction to Adam Smith's Theory of Moral Sentiments, Indianapolis: Liberty Classics

Rima IH (1991) Development of Economic Analysis, Fifth Edition, Homewood Ill: Richard D Irwin, Inc.

Ross IS (2010) *The Life of Adam Smith.* Second edition, Oxford: Oxford University Press Rousseau J-J (1968 [1762]) The Social Contract. Edited with an introduction by M Cranston. Harmondsworth UK: Penguin Books Ltd.

Rousseau J-J (2007 [1762]) The Social Contract and other later political writings. Edited and translated by V Gourevitch. Cambridge: Cambridge University Press

Rousseau J-J (2008 [1750]) The Discourses and other early political writings. Edited and translated by V Gourevitch. Cambridge: Cambridge University Press
Rousseau J-J (2014 [1762]) Emile or Education. Translated by B Foxley. London & Toronto: Online Library of Liberty Fund
Schabas M (2014) 30. Philosophy of the Human Sciences. In Garret (2014), pp. 731-752
Scott WR (1900) Francis Hutcheson. His Life, Teaching and Position in the History of Philosophy. Cambridge: The University Press
Scott WR (1965 [1937]) Adam Smith as a Student and Professor, Glasgow: Jackson, Son &Company
Shackleton, R (1961) Montesquieu, A Critical Bibliography, Oxford: Oxford University Press
Smith A (1982a [1759]) The Theory of Moral Sentiments, Glasgow, sixth edition 1790, edited by DD Raphael and AL Macfie (1976), Oxford: Oxford University Press. Published as Liberty Classics, Indianapolis 1982
Smith A (1982b [1762-63]) Lectures on Jurisprudence, Report of 1762-3 and Report dated1766 together with an Appendix containing the "Early Draft" of the Wealth of Nations from the 1760's. Edited by R L Meek, DD Raphael and PG Stein, Oxford University Press 1978. Published as Liberty Classic, Indianapolis 1982
Smith A (1976[1904/1789/1776]) An Inquiry into the Nature and Causes of the Wealth of Nations. Fifth edition, Edinburgh. Reprint of the 1904 Cannan edition with a new Preface by G J Stigler. Chicago: The University of Chicago Press
Spiegel HW (1983) The Growth of Economic Thought. Revised and expanded edition. Durham NC: Duke University Press
Stein PG (1982) From Pufendorf to Adam Smith: the natural law tradition in Scotland. In Norbert Horn [Hrsg.] Europäisches Rechtsdenken in Geschichte und Gegenwart. pp. 667-679, Festschrift für H Coing (1982). Band 1. München: CH Becksche'Verlagsbuchhandlung.
Sæther A (2017a) Samuel Pufendorf – The Grandfather of Modern Political Economy. Doctor Philosophy thesis. Bergen: Norwegian School of Economics
Sæther A (2017b) Natural Law and the Origin of Political Economy. Samuel Pufendorf and the History of Economics. London and New York: Routledge. Taylor & Francis Group
Taylor W (1965) Francis Hutcheson and David Hume as predecessors of Adam Smith. Duke University Press, Durham, North Carolina
Vaughn KI (1980) John Locke Economist and Social Scientist. Chicago and London: The University of Chicago Press
Waddicor MH (1970) Montesquieu and the Philosophy of Natural Law. The Hague: Niijhoff
Walras L (1977 [1926,1874]) Elements of Pure Economics or The Theory of Social

Pufendorf's Theory of the Origin of Property Rights and Its Relationship to Locke's Ideas

Nicolaus Tideman

Abstract Samuel von Pufendorf's theory of the origin of property rights is a strictly positive theory, not at all normative. It has three central propositions: (1) Ownership requires implicit or explicit agreement. (2) Ownership institutions will be whatever people decide they will be. (3) People are motivated to establish ownership institutions by considerations of efficiency. John Locke's theory of property seems intended as a commentary on Pufendorf's theory, though Locke does not mention Pufendorf by name. The key difference between Locke and Pufendorf arises because Locke treats Pufendorf's first proposition as if it was intended to be normative, so that Pufendorf would have been claiming rightful ownership requires agreement. Locke then argues that agreement is not needed for rightful ownership when natural opportunities are abundant and, implicitly, people are not in community with one another. Locke's normative argument is valid under these conditions, but not otherwise.

Keywords Pufendorf · Locke · Origin of property · Natural law · History of economic thought

JEL Codes A13, B11, B31, K11

1 Introduction

Samuel von Pufendorf had interesting things to say about the origin of property rights. It seems likely that his ideas had an unappreciated significant influence on the more widely known ideas of John Locke on property. Pufendorf wrote in Latin, which might have made his ideas obscure if there were no translations. However, his

N. Tideman (✉)
Virginia Polytechnic Institute and State University, Blacksburg, VA, USA
e-mail: ntideman@vt.edu

J. G. Backhaus et al. (eds.), *Samuel Pufendorf and the Emergence of Economics as a Social Science*, The European Heritage in Economics and the Social Sciences 24, https://doi.org/10.1007/978-3-030-49791-0_5

ideas were translated into English very early on, so that is not an issue. On the other hand, the translations are cumbersome and full of technical terms, making it hard to grasp his meaning. Furthermore, he wrote at a time when Christian theology was an accepted part of philosophical reasoning, which makes his ideas seem quaint and not relevant today, when atheism or agnosticism is the philosophical norm. In this paper, I make an effort to update Pufendorf's ideas, suggesting what he would say if he wanted to convey his ideas to a modern audience. After presenting a modernized version of Pufendorf's ideas, I evaluate, from Pufendorf's perspective, the framework that Locke seems to have developed in response to Pufendorf's ideas.

2 What Pufendorf Said

Omitting Pufendorf's comments on the ideas of others, what Pufendorf said about the origin of property (Pufendorf 1934 [1672], Book IV, Chapter 4, Sections 4 and 5) was as follows:

> The further point should be carefully observed, that the grant of God, by which He allowed men to use the products of the earth, is not the immediate cause of dominion, as it has its effect in relation to other men (a proof of which is to be found in the fact that brute creatures use and consume them as if it were God's will, although no dominion is recognized among them); but that dominion presupposes absolutely an act of man and agreement, whether tacit or express. It is true that God allowed man to turn the earth, its products, and its creatures, to his own use and convenience, that is, He gave men an indefinite right to them, yet the manner, intensity, and extent of this power were left to the judgement and disposition of men; whether, in other words, they would confine it within certain limits, or within none at all, and whether they wanted every man to have a right to everything, or only to a certain and fixed part of things, or to be assigned his definite portion with which he should rest content and claim no right to anything else….
>
> It is idle, therefore, to discuss the question of whether God gave dominion over things to the first pair, as personifying the whole race of men, or assigned it to them is a special way as individuals, so that they were masters of the whole world on their own proper right, to whom the rest of mankind owe their possessions by receiving it from their hands. For that divine gift only rendered men more certain of the mercy of God towards them, and assured them that it was with His approval that they turned other creatures to their use and service. But it was left to men themselves, to determine by the forethought of sane reason what measures must be taken to prevent discord from arising among mankind for the use of that right. Yet it was far from God to prescribe a universal manner of possessing things, which all men were bound to observe. And so things were created neither proper nor common (in positive community) by any express command of God, but these distinctions were later created by men as the peace of human society demanded….
>
> And yet there is no precept of natural law whereby all things are commended to be proper to men in such a way, that every man should be allotted his own separate and distinct portion. Although natural law clearly advised that men should by convention introduce the assignment of such things to individuals, according as it might be of advantage to human society, yet on the condition that it would rest with the judgement of men, whether they wanted all things to be proper or only some, or would hold some things indivisible and leave the rest open to all, yet in such a way that no one might claim them for himself alone. From this it is further understood, that the law of nature approves all conventions which have been introduced about things by men, provided they involve no contradiction or do not

overturn society. Therefore, the proprietorship of things has resulted immediately from the convention of men, either tacit or express. For although after God had made the gift, nothing remained to prevent man from appropriating things to himself, yet there was a need of some sort of convention if it was to be understood that by such appropriation or seizure the right of others to that thing was excluded. But the fact that right reason suggested the introduction of separate dominions does not prevent them from going back to a human pact.

From such remarks as these it is clear that before any convention of men existed there was a community of all things, not, indeed, such as we have called positive, but a negative one, that is, that all things lay open to all men, and belonged no more to one than to another. But since things are of no use to men unless at least their fruits may be appropriated, and this is impossible if others as well can take what we have already by our own act selected for our uses, it follows that the first convention between men was about these very concerns, to the effect that whatever one of these things which were left open to all, and of their fruits, a man had laid his hands upon, the intent to turn it to his uses, could not be taken from him by another. ... This can be illustrated by the special case of animals, no one of which, of course, can claim a special right above others to anything, but every one takes for his own nourishment everything he first happens upon. And even if any one of them has stored up some things for his future use, others are not prevented from seizing them, for the reason that there is no convention among animals which confers a special right over a thing to the one that first got it.

3 A Modern Understanding of Pufendorf

In presenting Pufendorf's ideas to a modern audience, the issue arises of how to deal with Pufendorf's theism, when modern scholarship is atheistic or agnostic. Arguably, theism is not essential to Pufendorf's thinking. When Pufendorf writes 'the grand of God' or 'God's will', we can understand him to mean what a utilitarian would express as 'the arrangements that are most conducive to overall well-being'. I interpret him in this way. Thus, what I think Pufendorf would say about the origin of ownership to a modern audience would be as follows:

Ownership is not inherent in the usefulness of things, which can be seen in the fact that animals use things, without any concept of ownership. Ownership requires agreement, either explicit or implicit. When people first sought to develop agreed institutions of ownership, they had no source to tell them what was right. The fact that they were initially unconstrained told them nothing about what constraints might be appropriate. They needed to reach understandings among themselves. What would be would be whatever they agreed to. They could agree on restrictions on how things could be used, or they could allow everyone to use everything in whatever way they wished. They could have constraints on some things and not on others. They could divide things among people, giving everyone his or her share.

It was not necessary to divide everything into individually owned shares. While there are clear advantages of private ownership, it was up to people to decide whether private ownership would apply to everything or only to some things, with other thing available for use, but not in such a way as to exclude use by others. Whatever internally consistent rules people agreed to would be acceptable, as long as they did not destroy society. Therefore, ownership resulted from tacit or explicit agreements about things being owned. The fact that such agreements were in the general interest did not make it possible for ownership to arise without agreements.

Prior to such agreements, everything belonged to everyone. To make it worthwhile for people to invest in things, there had to be agreement that when someone invested in a thing it belonged to him or her. Animals, on the other hand, have no such convention.

Pufendorf's original argument is quite repetitive, and even my modernized summary is not as succinct as it might be. The essence of Pufendorf's argument is:

1. Ownership requires implicit or explicit agreement.
2. Ownership institutions will be whatever people decide they will be.
3. People are motivated to establish ownership institutions by considerations of efficiency.

A notable feature of this argument is that it is entirely positive, not at all normative.

If there is a place where the argument would be challenged, it is probably in the statement that ownership arises from agreement. There are two possible challenges:

1. Universal agreement is not feasible.
2. Agreement is sometimes coerced.

There are answers available to Pufendorf with respect to both of these challenges. With respect to the concern that universal agreement (agreement of all humans) is not feasible, Pufendorf can respond that universal agreement is not needed. All that is needed is agreement among those who encounter one another. Even then, if departures from full agreement are sufficiently infrequent, there will be ownership for most practical purposes. A reasonable understanding of what Pufendorf means by agreement is the development of a generally observed convention among the preponderance of a group of people who interact regularly.

With respect to the challenge that agreement is sometimes coerced, Pufendorf could say that he is not arguing that it is agreement that *justifies* private ownership. Rather, agreement is what *achieves* private ownership. It is true that agreement is sometimes coerced, but that does not prevent agreement from generating an institution of private property. Whatever the source of agreement may be, agreement on a convention of respect for what belongs to others is necessary for the creation of private property.

4 Locke's Variation and Pufendorf's Conjectured Response

John Locke offers a theory of property that makes no mention of Pufendorf and yet seems to echo Pufendorf. At the beginning of his chapter on property, Locke (2017 [1689], Section 25) says:

> … [I]t is very clear, that God … has given the earth to the children of men; given it to mankind in common. But this being supposed, it seems to some a very great difficulty, how any one should ever come to have a property in any thing: … I shall endeavour to shew, how men might come to have a property in several parts of that which God gave to mankind in common, and that without any express compact of all the commoners.

Pufendorf's reaction to this statement, as I see it would be, How very interesting. Mr. Locke claims that I am wrong in saying that private property requires agreement. I wonder how he defends this. And he seems to suggest that according to the view he opposes, a property right requires an "express compact of all the commoners". That is not my view. The compact can be either implicit or explicit. Furthermore, an "express compact of all the commoners" is almost impossible to imagine. What I discussed was a convention of respect for the things that belong to others, that is shared by enough of the people in a given society to create a sense of property that people are generally able to rely on'.

Since Locke does not mention Pufendorf by name, it might be argued that Locke is not denying Pufendorf's claim in particular. However, it is clear the Locke was well aware of Pufendorf.[1] Therefore, I treat Locke as responding to Pufendorf.

It is notable that Locke, like Pufendorf:

1. Mentions that God gave the earth to mankind.
2. Mentions agreement in connection with the creation of property rights.

Furthermore, Locke published *Two Treatises of Government* just 17 years after Pufendorf's publication of *Laws of Nature and of Nations* in 1672.

Locke begins his development of a view different from Pufendorf's (Locke 2017 [1689], Section 27) with:

> Though the earth, and all inferior creatures, be common to all men, yet every man has a property in his own person: this no body has any right to but himself.

Pufendorf might say, 'Is this the same John Locke who, in his previous chapter (Locke 2017 [1689], Section 24), wrote of "the perfect condition of slavery, which is nothing else, but the state of war continued, between a lawful conqueror and a captive"? Does the captive have a right to himself? And what about men who are feeble-minded, insane or suffering from dementia? What about prisoners or drafted soldiers? Do these people have rights to themselves?'

I imagine that Locke would say, 'You are right that there are men who do not have rights to themselves. But these are exceptions. Men generally have rights to themselves. I am offering a theory that applies to those who do have rights to themselves'. Pufendorf, I imagine, would accept this compromise.

Locke (2017 [1689], Section 27) goes on to say:

> The labour of his body, and the work of his hands, we may say, are properly his. Whatsoever then he removes out of the state that nature hath provided, and left it in, he hath mixed his labour with, and joined to it something that is his own, and thereby makes it his property. It being by him removed from the common state nature hath placed it in, it hath by this labour something annexed to it, that excludes the common right of other men: for this labour being the unquestionable property of the labourer, no man but he can have a right to what that is once joined to, at least where there is enough, and as good, left in common for others.

Pufendorf, I imagine, would say, 'I see. You are not discussing, as I was, a description of the process by which property rights originate, but rather the normative question of what rights ought to be recognized. I have not written about what rights *ought* to be recognized, but rather about what rights *are* recognized, that they are

[1] See "Pufendorf's Moral and Political Philosophy" in *The Stanford Encyclopedia of Philosophy*.

whatever people want them to be, with people generally guided by considerations of efficiency. So let us go from the positive to the normative. You say that, with respect to situations where there is "as much and as good left in common for others", that is, when the things being appropriated are not scarce, justice requires that those who add value the things that are not scarce be accorded ownership of those things.

'Consider the case of salt in the ocean. I presume that we may stipulate that it is not scarce, that however much any one person takes, there will be 'enough and as good left in common for others'. Suppose there is a community that has a salt-making festival, in which everyone participates, after which everyone is accorded a portion of salt adequate to his or her needs. But one person objects. He wants to make his own salt and keep it for himself. The community says to him, "We do not recognize a right of people to keep salt they make for themselves. If you want to be a member of this community, you will need to share any salt that you make with all of us. If you do not like this rule, you can depart from our community".

'The solitary salt maker may object, "My right to myself entails a right to keep what I produce when there is 'enough and as good left in common for others' of the resources I started with. Furthermore, it is inefficient to not allow me to keep what I have mixed my labor with in these circumstances. Why are you oppressing me?"

'The community can respond, "We are not oppressing you. We are exercising *our* rights to ourselves. We want to have a community in which everyone participates in the salt-making festival. We will be happy to let you join us if you share our idea of what a good community is, but if you do not share our ideals, your right to yourself is the right to go somewhere else. Whether or not our rule is inefficient depends on the value one assigns to the sense of community spirit that is engendered by the salt-making festival, compared to loss of incentive from not allowing individuals to keep the proceeds of their efforts".

'This illustrates', Pufendorf would continue, 'that not only is it true that people *can* choose whatever institutions of property they wish, but that there may be good reasons for them to choose institutions that might at first seem inappropriate to an outsider'.

I imagine that Locke would say, 'I concede your point. But you grant, at least, that if the solitary salt maker chooses to leave the community, then he ought to be accorded the right to keep the salt that he makes. Let's see where we can go with that'.

Continuing with an actual quote from Locke (2017 [1689], Section 36):

> [S]upposing a man, or family, in the state they were at first peopling of the world by the children of Adam, or Noah; let him plant in some inland, vacant places of America, we shall find that the possessions he could make himself, upon the measures we have given, would not be very large, nor, even to this day, prejudice the rest of mankind, or give them reason to complain, or think themselves injured by this man's incroachment, though the race of men have now spread themselves to all the corners of the world, and do infinitely exceed the small number was at the beginning.

Pufendorf, I imagine, would reply, 'Alright. For the sake of discussion, let us suppose that there are "inland, vacant places of America" where there is no competition for land. If a person wishes to plant in such a place, it is not clear that the word "property" has any meaning for him. If he never sees anyone else, there cannot be an issue of whether the land that he improves is his property. Perhaps you have in mind a somewhat less severe instance of isolation, where there are people who interact, but in an environment where they all agree that there is no scarcity of unimproved land. You want to argue that in that case, land that is improved belongs to the person who improves it. However, suppose that the persons in this locale are all members of the Hutterite faith, who hold all productive assets in common. Then the land that a person improved, by common agreement, would not be the property of that person.'

An exasperated Locke responds, 'Suppose that in this Hutterite community there is a young person who, upon attaining maturity, decides to reject the teachings of his elders and plant on land just beyond the territory occupied by the Hutterites. Do you agree that the Hutterites have an obligation to respect the land that he improves as his property?'

Pufendorf says, 'Yes. Since we have stipulated that land is not scarce, it would be unjust if the Hutterites were to attempt to remove him from the land where he planted (which they would not do since they are pacifists). It would also be unjust for them to treat his crops as common property. However, this is all on the supposition that there is no scarcity of land. I understand that it is your view (Locke 2017 [1689], Section 45) that,

> the several communities settled the bounds of their distinct territories, and by laws within themselves regulated the properties of the private men of their society, and so, by compact and agreement, settled the property which labour and industry began; and the leagues that have been made between several states and kingdoms, either expresly or tacitly disowning all claim and right to the land in the others possession, have, by common consent, given up their pretences to their natural common right, which originally they had to those countries, and so have, by positive agreement, settled a property amongst themselves, in distinct parts and parcels of the earth;

'Here, it seems, you are discussing a situation in which it is no longer true that there is "enough, and as good, left in common for others". You have *not* provided an explicit normative rationale for the justice of the process you describe. Rather, you have offered, as I did, a positive description. There is a hint of a normative justification in phrase, "by compact and agreement, settled the property which labour and industry began". However, to make this a satisfying normative justification, one would need to establish either that the agreements were unanimous, or that non-unanimous "agreements" ought to be binding. If the agreements actually were unanimous, one would need to establish that agreements that are unanimous at the time that they are initially made are binding on those who are born later.

'Mr. Locke, you have established the moral proposition that when natural opportunities are not scarce, justice requires those who are not in community with one another to respect the property claims of those who have made natural opportunities valuable by their efforts. However, this proposition does not compel those who *are* in community with one another to treat improved natural opportunities as the private property of those who have done the improving. Furthermore, your moral proposition has no moral implication for times when natural opportunities that were initially abundant have become scarce'.

Locke has no adequate rejoinder to this summary by Pufendorf.

5 Conclusion

Pufendorf has offered a positive theory of the origin of property rights. Property rights require agreement. They can be whatever a community wants them to be. And people are guided by utilitarian considerations in choosing a property rights regime.

Locke has established the moral proposition that people who are not in community with one another should respect the property claims of those who improve natural opportunities that are not scarce. This proposition has no implication for people who *are* in community with one another or for times when natural opportunities *are* scarce.

References

Locke, J. (2017 [1689]), Second treatise of government, The Gutenberg project, http://www.gutenberg.org/files/7370/7370-h/7370-h.htm

von Pufendorf, S. (1934 [1672]), De jure naturae et gentium, libri octo, translated into English (using the 2nd ed. of 1688) by C.H. and W.A. Oldfather, Vol. 2 (2 Vols.), Oxford, Clarendon Press

The Stanford Encyclopedia of Philosophy, https://plato.stanford.edu/

How to Shape Societies: Pufendorf on Organizing Individual Interests and Social Interaction

Hans A. Frambach

Abstract Samuel von Pufendorf, one of the most influential natural law theorists of the seventeenth century, contributed decisively to the conceptual foundations of the modern state with its specific tasks and responsibilities. He remains today an example of a profound and differentiated thinker who combined intellectual acuity with recommendations for action. Especially, his insights into decision-making mechanisms are, from a contemporary point of view, still of far-reaching significance. The article sees modern fields of application of Pufendorf's thought as extending to socioeconomic problems of selfishness and the societal challenges of ever-increasing variety and heterogeneity. For this purpose, reference is made to models such as Amitai Etzioni's "communitarian paradigm" and Ian Ayres and John Braithwaite's "responsive regulation."

Keywords Pufendorf · Natural law · Individual action · Social choice · Decision rules · Golden rule · New golden rule · Tripartism · Communitarianism · History of economic thought

JEL Codes A13, B11, B310, D70

1 Some Background

Samuel von Pufendorf (1632–1694) grew up during the turmoil of the Thirty Years War. He was educated in theology, law, history, and philosophy (especially neo-Scholastic philosophy), cameralistics, and political theory.

Pufendorf started out from a purely secular conception of law, understanding natural law as an empirical science; in that sense, he can be thought of as a forerunner of the Enlightenment. Already as a student, he was interested in issues of the

H. A. Frambach (✉)
Universität Wuppertal, Wuppertal, Germany
e-mail: Frambach@wiwi.uni-wuppertal.de

J. G. Backhaus et al. (eds.), *Samuel Pufendorf and the Emergence of Economics as a Social Science*, The European Heritage in Economics and the Social Sciences 24, https://doi.org/10.1007/978-3-030-49791-0_6

origin of the state, and his doctrine of natural law constituted the foundation of his later systems of state theory, rationalism, and moral philosophy (Döring 1989, 27–28). His call for a unified system of international law was formative both for German philosophy of law and for its European development toward the end of the seventeenth and eighteenth centuries. Standing squarely in the European tradition, Pufendorf saw the dignity of man as the basis of the constitution of the state, and hence, too, of its legislation—a perspective that enabled him to combine the primacy of the human with a fundamentally pragmatic legal approach (Hunger, 53–55; Maihofer 1996, 263; Welzel 1986, 104). His central work *De jure naturae et gentium libri octo* ("The Law of Nature and Nations: Eight Books"), was published in 1672 (a German translation titled "Acht Bücher von Natur und Völkerrecht" appeared in 1711); a year later an abbreviated version titled *De Officio Hominis et Civis* ("The Duty of Man as Citizen") was published.

In contrast to his precursors in the field of natural law, Hugo Grotius and Thomas Hobbes, Pufendorf found a way to reconcile the role of the individual and the state and, moreover, to locate the position of theology within his system: in this respect, he advocated religious tolerance and the scientific separation of theology and philosophy. He distinguished between natural law, civil state law, and moral theology: natural law is concerned with what is necessary for the community of human beings under the dictates of reason, the precepts of positive law are justified because they are determined by a legislator and, for the moral theologian, the divine commands recorded in the Bible must suffice (Pufendorf 1943 [1673], 6). Natural law[1] is understood as the fundamental order of community life that teaches man how to behave as an upright member of society; its main ordinance is to maintain and foster the life of the community and to serve the whole as best one can (Pufendorf 1943 [1673]), 17). The tripartite role of duties in Pufendorf's thinking comes through clearly as (i) the duties necessary to render man capable of society with other men [*sociabilis*]; (ii) the duties of the citizen living in a particular, defined state [*civitas*]; and (iii) the duties imposed by Christian values (Pufendorf 1943 [1673], 5–6).

2 Man as Selfish and Social

Pufendorf also considered many fields of political economy to be an integral part of natural law, and contributed decisively to the foundations of the modern state and its tasks and responsibilities. Like many later economists, he begins his analysis with the individual. Summarizing the second paragraph of his chapter "On the motive leading to the establishment of a state" in *The Law of Nature and Nations,* he sees man's first goal as striving for his own well-being: "Man, by nature, loves himself more than society" (Pufendorf 1934 [1672], VII, I, 949; Sæter 2017a, 107). He backs his argument with references on one hand to those writers who explain that

[1] Pufendorf uses the notions 'natural law' and 'natural right' synonymously (Hunger 1991, 51).

without civil society man "neither wishes to nor can exist," and on the other to those who show "that man is in fact an animal which loves first and foremost himself and his own advantage," citing Hobbes and Isaeus that no man cares more for others than he does for himself (Pufendorf 1934 [1672], VII, I, 949).

Between these extremes, Pufendorf realizes that man is a living being, capably of desire. Unlike the animal, he strives for more than just a sated stomach: he longs for delights such as clothes—and this not only for protection from cold, but also for purposes of conspicuous consumption. He has the desire for abundance, glory, a craving for recognition, and he experiences envy and jealousy, disagreement and quarrels. People wage war against each other, which is totally unknown to animals. But (anticipating the Enlightenment) man is endowed with intelligence and reason, enabling him to reach his aims. In Pufendorf's thinking, God has given man both his nature and the ways and means to fulfill it through the use of reason (Denzer 1972, 24–25; Hunger 1991, 51–52; Welzel 1986, 101). Man recognizes that cohabitation in society is the only way to escape from natural threats and to make humanity as a collective vision come true. Thus, it can be no surprise that Pufendorf

> derives the natural law norms of sociability solely from the need to achieve civil peace, exclusive of the requirement to perfect man's moral nature or respect the enactments of his "higher" rational being. In this way he sought to exclude moral theology and philosophy from the domain of natural law. (Hunter 2001, 157)

To an economist, the dominant theme of Pufendorf's thought is the "economic" conception of man—an idea well known since Adam Smith but for the most part derived from Thomas Hobbes (1588–1679). According to this, all men seek to maximize their personal benefit: in the natural state man possesses every right, even over the life of his fellow man, and there is nothing to prevent him from committing the most serious of all evil, namely bringing about another person's death (Hobbes 1962 [1651], Cap. XIII, 63). Freedom at this first stage is freedom to act, the absence of external impediments (Hobbes 1962 [1651], Cap. XIV, 66)—a radically liberal political concept that became decisive for other philosophers from John Locke (1632–1704) to Voltaire (1694–1768). However, at a further stage, freedom is not unlimited but restricted by law—the law made by rightful authority. Law, in his thinking, is basically enacted by power, not by truth, for no law can issue from opinion alone—however correct—without state authority (Hobbes 1962 [1651], Cap. XXVI, 146–147). Fundamental for Hobbes is the human instinct of self-preservation, an irreducible, vital incentive, combined with the individual desire to increase and heighten life's possibilities.

In contrast to Hobbes, Samuel Pufendorf did not derive the right of everyone to everything in man's natural state—and consequently the idea of the war of all against all—and on this base his idea of the necessity of the state. Clearly, man is primarily driven by self-interest, but at the same time he realizes his dependence on other people, because he is simply not built to live alone: as a single being, he is incapable of survival. Man is too weak alone, incapable of maintaining himself without receiving help from others, but, conversely, able to grant mutual assistance. If he wants to remain unhurt, he must combine for his own advantage with people like him, he must cohabit sociably with others (Pufendorf 1934 [1672], e.g., VII, I, 959; 1943 [1673], 14–18).

For Pufendorf, human nature is fundamentally determined first by its inability (*imbecillitas*) to live in accordance with its own survival instinct (man is not equipped by nature to maintain himself as an isolated individual), and secondly by the need for sociability (*socialitas*) (Pufendorf ibid. II, III, 207–208, 210–212; see also, e.g., Hunger 1991, 53–54; Rabe 1958, 34). All human comforts come from humankind's mutual assistance. The urge toward sociability is elementally linked to the survival instinct: instead of wolves baring their teeth, social people treat each other with respect (Sprenger 1996, 253, 265). The need for sociability follows from the anthropological finding of the simultaneity of the survival instinct and the incapability of its fulfillment. This is consistent with Ian Hunter's comment (2001, 178) on Pufendorf that "man is only observing his moral end from within the limits of his worldly nature" and the desire for sociability (and hence society) is disconnected from all higher rational and moral law.

3 The State

The state as conceived by Pufendorf enables the individual to multiply strengths and fend off outer and inner dangers. In order to achieve their aims, people explicitly (or tacitly) subordinate their strengths to a single person, council, or committee that represents the sovereign power:

> All the persons in the state submit their will to that of one man, or of a council, in whom the supreme sovereignty has been vested. And since the individual citizens must comport themselves in accordance with the will of the state, that will must be set before them by clear signs. Therefore, it is understood to be the task of the supreme sovereignty to make clear and to prescribe what should be done or avoided. And since it would be impossible to issue special commands for each act of each citizen in so great a multitude of men, general rules are prescribed whereby what must be done, or what must be avoided, is made known to all men and for all time. (Pufendorf ibid. VII, IV, 1010–1011)

The state is the result of a willed imposition, the sovereignty pact, and not an expression of man's rational and moral being (Hunter 2001, 181). To put it differently, society is based on contractual relations, which involve coordination. Initially society is established without any specific form of organization, but in a second step, a contract about the form of government is required, and this is specified in further steps (Behme 1995, 120; Lagerspetz 1986, 180). However, with the assignment of power and rights people are willing to submit themselves without resistance. They voluntarily embrace a state to avoid greater evils. Two agreements, one of association and one of subjection are needed to create a state and these are required under all forms of government (Behme 1995, 123–130; Sæther 2017b, 4). States are established to gain security and protection from the evil or wickedness of men; the safety and preservation of humankind can be secured only by civil societies (Sæther 2017a, 108).

But to establish a state is more than merely to have a number of people with similar temporary interests in avoiding wars and disputes and enjoying peace. A state requires the deep insight and unconditional conviction of a vast majority of people to subordinate the will of every individual to a single council or government. Pufendorf speaks of a "union of wills" which "cannot possibly be encompassed by the wills of all being naturally lumped into one, or by only one person willing, and all the rest ceasing to will […]." On the contrary:

> the only final way in which many wills are understood to be united is for every individual to subordinate his will to that of one man, or of a single council, so that whatever that man or council shall decree on matters necessary to the common security, must be regarded as the will of each and every person. […] When such a union of wills and strength has been made, then there finally arises a state, the most powerful of moral societies and persons. (Pufendorf ibid. VII, II, 972; see also Hunter 2001, 186; Saeter 2017a, 110)

But in order to build a state, people must reach a common agreement, and to do this they must take note of differences between "their own private advantage [and] that of the group" (Pufendorf ibid. VII, II, 969)—a statement that goes beyond some approaches of modern social choice theory in which collective decisions are reached by different decision rules and are to that extent determined by a mechanism. Pufendorf emphatically assumes people to have some understanding of what they are doing, the human will being, in his philosophy, by definition informed by reason.

Once individuals have agreed to administer their desires for safety and security through common council and leadership (Pufendorf ibid. VII, II, 974)—that is, to constitute a state—they then have to decide on how exactly to be governed. Pufendorf distinguishes "three forms of a regular state, based upon the subject proper of the supreme sovereignty, according as that subject is one simple person, or one council, composed of a few, or of all the citizens" (Pufendorf ibid. VII, V, 1024). In other words, the supreme sovereignty can be organized as a council consisting of all citizens with the same right to vote (a democracy), a council consisting of selected citizen (an aristocracy), or as a single person as executive decision-maker (a monarchy) (Pufendorf ibid. VII, V, 1024–1025).

Once this has been decreed, the relationship of the state to its members has to be clarified by means of rules and laws. As the people have transferred their rights and natural liberty to the supreme sovereignty without reservation, the latter has the right to decide what is of national interest: in modern terms, the welfare of the nation. In a conflict situation between the government and its subjects, Pufendorf always recommended subjects to submit. If the situation became unbearable, he recommended that they flee abroad—and this not only for the subject but also for the ruler. If no opportunity for flight offers itself, then it is better to die than to kill, so that the state may be protected from worse (Saether 2017a, 123–125). This is just one example of Pufendorf's pragmatic approach to a problem-solving, his understanding of politics as the "art of finding reasonable compromises and of solving practical problems" from what amounts to a set of rules of thumb (Lagerspetz 1986, 180).

4 Decision Rules or the Art of Reasonable Compromise

The simplest case of a collective decision is unanimity. Pufendorf considers the possibility of a veto, when council members explain from the start that they do not feel bound to other decisions that have been taken. In this case, the dissent of one person can render void an agreement of all the rest, and Pufendorf appeals to the understanding of the individual member and their agreement for the good of the whole (Pufendorf ibid. VII, II, 986–987). It is obvious that under such circumstances it is difficult to make decisions, so all members of a decision group (i.e., the council) have to oblige themselves without exception to submit to majority decisions (Pufendorf ibid. VII, II, 988). If somebody was outvoted, then it can be expected that he supports the decision as taken; the number of votes is decisive:

> Therefore, in all councils, the votes of a majority have the force of those of all the members, not because there is any necessity by nature for it to be so, but because there is scarcely any other way for them to carry on their business. (Pufendorf ibid. VII, II, 988)

In terms of social choice theory, Pufendorf considered the cases of *unanimity* and *simple majority* (Gaertner 2005, 235). In the case of simple majority voting, he is aware that the more prudent may be outnumbered by the less—a phenomenon that seems today more topical than ever. On this (or an allied) point, he makes the incisive comment: "Indeed, in deciding upon the theoretical truths opinions are rated not by number but by weights. Nay, the very multitude of those who approve is treated as an indication of error" (Pufendorf ibid. VII, II, 988). What Pufendorf suggests here is a system of *weighted voting*, where people with more knowledge about the decision should have greater influence. Consequently, he considers it appropriate and practicable to count the number of opinions (Pufendorf ibid. VII, II, 989–990). However, in a situation of equal rights for everybody, special weight cannot be attached to such opinions by rule; this would only be possible in a kind of dictatorship. He concludes that important decisions should only be adopted if they are backed by a great number of votes—what we call a *qualified majority* (Pufendorf ibid. VII, II, 989–990; see also Gaertner 2005, 236). When it is a question of voting about more than two alternatives, aggregation rules become relevant.[2]

---

[2] Pufendorf (1934 [1672], VII, II, 991–992) describes the underlying problem as follows: "Finally, when there are more than two opinions, the question arises as to whether they are to be voted upon separately, so that the one is carried which commands more votes than each of the others, or whether two or more, though opposed, may be combined to beat a third, upon the elimination of which the others may then be taken up, so that the one of the remaining questions is carried which has the majority of the votes. If we fix our eyes upon mere natural equity, without reference to agreements or special laws, it appears that we should distinguish between opinions which are entirely different from one another, and those where one includes a part of another, or which, in other words, differ only in quantity, so that they can be united on the points in which they agree, while the former cannot. Thus those who fix a fine upon a man, at twenty units of value, may be united with those who fix it at ten units, against such as would acquit him altogether, and the defendant will be fined ten units, because this is agreeable to the majority of the judges, in view of the fact that those in favor of the twenty, are included with those in favor of the ten […] (p. 991) But

In terms of social choice theory, two rules can be distinguished (Gaertner 2005, 236; Lagerspetz 1986, 180–181): Firstly, each voter gives a positive vote for the preferred alternative and zero vote for all other alternatives. The alternative with most votes will be imposed as the result of a *plurality rule*. Secondly, two or more alternatives may be bundled into one alternative, especially when they are compatible in some way, or even mutually inclusive, in order to outvote other options[3] (Pufendorf ibid. VII, II, 991). Pufendorf gives the example of three judges who have to decide on a fine for a particular defendant. The first judge pleads for acquittal, the second for a fine of 10 units of value and the third for a fine of 20. Because the third judge must prefer ten units to acquittal, a majority can be found for this option and against acquittal. One could go so far to argue that the first judge will prefer the 10-unit penalty to the 20, so they can all agree to 10. In other words—in terms of modern collective decision-making theory (see Gaertner 2005, 237; Lagerspetz 1986, 181)—in cases of "single-peaked preferences" the median voter wins.

From the viewpoint of social choice theory, what Pufendorf proposes is no less than procedures for aggregating individual preference orderings into a social ordering of alternative social states—that is, precisely the idea of an Arrow type social welfare function. In contrast to a Bergsonian social welfare function—where a real number (of votes) is associated with each social state and put in a sequence that reflects the order of preference of those states—an Arrow type social welfare function is a function (strictly functional) of the set of individual preference orderings associating a social preference ordering with each possible configuration of that set. Thus, the concept of a social welfare function of the Arrow type is more fundamental and more general than a function of the Bergson type: a Bergsonian welfare function depends on utility functions, and Arrow makes the concept much more livable and tangible. The link to Pufendorf lies in the attempt to determine the ordering of alternative social states from individual preferences—in other words, to create a mechanism or procedure (e.g., a voting scheme) in which the following conditions prevail: (i) each individual may cast a vote for one of the alternative social states; (ii) individual votes are determined by personal preference orderings, which also entail ethical convictions; (iii) social states are ordered by the total number of votes each state receives; and (iv) the state with the most votes is chosen (see below).

if, for example, the judges be divided about a defendant, a part voting to banish, a part to execute, and a part to free him, surely those in favor of banishment will not be able to unite with those who would condemn him to death, against those who would free him; nor these last with the one in favor of banishment, against those who would have him die. For these sentences are entirely different from each other, since there is no banishment in death, nor is it a part of death. And although the banishers and acquitters should agree that the accused should not be slain, their sentence does not produce this effect directly, but only by consequence. Yet they are in themselves, as a matter of fact, different, for whoever votes for acquittal frees him of all punishment, while a banisher favors a punishment."

[3] Gaertner (2005, 236) speaks in this case of a variant of successive pairwise majority voting.

5 Paradox of Majority Voting and Impossibility Theorem

In trying to find a procedure for social ordering, one is faced with the well-known paradox of majority voting. Consider a group of three individuals, labeled 1, 2, 3, and three possible social states, *a, b, c*. Assuming that preferences over states are strict (no individual is indifferent between any two states), and that the individual preference orderings are $(a, b, c)_1$, $(b, c, a)_2$, and $(c, a, b)_3$, if individuals now vote on each pair of alternatives and the social order is to be determined by majority outcomes,

- Taking the first pair *(a, b)* from the preference order we have: $(a, b)_1$, $(b, a)_2$ and $(a, b)_3 \rightarrow [a, b]$, that is, person 2 is outvoted by persons 1 and 3.
- Taking the pair *(a, c)* we have: $(a, c)_1$, $(c, a)_2$ and $(c, a)_3 \rightarrow$ [c, a], that is, person 1 is outvoted by 2 and 3.
- Taking the pair *(b, c)* we have: $(b, c)_1$, $(b, c)_2$ and $(c, b)_3$, $\rightarrow [b, c]$, that is, person 3 is outvoted by 1 and 2.

Comparing the three social states obtained *[a, b], [c, a], [b, c]*, it follows directly that *a* is apparently socially preferred to *b*, *b* is socially preferred to *c*—from which would follow by transitivity that *a* is also socially preferred to *c*—but this contradicts the fact that *c* is socially preferred to *a*. Hence, the voting is intransitive and no social ordering of the three states transpires. A natural response to this "paradox of majority voting" or "Condorcet paradox" is to design an Arrow-type social welfare function which does yield transitive social choices.

For a general solution to aggregating social preferences, Kenneth Arrow (1951) suggested four minimal properties, which (under the condition of complete and transitive individual preference ordering) the social welfare function should possess:

1. *Universality* (the welfare function is suitable for all conceivable individual preference orderings).
2. *Rationality* (*Pareto Principle*) (if everyone prefers an alternative *a* to *b* then *a* should be preferred to *b* in the social ordering).
3. *Nondictatorship* (nobody shall be allowed to determine the decisions of others, that is, there is nobody whose individual preference ordering also determines the social ranking).
4. *Independence of irrelevant alternatives* (to socially assess two alternatives *a* and *b*, it is sufficient to ask individuals about their preferences toward *a* and *b*, and it is not necessary to look at the complete individual preference ordering concerning all alternatives).

Unfortunately, Arrow's impossibility theorem states that no social choice or voting system can simultaneously satisfy all requirements (at least if the number of alternatives is equal to or greater than three). This is not the place for demonstrating the general proof of this theorem (see, e.g., Sen 1970), nor is there room here to discuss details of the modern theory of social choice. Nonetheless, it is worth focusing for a moment on the social welfare theory issues Pufendorf was most concerned with.

In other words, what does Arrow's fundamental impossibility theorem mean for the two common voting systems, majority rule and plurality rule?

As regards both voting systems, it is commonly agreed—and also applied in the international institutional law—that a (simple) majority is more than half of the votes cast. A plurality vote is just another name for what is frequently called a relative majority: the situation when one alternative receives more votes than any other, but not an absolute majority. For example, if 100 votes are cast, 45 for alternative *a*, 30 for *b* and 25 for *c*, then *a* receives a plurality of votes, but not the majority. Henry Watson Fowler suggested that the American terms *plurality* and *majority* offer single-word alternatives for the corresponding two-word terms in British English, *relative majority* and *absolute majority* (Fowler 1965, 725).

Considering the implications of Arrow's theorem in a voting scheme of three and more alternatives, contradictions can appear in certain circumstances. For example, if 100 votes are cast, 45 for alternative *a*, 30 for *b* and 25 for *c*, and all alternatives are compared pairwise, what is called the *Condorcet paradox* or *paradox of majority voting* can arise:

$a > b > c$ 45
$b > c > a$ 30
$c > b > a$ 25

Alternative *b* wins with 75 votes over *c* and 55 over *a*, a clear contradiction to $a > b$ of 45 in the first step.[4]

Applied to the four apparent properties of an (Arrow) social welfare function, a situation is assumed where one-third of the voters prefer the alternatives along the following orderings:

$a > b > c$ 1/3
$b > c > a$ 1/3
$c > a > b$ 1/3.[5]

[4] All pairwise possibilities:
$a > b$ 45
$a > c$ 45
$b > a$ 55
$b > c$ 75
$c > a$ 55
$c > b$ 25

[5] All pairwise possibilities:
$a > b$ 2/3
$a > c$ 1/3
$b > a$ 1/3
$b > c$ 2/3
$c > a$ 2/3
$c > b$ 1/3

Majorities are given in the cases $a > b$, $b > c$, and $c > a$. Transitivity of this last to relation $b > a$ is a direct contradiction to $a > b$, that is, the social ordering is intransitive.

The plurality rule, a widely used voting system in many countries of the world, determines the winning alternative as that which is ranked first by most voters (a relative majority).

$a > b > c$	45
$b > c > a$	30
$c > b > a$	25

In this case, *a* is clearly the winning option because it achieves a majority over the other alternatives: *a* has the plurality of 45 per cent of the votes. This contrasts with alternative *b* when using the majority rule in a pairwise comparison. But referring to the impossibility theorem, a contradiction could also appear, if, for example, alternative *c* is substantially more closely related to *b* than to *a*. That means, if a round of elections only votes on the alternatives *a* and *b*, most of the votes of *c* will go to *b* and bring the majority to *b* (over *a*). In this case, the condition of the *independence of irrelevant alternatives* is violated, because the removal of a supposedly irrelevant alternative would have changed the outcome of the election.

Although certainly far from solving precisely these problems, Pufendorf nonetheless accurately anticipated the general problem of aggregating individual preferences. Arild Sæther (2017a, 117, fn. 2 and 3; see also his reference to John Chipman) argues that Pufendorf anticipated Arrow's impossibility theorem on aggregating individual preferences. For Pufendorf, people seek agreement to transfer decision-making power to a government body to avoid the chaos that would otherwise arise. He did not believe people could achieve a perfect union of wills by aggregating preferences effectively (and thus avoid the "impossibilities" Arrow later demonstrated) (Saether 2017a, 117–118, fn. 3).

Of course, Pufendorf was not the first to discover the problem of aggregating votes, obtaining majorities, etc. Even in Greek and Roman Antiquity such issues were considered and put into practice (e.g., Cicero 2019). Pufendorf knew about the difficulty when different alternatives have no common element. He was also aware of the fact that voting agendas can be manipulated and situations can have completely incompatible interests. For all that, my impression is that Pufendorf argued in favor of finding and separating common elements in alternative arguments and using these elements to ease voting processes. In this, I see him as a forerunner, advocating the pragmatic facilitation of decisions by looking for commonalities.

Pufendorf saw the state as the basic requirement of civilized society and as indispensable for every individual. Its main task was to educate and direct people through civil law to contribute to the welfare of society (Pufendorf ibid. III, III, 346, 350; 1943 [1673], 17; especially for the civil law aspect, see Luig 1996, 86).

6 Outlook for the Future on Pufendorf Fundamentals

Even though Pufendorf's conception of the state is of an absolute entity, he rejected its legitimization through the political theology of a divine kingdom. A state is a moral body, understood to have a single will, despite all the difficulties accompanying the voting procedures that constitute it. Because of their naturally restricted capabilities on the one hand and their sociability on the other, people agree to be organized in a community and rely on the assistance of their fellows. But sociability entails certain fundamental duties, which Pufendorf lists as follows: Nobody should hurt another; everybody should respect and treat their fellows as equals; and everybody should as far as possible be useful to others (Pufendorf 1943 [1673], 20, 26, 30; 1934 [1672], III, I, 313–314; III, II, 330–333, 335–337; III, III, 346–351). This clearly realizes the different tradeoffs between individual power and weakness, self-interest and social responsibility, freedom and duty, and is closely related to the "golden rule" *do as you would be done by*. To what extent, however, can Pufendorf's fundamental considerations be transposed, and possibly enhanced in a fruitful way, to meet present-day circumstances?

In its traditional understanding, the golden rule involves a tension between behavioral aspirations at the purely interpersonal and at the wider communal level. In the modern world, with its growing variety and heterogeneity, this problem has become increasingly acute, and ways must be found to cope with rampant selfishness and the future challenges of mass societies. While being aware that the tension between the poles of "personal behavior" and "virtuous conduct" cannot be completely eliminated, the sociologist Amitai Etzioni seeks to reduce the distance between them (Etzioni 1996, xviii, 193–196) by postulating what he calls a "communitarian paradigm." This means that people must learn to maintain relationships within a broader encompassing community without suppressing the member communities: "Individual rights must be balanced with a commitment to a shared core of values, so the commitment to one's community (or communities) must be balanced with commitments to the more encompassing society" (ibid. 191).

What do I want and what is expected from me? This field of tension can be eased by increased individual awareness of the values, rights, and duties of society on the one hand and a better understanding and greater respect on the part of society for individual rights on the other. This amounts to an expansion of the golden rule in both directions: people have to be more intensely aware of society and society of people—or as Etzioni (ibid. xviii) puts it in what he calls the "new golden rule": "Respect and uphold society's moral order as you would have society respect and uphold your autonomy":

> In short, a person should hold on to the values he or she finds most compelling, seeking to be joined by the community but steadfast even if others initially or ultimately do not approve. The community provides one with a normative foundation, a starting point, culture and tradition, fellowship, and place for moral dialogue, but is not the ultimate moral arbitrator. The members are. This is the ultimate reason that the communitarian paradigm entails a profound commitment to moral order that is basically voluntary, and to a social order that is well balanced with socially secured autonomy—the new golden rule. (ibid. 257)

In the new golden rule, society as well as the individual is under obligation. The state must respect and protect the autonomy of its members just as they are called upon to contribute, on their own initiative, to the moral order of society. For the new golden rule to work, it is not enough to voice moral pleas and demands: Concrete measures must be enacted to enhance the social awareness of individuals in their decisions; and, conversely, the state must consider and support the social incentives of individuals.

Etzioni argues for the meaning of morality, the sharing of core values, the adherence to pluralism within unity. For him, the community is always the final arbiter of values, consensus building is a social and democratic process, societal values must be seen as moral frameworks, dialogue about individual convictions must take place in a cross-societal manner encompassing global moral values and virtues (see Etzioni 1996, Chapter 8). Allowing for the different circumstances of seventeenth-century societies, these principles unmistakably overlap with Pufendorf's universal ethics (see, e.g., Hunger 1991, Chapter 6).

Without wanting to pursue these basic sociological questions further at this point, an interesting issue of current economic relevance remains: Can efforts to improve the relationship between the state and the individual in the sense of the new golden rule reduce the increasing scope of state intervention?

In this context, the model of "responsive regulation" proposed by Ian Ayres and John Braithwaite shifts the regulatory enforcement debate away from a stale dispute between proponents of free market and regulation, and between the deterrence and compliance models of enforcement. They suggest a process described as a "republican form of tripartism, […] a process in which relevant public interest groups (PIGs) become the fully fledged third player in the game" (Ayres and Braithwaite 1992, 56). Tripartism is defined as a regulatory policy that fosters the participation of interest groups in three ways: First, public interest groups grant all their members access to all the information that is available to the regulator. Secondly, public interest groups have a seat at the negotiating table: they are relevant decision makers. Thirdly, regulatory policy grants public interest groups the same rights as the regulator (ibid. 57–58). Ayres and Braithwaite understand public interest groups as striving for the improvement of public welfare, for example, environmental groups like the Sierra Club, animal welfare groups like the National Wildlife Federation, civil liberties groups, and women's groups for affirmative action and legislation (ibid. 74, 159); but the list can be extended to groups within enterprises seeking to better the situation of workers, or with other social aims (see, e.g., ibid. 159). The authors' overall aim is to support underrepresented interests by installing an institutional procedure that helps direct governmental regulation in fulfilling required tasks. The state should nurture the growth and empowerment of public interest groups, and may in turn hope to benefit from the self-regulation effects generated by improved participation and consequent reduction of the need for external intervention (ibid. 103, 159–160).

An important function of tripartism is empowerment. For Ayres and Braithwaite, tripartism plays an important role as an effective realization of countervailing power (ibid. 81), remedying existing inequalities of power and allowing representation of interests on a level playing field—as in the case, for example, of unionized labor. They also suggest that certain regulatory tasks might be delegated to private parties for the sake of market efficiency, but that such delegation be reinforced by traditional forms of regulatory fiat to take account of possible failure. As well as public interest groups, this role could be taken by firms, industrial associations, and commercial competitors (ibid. 158).

What follows from such considerations? The fundamental issue is to seek ways of steadily improving social interaction in light of ever-increasing requirements. Following the principle of proportionality, regulation observes and intervenes wherever needed and useful. Where individuals develop alternative solutions, regulation will withdraw. The state does not withdraw in principle; it appeals to individuals, who contribute of their own accord to its social aims. The motivation of those individuals should not be affected.

From a modern point of view, such ideas of regulation and self-responsibility can only be applied if the motivation situation of individuals allows the state to assume the achievement of its aims. Hence, self-responsibility has to be embedded in a suitable regulatory setting—a lot of typical applications already exist in environmental laws, healthcare, public supply, insurance, utilities provision, etc. Other absolute imperatives for the viability of this model are transparency—both of self-responsible behavior and its impact—and cooperation. The state has to provide the regulatory framework in which market power can unfold, and has to monitor and direct the process. In all of this, Pufendorf's considerations in the field of tension between self-interest and social responsibility, freedom and obligation, individual power and individual weakness provide an extended understanding of social processes and the workings of regulatory frameworks. His fundamental thoughts are, in fact, a helpful response to the functioning of modern democracies: Civic virtue and deep insight and trust in the state are necessary for its survival; negative attitudes toward the state destroy the basis of a functioning democracy.

For years, social and political scientists have drawn attention to the (mal-)functioning of democracies. Increasing revenue-seeking activities in a society, for example, foster socially unproductive energies and the demand for increased benefits from society in recompense. In such a mental environment, Bruno S. Frey sees the danger that civic virtue can be crowded out by the state's need to raise revenue (Frey 1997, 113). His insights into the crowding-out effects of economic policies are in line with the argumentation presented here. Policymakers, Frey argues, should be aware of the limited impact of price effects: The more avidly solutions are sought via price mechanisms, the less intensely will personal interest, responsibility, and motivation be involved (ibid. Chapter 11). Examples of the meaning of crowding out can be found in governmental tax and subsidies policy, as well as in such areas as work morale, blood donation, crime prevention, and environmental policy. A prime example is the NIMBY problem cited by Frey and Oberholzer-Gee (Frey 1997, 67) that typically occurs in with the context of hazardous waste disposal, construction of freeways, airports, prisons, and clinics for the physically or mentally handicapped, where the projects are generally supported by society but not wanted in the respondents' neighborhood (ibid.). People fear the risks of damage from chemical leaks, emissions, noise, reduction in amenities, and so on. A common instrument used by economists to solve this problem is monetary compensation. But this underestimates the true costs because the detrimental effects of crowding out in terms of motivation are not taken into account—not everything can be balanced by money. Frey and Oberholzer-Gee support their argument with three hypotheses:

1. The higher a citizen's initial sense of civic duty, the more strongly intrinsic motivation is crowded out when compensation is introduced. [...]
2. If citizens are to remain intrinsically motivated to serve their country and accept thankless tasks, they must be convinced that the burdens are generally shared in a fair manner. [...] If the site selection process is perceived to be fair, we can expect more intrinsically motivated citizens. [...]
3. In order to preserve one's intrinsic motivation, it is essential to believe that the action undertaken corresponds with one's personal conviction. We expect citizens who emphasize the importance of technically and socially sound solutions to react negatively to the introduction of price incentives if they feel that money is being used to cover up technical or social weaknesses. (ibid. 68–69)

How, then, can the state fulfill its duty to ensure and increase the welfare of its citizens? The answer lies in the extent to which—over and above all binding rules and regulations—it can attract, motivate, and actively involve people to work for society. Measures to be undertaken in this respect are as follows:

- Responsive regulation
- Self-awareness
- Self-responsibility
- Civil virtue and morality
- Deeper insights into societal processes
- Economic policies that do not neglect the factor of intrinsic motivation
- Avoidance of economic policies with dangerous crowding-out effects
- A special imperative for economists—taking account of the insights of the neighboring social sciences: sociology, psychology, political science, and history.

All these measures reflect and fulfill Pufendorf's fundamental principles as we have already seen them: That nobody should hurt another, that everybody should respect and treat their fellows as equals, and that everybody should, as far as possible, be useful to others.

References

Arrow K (1951) Social Choice and Individual Values, New York: John Wiley

Ayres I and Braithwaite J (1992) Responsive Regulation. Transcending the Deregulation Debate, New York, Oxford: Oxford University Press

Behme T (1995) Samuel von Pufendorf. Eine Analyse und Interpretation seiner Theorie, ihrer Grundlagen und Probleme, Göttingen: Vandenhoeck & Ruprecht

Cicero MT (2019) De Legibus, Loeb Classical Digital Library, Harvard, https://www.loebclassics.com/view/marcus_tullius_cicero-de_legibus/1928/pb_LCL213.467.xml [06.01.2019]

Denzer, H (1972) Moralphilosophie und Naturrecht bei Samuel Pufendorf. Eine geistes- und wissenschaftsgeschichtliche Untersuchung zur Geburt des Naturrechts aus der praktischen Philosophie, Munich: Beck

Döring D (1989) Samuel Pufendorf und die Leipziger Gelehrtengesellschaften in der Mitte des 17. Jahrhunderts, Berlin: Akademie-Verlag

Etzioni A (1996) The New Golden Rule – Community and Morality in a Democratic Society, New York: BasicBooks (HarperCollins)

Fowler, Henry Watson (1965). A Dictionary of Modern English Usage, 2. ed, Oxford: Oxford University Press

Frey BS (1997) Not Just For the Money. An Economic Theory of Personal Motivation, Cheltenham, UK: Edward Elgar

Gaertner W (2005) De jure naturae et gentium: Samuel von Pufendorf's contribution to social choice theory and economics, in: Social Choice and Welfare, December 2005, Vol. 25, Issue 2–3, Springer, pp. 231–241

Hobbes T (1962 [1651]) *Leviathan*: or the matter, form and power of a commonwealth, ecclesiastical and civil, introd. by A. D. Lindsay, London, New York: Dent & Sons, Dutton

Hunger W (1991) Samuel von Pufendorf. Aus dem Leben und Werk eines deutschen Frühaufklärers, Flöha: Verlag Druck & design

Hunter I (2001) Rival enlightenments. Civil and metaphysical philosophy in early modern Germany. Cambridge University Press, Cambridge

Lagerspetz E (1986) Pufendorf on Collective Decisions, Public choice, Vol. 49, No. 2, pp 179–182

Luig K (1996) Pufendorfs Lehre von der Wirksamkeit des Staates und das Privatrecht, in Geyer B and Goerlich H (eds.) Samuel Pufendorf und seine Wirkungen bis auf die heutige Zeit, Baden-Baden: Nomos, pp 85–98

Maihofer W (1996) Schlusswort: Was uns Pufendorf noch heute zu sagen hat, in Geyer B and Goerlich H (eds.) Samuel Pufendorf und seine Wirkungen bis auf die heutige Zeit, Baden-Baden: Nomos, pp 223–282

von Pufendorf S (1934 [1672]) De jure naturae et gentium, libri octo, translated into English (using the 2nd ed. of 1688) by C.H. and W.A. Oldfather, Vol. 2 (2 Vols.), Oxford, Clarendon Press.

von Pufendorf S (1943 [1673]) Die Gemeinschaftspflichten des Naturrechts – Ausgewählte Stücke aus "De officio hominis et civis" 1673, Frankfurt a.M.: Klostermann

Rabe H (1958) Naturrecht und Kirche bei Samuel von Pufendorf. Eine Untersuchung der naturrechtlichen Einflüsse auf den Kirchenbegriff Pufendorfs als Studie zur Entstehung d. modernen Denkens, Tübingen: Ekkehart Fabian

Sæther A (2017a) Natural Law and the Origin of Political Economy. Samuel Pufendorf and the History of Economics, London and New York: Routledge

Sæther A (2017b) Samuel Pufendorf and Ludvig Holberg on Political Economy, Norwegian School of Economics, Department of Economics, discussion paper August 2017

Sen AK (1970) Collective Choice and Social Welfare, San Francisco: Holden-Day

Sprenger G (1996) Die Bedeutung der Lehre von der Imbecellitas bei Samuel Pufendorf. Einige anthropologische Anmerkungen, in Vanda Fiorillo. Samuel Pufendorf – Filosofo del diritto e della politica, La città del sole, Naples: Città del sole, pp. 251—267.

Welzel H (1986) Die Naturrechtslehre Samuel Pufendorfs. Ein Beitrag zur Ideengeschichte des 17. und 18. Jahrhunderts, 3rd edn., 1st edn. 1958, Berlin, New York: de Gruyter

Samuel Pufendorf's Contractarian Corporate Governance Principles. A New Perspective for Business Economics and Ethics Studies

Francesco Forte and Sabato Vinci

Abstract Pufendorf's theory of justice is extremely important not only for government organizations but, more generally, for research about all organizations made up for man for achieving a common objective. These include, first of all, companies. So, Pufendorf's theory represents a theoretical basis both in the area of public finance and in the area of business economics. In this paper, we focus above all on an application of Pufendorf's theory to corporate governance, in particular relating to the problem of prevalence between shareholders' objectives and company objectives, in case of conflict between them. This question can be interpreted, bearing in mind Pufendorf's theory, in the light of the distinction between universal and distributive justice: the first (universal justice) based on a natural law commutative concept and the second (distributive justice) based on a compensatory concept. So, Pufendorf's thought about contractual relations can be applied fruitfully to the problem of the company's relations, as an association of individuals for the realization of a superior business activity and, at the same time, itself as autonomous entity. The same basic postulate of Pufendorf about men as "moral subjects" which can represents, for business and economic studies, the basis for a renewed conception of the enterprise, as institution that puts man, his needs and his vocation to sociality at the centre of it. Pufendorf's ideas, then, give interesting insights to the social and academic debate about modern ethics studies and modern business economics, about topics such as the relationship between natural law and positive law, public goods and the relationship between private company ownership and its social responsibility, and therefore the ethicality of business and economic behaviour of owners and managers.

F. Forte (✉)
Department of Economics and Law, Sapienza – University of Rome, Rome, Italy

Mediterranea University of Reggio Calabria, Reggio Calabria, Italy

S. Vinci
Department of Political Sciences, University of Roma Tre, Rome, Italy
e-mail: sabato.vinci@uniroma3.it

J. G. Backhaus et al. (eds.), *Samuel Pufendorf and the Emergence of Economics as a Social Science*, The European Heritage in Economics and the Social Sciences 24, https://doi.org/10.1007/978-3-030-49791-0_7

Keywords Samuel Pufendorf · Contractarian corporation · Corporate governance · Business ethics · Business economics · Law and economics

JEL Codes B11 · B30 · B52M20 · M14

1 General Principles

Francesco Forte

1.1 The Importance of Pufendorf's Theory of Justice in the Area of Business Economics

Pufendorf's theory of justice is extremely important not only in the area of public finance, but more generally in the area of business economics. Indeed Pufendorf, in his opus magnum *De Jure Naturae et Gentium* of 1672 and in his shorter book *De Officio Hominis et Civis* of 1673 on the principles of natural law which aims to provide a synthesis of his previous book focused on its main topic, had the ambition of creating a general theory of human behaviour in the public and private life similar to those of the great catholic philosophers and jurists of the Middle Ages and Renaissance, but laic (Gihl 1932, 53). He did it by adopting a scientific methodology similar to that of physics of Galileus and Newton, separated from religion. As has been noted by Bobbio (1943, V), between the two basic approaches to modern philosophy, *Novum Organum*, the empirical approach by Roger Bacon, and *Discourse on Method* by René Descartes, Pufendorf chose the second. It must be added that Pufendorf, to develop this method, chose a scientific methodology whose theoretical rules, or better: cognitive paradigms, had been tested empirically with the first method.

Thus, he succeeded in this ambitious work, however at the price of an oversimplification, which may be defined with three words: perfectionism, reductionism, anti-historicism. But proceeding in this way, he did not an un-useful work. On the contrary, given the high level of abstraction, most of the conceptual paradigms which he presented had the property of surviving the great changes in our societies from that time and are useful conceptual boxes in the third millennium too, also in economics which, at that time, was merely a part of political philosophy.

1.2 What Pufendorf Means by Natural Law

By Natural Law, Pufendorf means a natural law pertaining to humans, as a 'scientific', therefore laic, interdisciplinary general theory of political philosophy and legal universal principles. As economics at his time was a part of political philosophy of great, increasing importance, because of the intense economic developments then taking place, Pufendorf's natural law basic paradigms, both in his opus magnum *De Jure Naturae et Gentium* and in *De Officio Hominis et Civis*, more than often, are basic paradigms of business economics and of public economics and of their mutual relations, and are important in this millennium.

According to a current interpretation the 'laic ethics' manual of Pufendorf was intended to be a sort of 'scientific construct' against Catholic thinking. However, de facto this is not true at all, because in the doctrine of the Catholic Church, at least from the middle of the XIX century, when the Encyclical *Rerum Novarum* was promulgated by Pope Leo XIII, the Catholic quasi-natural laws at the basis of the social, political and economic principles do have a clear laic nature.

Thus, it frequently happens that important thinkers of Protestant faith, as Walter Eucken, leader of the Ordo-liberal School of economics, Alfred Müller-Armack, who developed the social wing of the school, and Wilhelm Röpke, who developed a parallel economic-political sociological theory, make explicit reference to *Rerum Novarum* and to other papal encyclicals. Thus, we can safely say that Pufendorf's paradigms are relevant for business economics and public economics, and their mutual relations have a general validity, at least in Europe.

It must be added that Pufendorf's theory was based on the theory of Grotius, in opposition to that of Hobbes, however often adopting principles and intuitions of Hobbes (Pufendorf 1672, 7) in order to complement, broaden and correct Grotius' oversimplified deductive postulates.

1.3 The Basic Postulate of Pufendorf About Men as Moral Subjects

The basic postulate of Pufendorf about men as moral subjects different from animals is that they have will and knowledge. As we shall see, this reductionistic dichotomy conceals the potential richness of the content of will. This is particularly true for the basic postulate which Pufendorf adopts for his reasoning, considering it as a self-evident fact: that humans as single individuals are too weak for the realization of their ends (Pufendorf 1672, 2, 2, §2), from surviving animal attacks and violence by enemies, to the development of the means to improve their condition, to satisfy their potential will and to increase their knowledge. Thus, they need an association with other human beings, possibly permanently and possibly with a large number of people, giving origin to permanent, strong composite moral persons, capable of realizing efficiently the above-mentioned objectives (Pufendorf 1672, 2, 3, §19).

It is wrong to assume, as Bobbio did, that the basis of Pufendorf's ethics is utilitarian, merely because the reason of the need of humans to associate with others is to realize their wills of survival and development. Actually, the big box of 'wills' is an open box. Many ends are not utilitarian in terms of hedonic material utility. Indeed, as Pufendorf himself accurately states in his *De Jure Naturae et Gentium*, Liber I, Ch. VII on the quality of moral action, § III on the goodness of moral actions, § V on the goodness or malice of moral action, § VI on Justice among persons, § VII on the difference between Justice and goodness, and § VIII on the imperfect rights, many ends of will are not quantitative, but are merely qualitative. In Paretian terminology, one may qualify them as preferences with given ordering ranks, such as freedom of choice, which is certainly the first-order preference of will, but also the presence of other persons, to communicate with each other, preservation of basic elements of nature of which humans are part, aesthetic sentiments, love for our own parents and grand-parents and for our children and grandchildren with empathic sentiments. People's wills may include and normally do include the need of an environment of vegetal and animal entities unappropriated in which to live. The broadening of knowledge, too, may be a per-se objective (Darwall 2012, 213ff.). Therefore, it is correct to say that Pufendorf's ethics is a nonutilitarian one.

1.4 The Complexity of Pufendorf's Laic Ethics

A very complex itinerary of Pufendorf's laic ethics consists in his theory according to which the state as a moral person with a sovereign power enduring in the long run is a gift of God to the humans, which belongs to the laic ethics, because reason is the source of the information that God approves the state as a divine gift if there is a will of the people to form it, leaving to them the freedom of making mistakes.

Let us, then, consider a contribution of Pufendorf to market micro economics with its dual theory of natural common goods (Pufendorf 1672, Liber III): a positive natural class and a natural law theory of common goods (ibid., Liber III, Chaps. II–IX) and a negative common goods natural class and a negative theory of natural law of common goods (ibid., Liber III, Chap. I), which he develops in two different ways.

The positive class paradigm and its theory of natural law derives from the postulate of weakness of the individual: it is natural for them to own goods and to produce them in common with others, as single or complex persons in corporations or any other association to increase the robustness of the property nexus of the persons with the goods.

The negative class paradigm and natural law theory of common goods of Pufendorf arise from his controversy with Thomas Hobbes who maintains that in the natural state every human individual owns everything, so that they are entitled to fight to get a share, taking from all the other owners, by use of their power. Pufendorf correctly argues that in the natural state, before a social organization exists, all goods are common, in the sense that they are 'res nullius' – nobody owns them (ibid., Liber IV, Chaps. III and IV).

They are undivided in properties of simple or complex persons, formed by single persons. Let us first consider Pufendorf's positive common goods class and natural law theory. Here, principles of justice intervene, as for the rights and duties of the members of the community, which own the goods. God approves the appropriation of the goods of nature that he created by humans to cope with their weakness and to realize their wills more effectively and broadly than if they act alone. But God did not give any divine principle of justice to share the costs and fruits of the common properties. These are rules of human laic natural law based on human conventions. There may be a variety of them. Basically, this variety may be scientifically reduced to two main mathematic principles of justice: as 'do ut des' or commutative or exchange or equivalence justice, and distributive or proportional equality, i.e. the identical ratio between dignity and merits of the different members of the community. In the economic communities, clearly it is not dignity, but merit that matters, that determines the ratio of distributive justice; dignity however is not irrelevant because in a human complex community each member is equal to the other. Therefore, each member in the community has equal dignity. But if a member of a community is not capable of satisfying his minimal survival wants with his capabilities, he loses dignity and according to Pufendorf, out of the equal dignity principle arises the principle of assuring to everybody a minimum for basic necessities. Merit comes first to promote the development, basic wants to come at the second place, as constraint to the maximization of the first, but the level of satisfaction increases as development leads to more resources as object of distribution.

1.5 The Implications of Pufendorf's Negative Common Goods Natural Law Theory

Pufendorf does not examine a further implication of his 'negative' theory of common goods as 'res nullius', i.e. whether they may be divided, by excluding those who do not have a title to benefit of them, or they cannot be divided because they are intrinsically able to satisfy anybody, i. e. are common goods with an existence value independent from their use and, further, whether in case of common non-divisible existence goods, those who add their fruition to that of the others may provide a benefit to the other beneficiaries, i.e. a positive externality which can be object of appropriation or not.

Furthermore, an additional fruition in some cases may reduce the benefits of others, because the existence value is not independent from the use value, but in a sense rival, with a possibility of putting a remedy to the damage of the use to the existence or not. As one can see, this simple theoretical paradigm or theoretical box may be enriched by many variables of extraordinary relevance for the ethics and economics of business in general, and more specifically for corporate governance economics. Themes as the effects of corporations' behaviour on climate change, on the environment, on the cultural and historical patrimony have thus a basic tool of analysis in Pufendorf's negative common goods natural law theory. It is also important for the foundations of the rules of corporate governance. Corporations belong to the category of the composite moral person, which are made by single persons, the human individual. They may be private companies or public companies of the market sector (see also, Young 2008, 283ff.).

Pufendorf (1672, Vol. I, Liber I, Chap. VI) distinguishes two types of justice: the universal one, which is a mere natural law justice (commutative concept), and the particular justice, which consists of distributive justice (compensatory concept). The universal justice pertains to actions which are not due or, more generally, are supported only by an imperfect right of obligation or of punishment. Typically, stakeholder rights belong to this category, unless particular conventions are made with representatives of some of them. The other three kinds of justice, those of particular justice, consisting in compensatory justice, exchange justice and distributive justice pertain to obligations which the societies have:

1. With their members, their workers and managers.
2. With their private creditors and debtors.
3. With the public sector.
4. With the simple and complex persons damaged by them without a legal title to do so: here and in the situations of item 3, we find the compensatory justice, which implies to pay for damages done or to ask of being paid for damages received.

Pufendorf does not mention compensatory justice in the universal justice area, but this could be easily done, by considering the external economies and diseconomies, in the frame of the existing rules on property rights (Korkman 2003, 195ff.; Hunter 2013, 289ff.).

2 Corporate Governance

Sabato Vinci

2.1 The Company as an Artificial Individual Born from the Association of Single Individuals

Here, we focus on corporate governance, a sector of business economics and industrial economics, which is becoming more and more important. Let us first consider the nature of the enterprises as single persons or composite persons. In both cases, Pufendorf adopts the model of the 'artificial man' being bigger than an individual man (Pufendorf 1672, 12, §7), who, like the individual man, has not an endless life, unlike the state as moral permanent person, however with a life generally potentially much longer than that of individuals, because of the possibility of replacing the members who disappear, as a river that remains even if its waters flow from the source to the end in another river or in a lake or in a sea or in the surface of the ground or back down.

Obviously, while individuals cannot be simultaneously in one place and in another, corporations easily do this and may reside in several different places in the same town, region, nation, and may become multinational. Additionally, they may be both on the ground and in the web in the same moment, as individuals too can and may be present in different places in the web, with different languages, as individuals too; however, because of their greater dimensions they may enjoy economies of large scale and increasing returns on a dimension impossible for individuals, with a much greater market power that may result in oligopoly and monopoly situations, but with an unstable situation, if the market is open. For the giant public economic 'personae fictae' Hobbes speaks of Leviathans. However, Leviathans may exist in market-oriented economic corporations, too, and particularly as in the web (Gauthier 1979).

In particular, it can be said that, in line with Pufendorf's theory, the basic problem of corporate governance arises from the need for men to associate with each other (either personally or economically) in order to realize businesses that are beyond the reach of individuals. This leads to the overcoming of the small enterprise (artisan) model of the neoclassical style and to the birth of the modern 'big company' (Zanda 1974, 53ff.). This originally represents a sort of *longa manus* of the colonial power's governments (first of all, Great Britain and Holland) for missions of a commercial nature and then also of an administrative nature, with reference to overseas territories (Galgano 2007, 78ff.).

In particular, there are two specificities of the company with respect to a common enterprise:

1. The need for individuals to associate with each other (personally and/or economically) to achieve a collective goal
2. The recognition of limited liability to the new 'artificial individual' born from the association of individuals (Frigeni 2009, 6ff.)

However, while the first characteristic, in line with Pufendorf's theory, arises from a need for natural law which consists in the union of single weak individuals to create a strong artificial individual, the second characteristic arises instead from a need for artificial right, which consists in the government's desire to 'cover' part of the risk deriving from the crossing of the oceans with the recognition by the ship owners (the company members) of an economic responsibility for case of bankruptcy of the company (ship wreck and loss of cargo) equal to only the company's share capital.

2.2 *The Separation Between Ownership and Management in the Company*

The construction of large companies, born by the desire of individuals to bring together economic and intellectual resources, with a view to achieving a common goal, implies a certain degree of 'institutionalization' of the company itself. In this sense, the dialectical relationship extends beyond the spheres of 'capital' (property) and 'work' (workers), as a third subject also takes over: management. Thus, complex mechanisms of delegation, control, incentives and sanctions between proprietor and management are formed – which business economists interpret today primarily according to the alternative schemes of 'agency theory' (Williamson 2002, 171ff.) or 'stewardship theory' (Donaldson and Davis 1991, 50). Fundamentally, this complexity originates from the fact that the moral entity that Pufendorf defined as 'artificial individuals' (companies), due to its size, assumes a bureaucratic structural form, which splits the sphere of ownership from that of work and management.

2.3 *The Problem of the Company's Relations, as an Association of Individuals for the Realization of a Superior Business Activity, and the Institutional Theories of the Company*

In Pufendorf's logic, the men who associate with each other to have the strength to carry out an enterprise of dimensions unachievable for individuals enjoy a corresponding right to the distribution of profits. However, from this consideration a problem arises which is much debated in the current studies of business administration: which of the two instances will have to prevail in case of conflict between the objectives of the shareholders (natural single persons) and the objectives of the company (moral body or artificial composite person)? From this basic question, the distinction between a contractualist theory and an institutionalist theory arose within corporate governance. According to the first theory (contract theory), the interests of the members should prevail, since the purpose of the economic association is precisely the realization of a common enterprise in order to deliver benefits to the associates. According to the second theory (institutionalist theory), the interests of the company should prevail, because the company is a moral entity distinct from its shareholders and preordained for the realization of an economic activity not only higher to the individual shareholders interests but also more lasting than the existence of shareholders (Deger and Hettlage 2007; Pasquino 2010, 99ff.). The ideological contrast between contractualists and institutionalists has manifested itself not only within the academic communities of business and economic studies but also at the political level, producing the consequence that the legislator has found itself, practically in every modern economic system, to regulate the potential conflict by choosing between the prevalence of the corporate structure or the social function reasons. In general, a concept closer to the institutionalist idea seems to be predominant at the legislative level, in every system in the world. This vision has traditionally been dominant in the Italian school of business economics. In fact, the founder of business economics in Italy, Gino Zappa, defined the company as "an economic institution destined to last and which, for the satisfaction of human needs, orders and carries out in continuous coordination the production or procurement and consumption of wealth". On the basis of this assumption, the tradition of Italian business studies taken as its main staple the concept that the company itself goes beyond the interests of the owners (as it is an institution destined to "last") and it has as its institutional horizon the satisfaction of "human needs". However, it should be noted that, especially following the affirmation, since the 1980s, of a new type of capitalism strongly dominated by the finance role (in particular investment funds, investment banks and insurance companies), contract theory seems to have experienced a new golden age. In this perspective, the idea that the task of management should consist in maximising the value of shares and corporate profit has been reaffirmed, while any other behaviour (e.g. of social responsibility or towards the wider stakeholder landscape) would be considered questionable or not in line with the typical management mission. However, putting ideologically the interests of shareholders before those of other stakeholders may imply a mainly short-term view of the company. Indeed, if corporate profits tend to be distributed among shareholders, it will tend to decrease the company's ability to develop long-term investments to promote innovation, thus weakening its ability to compete in the market and exposing it to the risk of crisis and external acquisitions. Likewise, in economic phases where the company's profitability is unsatisfactory, making a contractual vision prevail may inducing managers to contract costs (moreover, the easiest to cut are personnel costs) in order to guarantee a certain margin of profitability to satisfy shareholders who are waiting for their dividends. Furthermore, managers will be encouraged to inspire their business choices more to a financial market-oriented logic than to a real economy-oriented logic. So, the company is certainly an asset owned by the shareholders, but a "property oriented" vision risks – beyond the short term – to be harmful not only for the company itself, but also for the owners, as well as for other important stakeholders such as workers and local communities. This ideology was called into question again after the great economic crisis of 2007–2008, which underlined the opportunity to look at the company as an asset with strong social relevance, which corresponds to a deep need for ethical behavior from owners and managers. In fact, the behaviour of companies strongly influences the social fabric, the local communities and their work, environmental and relational ecosystem.

Hence, the basic problem then becomes to understand that the association of men for the realization of companies so large as to be closed to individuals (the company) produces the consequence of a double split:

- A first split is internal to the company: it leads to the emergence of three types of fundamental actors in corporate life (shareholders, managers, workers), to which a more diverse and generic fourth one is added (the other stakeholders).
- A second split is between the objectives that the company must pursue: they can be the shareholders objectives or the objectives of the company as an artificial individual. The two types of objectives do not always coincide.

This question can be interpreted, bearing in mind Pufendorf's theory, in the light of the distinction between universal and distributive justice (Chroust 1979, 72). It would be possible to argue that the expectations of the shareholders towards the management aimed at remunerating their economic sacrifice (corresponding to the percentage of equity participation) finds legitimacy in a distributive justice perspective based on a compensatory concept, while the aspiration of the company to finalize its business activity to the realization of a purpose of social order (corresponding to the interest of the community to see its own need satisfied) finds legitimacy instead in a perspective of universal justice based on a natural law commutative concept (Schino 2014, 65ff.). This is because, unlike the right of shareholders to see their investment remunerated, the interest of the community to see its own needs fulfilled would not be envisaged in a natural law perspective (Wokler 1994, 373ff.). The various rules that, over the years, have projected the business activity into a 'social' dimension, removing it from a 'property oriented' dimension, are in fact placed mainly in a sphere of positive law (Gaertner 2005, 231ff.).

3 Conclusions

Considering the corporate phenomenon, Pufendorf adopts the model of the 'artificial man' being bigger than an individual man, who as the individual man has not an endless life, unlike the State as permanent moral person, however with a life generally potentially much longer than that of individuals, because of the possibility of replacing the members who disappear. The problem that arises with respect to the 'corporate' phenomenon, that it is at the same time an organization between single persons but also a composite person, can be summarized as follows: which of the two instances will have to prevail, in case of conflict between the objectives of the shareholders (natural single persons) and the objectives of the company (moral body or artificial composite person)? This question can be interpreted, bearing in mind Pufendorf's theory, in the light of the distinction between universal and distributive justice. So, Pufendorf's ideas give to the social and academic debate interesting insights for modern ethics studies and for modern business economics studies, about topics such as the relationship between natural law and positive law, the public goods and the relationship between private company ownership and its social responsibility, and, therefore, the ethicality of business and economic behaviour of owners and managers.

References

Bobbio N (1943) Prefazione a Samuel Pufendorf, Principi di Diritto Naturale, Torino: Piccola Biblioteca Paravia

Chroust A H (1979) Some Critical Remarks about Samuel Pufendorf and his Contributions to Jurisprudence, American Journal of Jurisprudence, 24/1, pp 72–85

Darwall S (2012) Pufendorf on Morality, Sociability, and Moral Powers, Journal of the History of Philosophy, 50(2), pp 213–238

Deger P and Hettlage R (eds.) (2007) Der europäische Raum: die Konstruktion europäischer Grenzen, Berlin: Springer

Donaldson L and Davis J H (1991) Stewardship Theory or Agency Theory: CEO Governance and Shareholder Returns, Australian Journal of Management, 16(1), pp 49–65

Frigeni C (2009) Partecipazione in società di capitali e diritto al disinvestimento, Milano: Giuffrè

Gaertner W (2005) De jure naturae et gentium: Samuel von Pufendorf's contribution to social choice theory and economics, Social Choice and Welfare, 25(2–3), pp 231–241

Galgano F (2007) John Locke azionista delle compagnie coloniali. Una chiave di lettura del Secondo trattato sul governo, Dimensioni e problemi della ricerca storica, 1, pp 77–91.

Gauthier D P (1979) The Logic of Leviathan: the Moral and Political Theory of Thomas Hobbes, Oxford: Clarendon Press

Gihl T (1932) Samuel Pufendorf och Jus Naturae et Gentium, Nordisk Tidsskrift for Internasjonal, Ret 2, pp 37–64

Hunter I (2013) The Figure of Man and the Territorialisation of Justice in 'Enlightenment' Natural Law: Pufendorf and Vattel, Intellectual History Review, 23(3), pp 289–307

Korkman P (2003) Voluntarism and Moral Obligation: Barbeyrac's Defence of Pufendorf Revisited, in Hochstrasser T J and Schröder P (eds.) Early Modern Natural Law Theories: Context and Strategies in the Early Enlightenment, Dordrecht, Boston: Kluwer Academic Publishers, pp 195–225

Pasquino P (2010) Samuel Pufendorf: majority rule (logic, justification and limits) and forms of government, Social Science Information, 49(1), pp 99–109

Pufendorf S (1672) De Jure Naturae et Gentium. Libri Octo, London 1934, Oxford: Clarendon Press

Schino A L (2014) Weigel e Pufendorf: metodo analitico e diritto naturale, Rivista di filosofia, CV(1), pp 65–90

Williamson O E (2002) The Theory of the Firm as Governance Structure: from Choice to Contract, Journal of Economic Perspectives, 16/3, pp 171–195

Wokler R (1994) Rousseau's Pufendorf: natural law and the foundations of commercial society, History of Political Thought, 15(3), pp 373–402

Young J T (2008) Law and economics in the Protestant natural law tradition: Samuel Pufendorf, Francis Hutcheson, and Adam Smith, Journal of the History of Economic Thought, 30(3), pp 283–296

Zanda G (1974) La grande impresa, Milano: Giuffrè

Late Scholastics as Predecessors of Natural Law Economics – The Viewpoint of Joseph Höffner

Daniel Eissrich

Abstract With the publication of Joseph Schumpeter's History of Economic Analysis, it became clear that the disdain expressed by many economists for scholastic economics was inappropriate and that the scholastics had a significant influence initially on Grotius and Pufendorf, and consequently also Adam Smith. Even before Schumpeter, Joseph Höffner had referred to the dependence of the philosophers of natural law on the Spanish late scholastics in the context of the law of nations. He also made important contributions to the rediscovery of the economics of the late scholastics. This chapter provides an overview of Höffner's work and shows connecting lines between the scholastics and Grotius and Pufendorf.

Keywords Höffner · Molina · Scholastic · School of Salamanca · Natural law · Just price · History of economic thought

JEL Codes A12 · B11 · B31

1 Joseph Höffner as a Scientist

The scientific career of Joseph Cardinal Höffner (1906–1987) began in 1926 with his studies at the Pontifical Gregorian University in Rome. Here, he received his doctorate in philosophy in 1929 and in theology in 1934 with a thesis on 'Soziale Gerechtigkeit und soziale Liebe' (Social Justice and Social Love). After his return to Germany, Höffner became chaplain in Saarbrücken, but decided to continue his scientific career. As his doctoral degree from a Roman university was not recognised in Germany at that time, Höffner went to the University of Freiburg to write

D. Eissrich (✉)
Deutsche Bundesbank, Frankfurt am Main, Germany

J. G. Backhaus et al. (eds.), *Samuel Pufendorf and the Emergence of Economics as a Social Science*, The European Heritage in Economics and the Social Sciences 24, https://doi.org/10.1007/978-3-030-49791-0_8

another theological dissertation on the subject of 'Peasant and Church in the German Middle Ages'. At the same time, he took the opportunity to study economics, which he completed with a diploma in 1938. After he attained a doctorate with Walter Eucken, his dissertation about 'Wirtschaftsethik und Monopole im fünfzehnten und sechzehnten Jahrhundert' (Business Ethics and Monopolies in the Fifteenth and Sixteenth Centuries) was published in 1941. Eucken had hoped that the economic ethical evaluation of monopolies in Höffner's work would lead to a contribution to the competitive order he represented (Rauscher 2007, 6–7). In his work 'Grundsätze der Wirtschaftspolitik' (Principles of Economic Policy), Eucken himself cited Joseph Höffner's dissertation as a reference for 'historical and fundamental' aspects of the monopoly issue (Eucken [1952] 1990, 359).

In 1942, Walter Eucken also wrote one of the expert opinions on Joseph Höffner's theological habilitation on 'Spanische Kolonialethik im 15. und 16. Jahrhundert' (Spanish Colonial Ethics in the Fifteenth and Sixteenth Centuries), which was first published in 1947 under the title 'Christentum und Menschenwürde: Das Anliegen der spanischen Kolonialethik im goldenen Zeitalter' (Christianity and Human Dignity: The concern of Spanish Colonial Ethics in the Golden Age). From 1951, Höffner taught at the University of Münster as Professor of Christian Social Sciences. He ended his academic career upon his appointment as Bishop of Münster in 1962.

Joseph Cardinal Höffner – Curriculum Vitae

24 December 1906	Born in Horhausen; eldest son of seven children of the farmer Paul Höffner and his wife Helene
1926–1934	Studies at the Pontifical Gregorian University in Rome
1932	Ordination
1929	PhD in Philosophy
1934	PhD in Theology
1935–1936	Chaplain in the Diocese of Trier
1937–1939	Studies at the University of Freiburg
1938	Renewed doctorate in theology
1940	PhD in economics
1944	Habilitation for Moral Theology
1945–1951	Professor at the Priesterseminar Trier
1951–1962	Professor of Christian Social Sciences at the University of Münster
1953–1962	Advisory Council in the Ministries of Labour, Family Affairs and Housing
1962–1969	Bishop of Münster
1969–1987	Archbishop of Cologne
1969	Appointment as Cardinal
1976–1987	Chairman of the German Bishops' Conference
16 October 1987	Joseph Cardinal Höffner dies in Cologne
2003	Award of the title 'Righteous Among the Nations' by the State of Israel

2 Views on the Economy at the Time of Scholasticism

Joseph Höffner opposed the portrayal of the medieval economy and economic convictions, that is, the view that the age of scholasticism had been shaped by the 'class-stationary ideal' of society and the all-dominant 'idea of food befitting one's rank', a misjudgement that was endorsed by well-known economists such as Wilhelm Endemann, Karl Bücher, Ernst Troeltsch, Werner Sombart and others (Höffner [1955] 2014, 251–252; Weber 1967, 12–13). Joseph Höffner himself cited examples such as the Hanseatic League, long-distance trade, mining in Hungary and Tyrol, and the large commercial centres such as Venice, Genoa, Antwerp or Augsburg as evidence of the dynamic economic life of the Middle Ages and the beginning of modern times (Höffner [1955] 2014, 252–253).

Joseph Höffner was not alone with this view by any means even at his time; renowned economists such as Joseph Schumpeter held similar views:

> Capitalist enterprise had not been absent before, but from the thirteenth century on it slowly began to attack the framework of feudal institutions that had for ages fettered but also sheltered the farmer and the artisan, and to evolve the contours of the economic pattern that still is, or until quite recently was, our own. By the end of the fifteenth century most of the phenomena that we are in the habit of associating with that vague word Capitalism had put in their appearance, including big business, stock and commodity speculation, and 'high finance,' to all of which people reacted much as we do ourselves. Even then these phenomena were not all of them new. Truly unprecedented was only their absolute and relative importance. (Schumpeter 1954, 74–75)

In recent times, the view of the dynamic economic development in Western Europe during the Middle Ages has gained more and more support. Thus, Douglass C. North and Robert Thomas noted in their work 'The Rise of the Western World': During the high Middle Ages, in Western Europe '… extensive growth continued apace, creating a market system where none had effectively existed' (North and Thomas 1973, 45). It was followed by the thirteenth century with '… population growth, which continued at an impressive rate. Urban places expanded. Trade and commerce flourished locally, regionally and internationally. In short, this was a dynamic era …' (North and Thomas 1973, 46). The following fourteenth and fifteenth centuries '… suffered contractions, crisis and perhaps even depression. The regions of Europe were repeatedly visited by famine, pestilence, war and revolution.' Nevertheless, it was also '… the time of the Renaissance – a rebirth of artistic and intellectual achievements. In short, it is difficult to give a simple assessment of these centuries' (North and Thomas 1973, 71). '… feudalism in Western Europe was buried by 1500, the following period of "nascent capitalism" was characterized by expansion during the sixteenth and crisis during the seventeenth century' (North and Thomas 1973, 102).

Ultimately, empirical studies of global economic development led OECD economist Angus Maddison to believe that Western Europe had the highest economic growth rates worldwide in the period between 1000 and 1500. During this period, per capita income in Western Europe had almost doubled, while it increased by about a third in China and less in other parts of Asia, and even declined in Africa. At the same time, the population in Western Europe had more than doubled (Maddison 2004, 34, 56).

More than the assessment of the economic development of the Middle Ages, however, Joseph Höffner was concerned with the distorted view of the economics of the scholastics, which was represented by the economists already mentioned; he notes '... that all these scientists hardly ever cite a passage from the writings of the scholastics, most of the time even fail to mention a name' (Höffner 1941, 4).

3 The Rediscovery of Scholastic Economics

The renaissance of scholastic economics began after the publication of Joseph Schumpeter's 'History of Economic Analysis' and his appreciation of the contributions of late scholastics to the development of economic theory. For Schumpeter, the economic doctrines of the scholastic doctors had a significant influence on Adam Smith through Hugo Grotius and Samuel von Pufendorf (Roover 1957, 119).

> In particular, no further explanation seems to be needed for the ease with which the economics of the doctors absorbed all the phenomena of nascent capitalism and, in consequence, for the fact that it served so well as a basis of the analytic work of their successors, not excluding A. Smith. (Schumpeter 1954, 90)

Schumpeter's work marked the culmination of a lengthy development in the rediscovery of scholastic economics, in which Joseph Höffner had also played an important role:

> After repeated attempts that date from over a hundred years ago, Spanish scholasticism has finally managed to find a place in the history of economic thought. The cumulative efforts by Dempsey, Höffner, Larraz ... culminated in its incorporation in Schumpeter's posthumous work, History of Economic Analysis. (Popescu 1997, 32)

In his appraisal of Joseph Höffner's work, Gustav Gundlach pointed out that 'most readers are surprised ... to recognize the scholastics' rich knowledge of economic life regarding the empirical reality and the theoretical contexts, and how poorly, sometimes even disparagingly, economic historians mostly judged scholastics'. However, Gundlach also noted that some experts had already been aware of these facts (Gundlach 1964, 583–584.). One example of the gradually changing view of scholastic economic knowledge can be found in Keynes' General Theory, which shows a certain sympathy for scholastic economic ethicists:

> I was brought up to believe that the attitude of the Medieval Church to the rate of interest was inherently absurd, and that the subtle discussions aimed at distinguishing the return on money-loans from the return to active investment were merely Jesuitical attempts to find a practical escape from a foolish theory. But I now read these discussions as an honest intellectual effort to keep separate what the classical theory has inextricably confused together, namely, the rate of interest and the marginal efficiency of capital. For it now seems clear that the disquisitions of the schoolmen were directed towards the elucidation of a formula

which should allow the schedule of the marginal efficiency of capital to be high, whilst using rule and custom and the moral law to keep down the rate of interest. (Keynes [1936] 2013, 351–352)

At times, Schumpeter's remarks on scholasticism were criticised as being excessively positive, whereby mostly the indirect effect of natural law philosophers on Adam Smith was debated rather than the direct effect of scholastics on natural law philosophers (Blaug 1971, 75–79). However, it was Schumpeter's History of Economic Analysis that drew the attention of many economists to the works of scholastics:

> But while the economic sociology of the scholastic doctors of this period was, in substance, not more than thirteenth-century doctrine worked out more fully, the 'pure' economics which they also handed down to those laical successors was, practically in its entirety, their own creation. It is within their systems of moral theology and law that economics gained definite if not separate existence, and it is they who come nearer than does any other group to having been the 'founders' of scientific economics. And not only that: it will appear, even, that the bases they laid for a serviceable and well-integrated body of analytic tools and propositions were sounder than was much subsequent work, in the sense that a considerable part of the economics of the later nineteenth century might have been developed from those bases more quickly and with less trouble than it actually cost to develop it, and that some of that subsequent work was therefore in the nature of a time- and labor-consuming detour. (Schumpeter 1954, 93)

4 Methodology and Issues of Scholastic Economics

The economic issues primarily concerning the scholastics were questions of private property, taxation, caring for the poor, trade, competition and monopolies, the just price, usury and money, interest, currency debasement and inflation, and exchange rates (Grice-Hutchinson 2015, 83; Roover 1955, 163). The economy was not seen as a separate system that encompasses the entirety of economic life and whose individual elements are interlinked in many ways. Rather, only individual aspects of economic activity were considered relatively isolated, resulting in a patchwork of individual theories. Although the aim of the scholastics was by no means to formulate a comprehensive economic theory, many fundamental economic questions were dealt with, some of which are still discussed in economic theory today (Grice-Hutchinson 2015, 85–86). Economics was not seen as an independent discipline, but as a branch of ethics and law, a state that prevailed until the eighteenth century, when Adam Smith took over the chair of moral philosophy at Glasgow College (Roover 1955, 162).

The scholastics always dealt with these economic questions from an economic-ethical perspective (Höffner [1955] 2014, 257). But the results were of considerable practical importance in everyday business life at their time. For example, the determination of the just price in court was decisive for the validity of contracts, for the determination of damages in the case of usury, for the decision in inheritance disputes and much more (Grice-Hutchinson 2015, 86).

The dialectical methodology of the scholastics remained largely unchanged over time. As in Thomas Aquinas summa theologiae, arguments were first put forward which contradict the desired solution (obiectiones); subsequently, the phrase sed contra announced the opposite view, usually with the utterance of an authority; it was then thetically presented in the main part of the article (corpusarticuli), which ultimately resulted in the answers to the initial counterarguments (Hirschberger 2000, 398). The works from the time of Thomas Aquinas to the late scholastics hardly changed in form: 'Questions, Articles, Objections, Distinctions, Solutions, and Conclusions follow one another in dutiful procession, and the most trivial statements are supported by a heavy apparatus of citations' (Grice-Hutchinson 2015, 97–98). The structure of the works of the various authors is also similar, '… in the great "sums" the first part of which is about God, the origin of all being, the second part about the way of man to God and the third part about Christ, the Redeemer and Completer, the economic ethical questions are found in the second part' (Höffner [1955] 2014, 257).

The economic teachings of the scholastics are by no means purely theoretical or ahistorical. Thomas Aquinas had already distinguished between the eternally unchangeable basic rules that God had made known through natural law and revelation and the changeable economic and social conditions (Höffner [1955] 2014, 255). Francisco Suarez attributes this changeability, following Thomas, to the variability of man, the change of customs and traditions, and the conditions of time (Höffner [1955] 2014, 256).

> There was the sacred precinct of the Catholic Church. But for the rest, society was treated as a thoroughly human affair, and moreover, as a mere agglomeration of individuals brought together by their mundane needs. Government, too, was thought of as arising from and existing for nothing but those utilitarian purposes that the individuals cannot realize without such an organization. Its raison d'être was the Public Good. The ruler's power was derived from the people, as we may say, by delegation. The people are the sovereign and an unworthy ruler may be deposed. Duns Scotus came still nearer to adopting a social-contract theory of the state. This mixture of sociological analysis and normative argument is remarkably individualist, utilitarian, and (in a sense) rationalist …. (Schumpeter 1954, 88)

The scholastic doctors were quite convinced that the answer to the questions of economic ethics had to be based on the concrete circumstances; Peter Binsfeld, for example, said that experience was the best rule in economic questions; Peter of Aragon recognised that the market had 'its own laws' and Dominikus Soto added that, apart from the merchants, there were only a few who could understand these mechanisms (Höffner [1955] 2014, 257f.). The Jesuit General Jakob Lainez (1512–1565) had emphasised that, due to the manifold tricks of the merchants, it is hardly possible to grasp economic facts, but above all that 'with the change of the slightest circumstance, the judgement with respect to the entire matter must be different' (Höffner 1953, 191). The precise analysis of economic facts thus became a core aspect in their ethical and legal assessment.

Joseph Höffner describes the approach of the late scholastics as a 'realistic method' to illustrate that the late scholastics aimed at the realistic observation of economic and social reality (Höffner 1953, 192; Franco 2018, 41–44). A similar description can also be found in Joseph Schumpeter's appreciation of scholastic methods:

> But it spelled an improved analysis of business facts that was, of course, partly induced by observation of the phenomena of rising capitalism. This realistic character of the work of the late scholastics should be particularly emphasized. They did not simply speculate. They did all the fact-finding that it was possible for them to do in an age without statistical services. Their generalizations invariably grew out of discussions of factual patterns and were copiously illustrated by practical examples. Lessius described the practice of the Antwerp exchange (bursa). Molina sallied forth from his study to interview businessmen about their methods. Some of his investigations into the economic conditions of his time and country, such as his study of the Spanish wool trade, amount to little monographs. (Schumpeter 1954, 95)

Höffner sees Luis de Molina's work as an example for the 'masterly' application of the 'inductive method of empirical investigation of economic facts' (Höffner [1955] 2014, 259). Höffner illustrates this empirical approach by using the example of Molina's study of the wool trade in the city of Cuenca in Castile, where a significant decline in the number of sheep flocks was observed at the time of Molina's study in 1592. By comparing historical prices and quantities, as well as interviewing merchants, Molina concluded that, although the monopolistic position of Genoese merchants in the purchase of wool was often accompanied by price agreements and this lead to a fall in prices, the increase in export duty and the increase in state pasture rents had contributed more to the decline in prices. Also the practice of forward transactions, whereby the wool was bought about a year before delivery with significant price discounts, meant that this was not usury even though interest was charged. Rather, in many cases, the maintenance of the herds would not be possible without the advances of forward transactions and other borrowing options would be even more expensive. In addition, the abolition of the guaranteed and scheduled acceptance would result in storage costs and the possibility that a part of the wool could not be sold. Molina concludes that a ban on forward transactions would only result in a further decline in the number of flocks of sheep (Höffner 1941, 67–71; [1955] 2014, 259–262).

An important characteristic of scholastic economics was the outstanding importance of natural law. Höffner quoted Gregory of Valentia, who emphasised in 1577 that natural law decides on the question of whether contracts are just or unfair, '… natural law in the scholastic sense, that is … the order placed into things by the one God …' (Höffner 1941, 66–67).

> Natural law contains the fundamental norms of human communal life, which are grounded in the natural order of being and thus ultimately in God and can be recognised by human reason. 'Originally,' writes Thomas Aquinas, 'natural law is contained in eternal law, but in second place in the natural judgement of human reason'. (Höffner 1972, 310–311)

In the economic context, this justice is expressed most clearly in the principle 'giving or letting each his own', and thus, Thomas von Aquinas exchange justice (iustitia commutativa) becomes the cardinal virtue, which became the supreme norm in economic life in the subsequent period, even before the virtues of distributive justice (iustitia distributiva) and common good justice (iustitia generalis) (Utz 2002, 23–24). Specifically, the scholastics started from the assumption of compensatory justice, that is, there must be equality between price and commodity in the exchange process (Höffner 1941, 158).

5 The Economic Teachings of a High Scholastic

Although Thomas Aquinas is the central point in the overall context of scholastic teaching, his importance for economics is limited.

> St. Thomas, in particular, was indeed interested in political sociology but all the economic questions put together mattered less to him than did the smallest point of theological or philosophical doctrine, and it is only where economic phenomena raise questions of moral theology that he touches upon them at all. Even where he does we do not feel, as we do elsewhere, that his powerful intellect is all there, passionately resolved to penetrate into the core of things but rather that he is writing in obedience to the requirements of systematic completeness. (Schumpeter 1954, 87)

'Thomas Aquinas is representative of scholasticism as a whole, but not of scholastic economics' (Weber 1962, 33–34). Raymound de Roover even described it as a methodological error to quote Aquinas without mentioning the successors (Roover 1957, 116–117). Nevertheless, Thomas has laid important foundations for later economic ethicists. These did not contradict Thomas either, but the development took place, as usual in scholasticism, by new and reinterpretations of the teachings of the great authority of Thomas Aquinas.

Thomas Aquinas assumes the right of private property: 'Private property corresponds to man's intellectual independence. It is "stimulus vitae", awakens personal initiative and strengthens personal responsibility, while the elimination of private property leads to inertia and unwillingness to work' (Höffner 1957, 121). Private property serves to clearly separate and delimit responsibilities within the economy (Höffner 1957, 122). For Thomas Aquinas, private property belongs to the Jus gentium, whereas for him the Jus gentium was still part of the natural law (Höffner 1975, 183; Utz 1953, 491–493, 2002, 98–99, 593). The right to private property was also defended by the later scholastics. For Francisco de Vitoria, the separation of things is based on human law, but in no way contradicts natural law, for God, knowing the sinful nature of man, did not enshrine a ban on private property in natural law. Private property serves the realisation of the natural law imperative for living in peace and thus becomes an implementation of natural law (Starck 2009, 127; Deckers 1991, 181–182).

> Molina adduces the reasons already named by Thomas ... in the case of man tainted by original sin, the introduction of a community of goods would lead to laziness, disinclination to work, disorder, discord, oppression, and general economic misery. Whereas Molina anchors in natural law the obligation to introduce a system of private ownership in this way, he ascribes the 'actual distribution of goods' to positive law ... Long before Molina, Juan

de Medina (1490–1546) professed the view 'that the distribution of goods is grounded in natural law,' if one understands natural law in the broad sense.

…. Luis de Molina (1535–1600) had declared … that the 'obligation' to introduce the system of private ownership 'could be derived from natural law … not always, but only then when serious evils would follow from the failure to introduce it, and only among those whom these evils would appear.' Here Molina must have been alluding to the distinction that was common in the traditional social teaching between the paradisiacal state … and the state of fallen humanity in which – if one excepts the family and the monastery – the system of private ownership is necessary. As proof of the natural-law obligation of realizing a system of private ownership, which is especially binding upon the leader of the state, Molina adduces the reasons already named by Thomas …. (Höffner 1975, 187f.)

Joseph Höffner is convinced that the importance of the interest rate problem for scholastic economic ethics is often overestimated (Höffner 1941, 65; cf. the interest problem, e.g., Dempsey 1943). 'Properly understood, the prohibition of interest did not pursue the aim of maintaining the economic conditions in a state of inertia, but to protect people in need, who were dependent on consumer credit, from exploitation' (Höffner [1955] 2014, 274). Until the sixteenth century, these consumer credits in times of need were the main loans in demand; it was not until the sixteenth century that they were gradually replaced by loans for investment purposes (Melé 1999, 176).

For a long time, Thomas Aquinas' comments on the question of interest were decisive:

Following Alexander of Hales and Albertus Magnus, St. Thomas condemned interest as contrary to commutative justice on a ground that proved a conundrum for almost all his scholastic successors: interest is a price paid for the use of money; but, viewed from the standpoint of the individual holder, money is consumed in the act of being used; therefore, like wine, it has no use that could be separated from its substance as has, for example, a house; therefore charging for its use is charging for something that does not exist, which is illegitimate (usurious). Whatever may be thought of this argument, which among other things neglects the possibility that 'pure' interest might be an element of the price of money itself – instead of being a charge for a separable use – one thing is clear: exactly like the somewhat different Aristotelian argument, it does not bear at all upon the question why interest is actually paid. Since this question, the only one that is relevant to economic analysis, was actually raised by the later scholastics, we defer the consideration of the clues for an answer, which St. Thomas' reasoning nevertheless suggests. (Schumpeter 1954, 90)

But even Thomas Aquinas recognised exceptions to the ban on interest: In the context of a partnership agreement, a return on the capital invested could be demanded. Also, if the lender missed out an advantage when granting a loan or suffered a loss, he could demand compensation for this, whereas the church interest theory required proof that the money could be invested productively. The more such investment opportunities arose in the late Middle Ages and early modern times, the more problematic became the ban on interest, which was increasingly watered down (Höffner [1955] 2014, 275; Utz 1994, 193–195).

By far the most important institutions, however, which enabled the economically fruitful investment of money in the Middle Ages and at the begin of the modern era, were the purchase of pensions and the social contract, which was widespread especially in the trading

> cities and was often concluded in the form of the so-called 'contractus trinus'. It is therefore not surprising that Antonin of Florence recognised the 'Monti' of the Arno city in the 15th century and moreover expressly confirmed that for the merchants money became 'capital character'.
>
> Luis de Molina calls it 'a general opinion of scholars' that merchants who could invest their capital profitably in trade could legally charge interest if they waived their own business and lend the capital. They were even more permitted to demand reasonable interest from princes, who compulsorily demanded the subscription of war bonds. Nor is it prohibited to account for any depreciation of money in the loan agreements. (Höffner [1955] 2014, 275–276)

Joseph Höffner did not go any further into the subject of the ban on interest. However, during his time as professor in Münster, he supervised Wilhelm Weber's doctor thesis on 'Money and Interest in Spanish Late Scholastics' (Weber 1962).

Of central importance for the economics of scholasticism is the question of the value and the just price of goods. An important point came from Augustine, but was cited by Thomas Aquinas and almost all scholastics: 'The goods are not valued according to the dignity of their nature; otherwise, a mouse, because it has life and senses, would be more expensive than a pearl that is lifeless. Things receive their prices based on the need of the people' (Höffner 1941, 72).

According to Thomas Aquinas, the price of goods is determined by the costs of production, the amount of labour, but also by the quantity of the goods and the number of buyers and sellers. Thomas stresses that a sale at the general market price must be regarded as just. The just price has a certain range and can vary over time and space. A resulting trade profit of the businessman is quite justified, however, only in as far as a necessary and honourable goal is pursued. This includes support for the family, support for the poor and service to the community. Apart from that, the mere pursuit of profit is nothing 'vicious or contrary to virtue', but it is associated with a 'certain ugliness'. But those who regard the pursuit of profit as the highest goal of their life and also pursue this through fraud, unlawful contracts and monopolistic machinations, act immorally (Höffner 1953, 186–187).

6 The Nominalists

According to Werner Sombart, the 'idea of food' was formative for the Middle Ages. Sombart argued that it was common among the peoples who settled down after the migration period for a peasant family to receive just enough land to enable them to earn a living. Sombart also transfers this basic idea that the economic activity serves only to cover the subsistence level to the areas of crafts and trade and sees it as a characteristic of the entire medieval, artisanal organised economy (Sombart 1916, 34). Numerous economists agreed with Sombart's view and it can still be found occasionally even today (e.g., Gabler-Wirtschaftslexikon 1988).

In the field of scholastic economic ethics, however, Joseph Höffner sees the 'idea of food' as limited only to the nominalism of the fourteenth and fifteenth centuries, as coined by Wilhelm von Ockham (1288–1347).

> One is accustomed to admiring the open mindedness of the nominalists and to draw parallels from Ockham to Locke, Berkeley and Hume. Strikingly, however, nominalist business ethics are by no means progressive, but much more guild-oriented than those of any other epoch of the Middle Ages. (Höffner 1953, 187–188)

Especially Heinrich Heinbuche von Langenstein (1325–1397), who can be attributed to nominalism, provides corresponding evidence (Höffner 1941, 79–84). The background is the advocacy of official price regulations and thus a critical position vis-à-vis competition (Höffner 1953, 188). According to von Langenstein, these officially fixed prices must be so high that they provide everyone with a living befitting one's rank. For the nominalists, the just price of the goods results from this income according to one's class. The attempt to acquire riches, to ascend to a higher class or to try to have one's children ascend to a higher class is considered damnable. Similar views can be found with Johannes Gerson, Gabriel Biel and also with Martin Luther (Höffner 1953, 189).

For the overall context of scholastic economics, the empirical approach of the nominalists to economic questions, which was adopted by later scholasticism, is of particular importance (Höffner 1941, 84).

7 The Fifteenth Century

Along with Johannes Nider (1380–1438), Gabriel Biel (1410–1495) and Archbishop Antonin of Florence (1389–1459), Konrad Summenhart (1450–1502), professor at the University of Tübingen, was the most influential economic ethicist of the fifteenth century. In his work 'On Contracts', he emphasises that the price of a product is not determined according to the natural 'dignity' of things, but by the utility or market value. The 'general market opinion' provides an indication for the determination of this value. He thus coincides with the saying, also quoted by him, 'a commodity is worth as much as you get for it'. On the other hand, Summenhart also cites 16 different factors that influence price formation in trade, with costs of production and trade, but also aspects of supply and demand as determining factors (Höffner 1941, 86–90).

Antonin of Florence had stated that the just price had a margin which he divided into three levels, describing the low range as gracious, the middle range as discreet and the high range as sharp (Höffner 1941, 91). Antonin of Florence had also stated that, if a contracting party is fully aware that he pays more or receives less than the just price and, nevertheless, agrees to the contract without being forced to do so due to a particular emergency, this contract is not objectionable (Illgner 1904, 62).

Already with Konrad Summenhart, Höffner recognises the idea that the best economic system is the one that gets by with a 'minimum of morality'. Here, a fundamental recognition of the competition takes place, because according to

Summenhart, somebody who stands in the competition 'has less the forehead and possibility to sell his goods at exorbitant prices' (Höffner 1953, 197). The activity of merchants is honourable if it takes place under the conditions of the free market. Summenhart emphasises that in an economy in which not everybody can be a winemaker, miller, blacksmith, shoemaker, butcher and farmer at the same time, the merchants assume important intermediary functions in such an economy with division of labour and accordingly have a right to an adequate trading profit (Höffner 1941, 91). However, this profit may not be driven by profit-seeking or generated by unfair machinations. This also leads Summenhart to reject any form of private monopoly, which he divides into six different categories (Höffner 1941, 92–94). Antonin of Florence argues that a price agreement, which is approved or stipulated by the public authorities and is based on the just price, would correspond to the conventional, officially regulated prices, and therefore is absolutely permissible. This would, however, also mean that entirely private agreements which reached the same result as the prices imposed by the authorities would have to be exempted from the strict monopoly ban. Remarkable here is the insight that private monopolies and state regulation can have similar effects. Despite the emphasis on the advantages of the free market, the scholastic doctors of the fifteenth century do not reject official price regulations and state monopolies as a whole, since both would serve the common good (Höffner 1941, 95–96).

8 The First Half of the Sixteenth Century

In the first half of the sixteenth century, scholasticism was marked by the rise of the school of San Esteban in Salamanca, founded by Francis of Vitoria (1483–1546). Höffner particularly identifies Dominikus Soto (1494–1560), a scholar of Vitoria, the Franciscan Johannes Medina (1490–1546) and Cardinal Thomas de vio Cajetanus (1469–1534) as important representatives of economic ethics (Höffner 1941, 102–103).

Johannes Medina identified three possibilities for price determination: official price fixing, general market opinion and calculation based on costs.

With respect to prices fixed by the authorities, Medina objects that the persons entrusted with this task can be bribed, inexperienced and without expertise. The reasons for determining a just price could also vary over time without this being reflected in the official fixed price. However, if none of these arguments apply, one would have to adhere to the fixed prices. Dominikus Soto also argued that it was virtually impossible to estimate all prices.

Medina classified the second option, the determination of the just price from the general market view, as more reliable than an official regulation. Against the objection that such a market price depended too much on the arbitrariness of the merchants, Medina argued that the price could not be determined entirely by the merchants, as it happens that they had to sell at a loss. Cajetan added that any fraud and coercion in determining the market price must be excluded.

Finally, as a third variant, it would be possible to estimate the price on the basis of the costs of the merchants, which Medina rejects, since each merchant has individual costs and different prices for the same goods are 'absurd'. Nevertheless, if previously unknown goods were offered for which there was no market price, this variant would be used, whereby the merchant could set a price which guaranteed him a moderate trading profit (Höffner 1941, 104–105).

At the beginning of the sixteenth century, opinions on trade became more moderate. Medina recognises that merchants can honestly acquire 'even the greatest riches'. Soto says that extensive trade speaks for progress of mankind from the imperfect to the perfect. In itself, trade is as 'indifferent as food' but can be misused because of 'human greed'. Above all, it is the monopolistic temptations that disgrace the trade, such as merchants who buy up all goods in order to deprive the market of its freedom and drive up prices. Soto demands that such merchants be driven out of the country. Similarly, Cajetan argues that monopolies are an 'attack on general freedom' and Medina claims that monopolists cause more damage 'than crop failures or locusts'. The attitude towards state monopoly privileges is less clear. While Medina advocates them when they serve the common good, Cajetan rejects them and Soto refers to the granting of monopoly privileges as a 'shameful act'. Particularly clear, the French lawyer Carolus Molinaeus (1500–1566) states that state monopolies are merely a way 'to drive the people into serfdom' (Höffner 1941, 105–109).

9 The Second Half of the Sixteenth Century

Among the 24 authors whose works Joseph Höffner cites to illustrate economic thought in the second half of the sixteenth century are the Dominican Bartolomé de Medina (1527–1580), the Jesuits Leonhard Lessius (1554–1623), Gregor de Valencia (1549–1603) and Francisco Suárez (1548–1617) and the Augustinian Martin de Azpilcueta (1492–1586) known as Doctor navarrus. However, the Castilian-born Jesuit Luis de Molina (1535–1600) is of outstanding importance.

Molina built his price theory on the basis of the free market. He distinguished between the 'natural price' (pretium naturale) and the price set by the authorities. The natural price is so called because it results from things themselves without human laws or decrees. The natural price, which comes about in a market with a multitude of suppliers and consumers, was seen by Molina as the just price. Due to a multitude of influencing factors, this price has a margin, resulting in a price range within which the just price can be said to exist. Like many scholastic doctors before him, such as Gabriel Biel or Johannes Medina, Molina distinguishes between the just price for known goods, for which a general market price exists, and for unknown goods, for example, from long-distance trade, for which the price is freely compatible.

According to Molina, the usual market price initially depends on the utility value of the goods. Like almost all scholastic doctors since Thomas Aquinas, Molina, reverts back to Augustine: the price determination depended on the usefulness and not on the order of being of things; otherwise, mice would be worth more than grain. In addition, there is human appreciation, which does not necessarily depend on the usefulness of the goods, as can be seen with many expensive luxury goods.

Important factors for price formation include the quantity of goods offered, an aspect previously ignored by scholasticism, the number of buyers, the urgency of the needs of the buyers and the competition between the various sellers and buyers. From the texts of Molina, Bañez and Gregory of Valentia, it becomes clear that the scholastic doctors only saw competition as a price formation factor, the effect on production costs remained unrecognised. However, the focus of the late scholastics was clearly on the area of trade; after all, the economic dynamics of the time was mainly in the long-distance trade, and aspects of production were not or only marginally considered (Höffner 1941, 117, [1955] 2014, 273; Franco 2018, 56f.).

Molina also presented the importance of the money supply for pricing for the first time (Franco 2018, 56). Although scholasticism had recognised the importance of the money supply for the exchange rate earlier, Nicolas Copernicus had already noted in 1526, 'money usually loses purchasing power when it is excessively increased' and in 1568, Jean Bodins had identified the massive imports of precious metals from the American colonies as the main cause for Spain's inflation; nevertheless, Molina first formulated a 'quantity theory of money': 'If there is a shortage of money somewhere, the price of other goods falls; if there is plenty of money, it rises. The lower the money supply, the higher the monetary value. In short, one can buy more goods for the same amount of money, all else being equal.' Wilhelm Weber noted that Molina uses here the term ceteris paribus; thus, the ceteris paribus clause already appears in late scholasticism. Molina also notes that the money supply is being increased by loans, influencing the prices also in this manner (Höffner 1941, 118–122; Weber 1962, 36).

If trade is 'done in the right manner and has a moral objective, it is allowed, morally good and useful and necessary to the nations'. It is quite permissible to make profits, even on a large scale, and the possibility of rising to a higher rank through the accumulation of wealth is also seen. 'All strata of the population in the country have the right to rise to a higher level if it so happens. For no one is owed a certain rank in such a way that he could neither descend nor ascend', says Molina (Höffner 1953, 199–200). But a certain ugliness and indecency adheres to the pure pursuit of profit itself, which then becomes something evil when perjuries, lies and usury are used as means. Höffner regards this view of trade as representative of the scholastic doctors of the time and quotes Dominikus Bañez (1528–1604) and Gregory of Valentia (1549–1603). Molina regards financial transactions as 'more dangerous' than trade, but admits that banking business can also be conducted honestly and meritoriously (Höffner 1941, 124–127).

Furthermore '… late scholastics observe the official price regulation increasingly critically from decade to decade, until finally Martin de Azpilcueta and Luis de Molina … began to sharply and openly reject the price policy of the authorities'. Molina 'is a clear advocate of free pricing on the free market' (Höffner 1941, 161). The scholastics of the time argue that a price tax would distort the entire price structure, and that an entire chain of measures would have to follow if a single price were to be fixed. If, for example, one wanted to regulate the price of shoes or bread, one would also have to set the prices of leather, grain, etc., at the same time. Molina therefore calls for the abolition of the price taxes 'which confuse the entire empire' and for confidence that the free market will result in a just price. Further concerns arise from the fact that, in the past, price regulations and other interventions in the market had often led to corruption among the authorities and that price fixing was rarely observed, resulting in constant violations of the law. Finally, against the argument that low official food prices are necessary for the poor in times of need, it is argued that one should support them by charity and not by enforced and unjust prices (Höffner 1953, 199–201).

10 The Scholastic Doctors and the Natural Law Philosophers

In the context of the development of economic theory, Joseph Schumpeter sees the immediate successors of the scholastic doctors in the natural law philosophers of the seventeenth century. He highlights Thomas Hobbes (1588–1679), John Locke (1632–1704), Hugo Grotius (1583–1645) and Samuel Pufendorf (1632–1694) as examples of natural law philosophers. The main works of the natural law philosophers – for example, Grotius De jure belli ac pacis from 1625, Hobbes Leviathan 1651 and Pufendorf's De jure naturae et gentium 1672 – followed shortly after the works of the late scholastics, the six volumes of Molina's De Iustitia et Iure appeared between 1593 and 1609, Azpilcueta's Comentario Resolutorio de Cambios 1556 and Lessius De Iustitia et Iure followed in 1605.

The scholastics' strong orientation towards natural law forms an important link to the subsequent philosophers of natural law, the late scholastics '... had an effect on the whole of Europe in the sense of an early Enlightenment and thus also on Hugo Grotius, on whose shoulders Pufendorf stood' (Starck 2009, 125). However, '... Samuel Pufendorf tried, turning away from both the Gospel and the Catholic tradition, to build the natural law on mere reason' (Höffner 1959 [2015], 174). Pufendorf himself rejected scholastic philosophy (Weizel 2012, 11–12). According to Joseph Höffner, the anthropocentric, individualistic way of thinking of many philosophers of natural law such as Hobbes, Locke or Pufendorf leads to a turning away from social-ethical topics, but also '... through the doctrine of the state, which as the sum of individuals simultaneously represents the concentration of all reason and all law, to the exaggeration of state ethics, which was practically equated with social ethics; from here the neglection of social ethics and the overemphasis on state ethical obligations can be explained...' (Höffner [1962] 2015, 217–218).

In addition to natural law, the law of nations represents a strong link between the scholastic doctors and natural law philosophers, in particular to Hugo Grotius, because late scholastics, especially the school of Salamanca, developed both the basic ideas of human rights and of the law of nations (Franco 2017, 359). The trigger was the discovery of America. This raised the question of the legal assignment of the new peoples and countries to the political and religious force field of Europe. The original approach of the 'conquistadors' proved to be increasingly questionable from day to day. The pioneers of the new ideas therefore turned away from the old theocratic concepts and founded a new ethics based on natural law (Weber 1967, 16–17).

> Now certain legal principles – 'like conclusions from principles' – can be derived from this natural law. They are different from natural law and from the scholastic jus gentium. For example, according to St. Thomas, by virtue of natural law, people are obliged to live sociably together. This is impossible, however, if purchase and sale are not introduced, which therefore go back to the jus gentium. … All scholastics agree that the laws of the jus gentium are different from natural law. After all, the jus gentium includes only those norms suggested by nature which are not natural law themselves, but are so plausible that they can be found in all nations. In all nations, not between all nations. (Höffner 1972, 310–311)

Francisco Suárez (1548–1617) had first referred to the double meaning of the Jus gentium, on the one hand, as was customary in scholasticism up to the sixteenth century, as the designation for legal institutions found among all peoples and, on the other hand, so Suárez, as the right 'to which all peoples and the various nations must adhere in their mutual relations' (Höffner 1947, 194–195). The scholastics developed a series of '… rules of international ethics that concerned the protection of personal freedom, private property, the right to political autonomy, immigration and settlement law, freedom of the seas and commerce … looking at the colonial-ethical efforts of the 16th-century Spanish scholastics, every unbiased person would have to admit that the colonial-ethical problems were never again discussed with such seriousness and zeal in the following centuries' (Weber 1967, 16–17). In Grotius' view of the Jus gentium, there are almost literal similarities with Suárez and Grotius extensively quoting several works of the Spanish scholastics in detail (Höffner 1947, 196–197). Ultimately, the conclusions of Grotius in relation to questions of the law of nations coincide almost without exception with the positions of late scholasticism (Höffner 1947, 198f.). The differences seem relatively limited. On the one hand, the Spanish late scholastics were unable to reach a liberal conception of missionary law. On the other hand, it '… provides food for thought when Hugo Grotius …, who otherwise likes to join the great Spaniards, unlike them, develops a pronounced "colonial people ideology" to give the Dutch East India Company moral backing …' (Weber 1967, 17).

Höffner emphasises that the science of the law of nations was founded by Spanish late scholasticism even before Grotius and that Grotius had most probably adopted the ideas of the law of nations from Suarez. Höffner admits, however, that Grotius has the merit of having expanded the law of nations into a system (Höffner 1947, 193, 1972, 410f.). 'The fame of Grotius is largely due to the inaccessibility of the works of the Spanish scholastics. Grotius himself is directly and essentially dependent on the Spanish theologians' (Höffner 1947, 193) Höffner's views on the effect of late scholastics on the further development of human rights and the law of nations are generally shared today (Honnefelder 2012, 8; Utz 2002, 78; Muha 2008, 274).

While Höffner clearly recognised the dependence of the natural law philosophers on the scholastic doctors with regard to the law of nations, he still assumed that scholastic economic ethics had only a small influence on the further development of economics (Höffner 1941, 163), an impression that was especially revised by Joseph Schumpeter:

> Pufendorf went much further into economics … though he still does not seem to me to have added much to the stock of knowledge and to the analytic apparatus of the late scholastics. … He was not much more than a follower of Grotius. (Schumpeter 1954, 113)

On pages 680 to 687 of the English translation of Pufendorf's De jure naturae et gentium, Wulf Gaertner found his central statements on markets and prices: Pufendorf thus distinguished between the natural price or the market price and the prices fixed by the authorities. He demanded that the prices set by the authorities should correspond to the natural price. The natural price may be subject to fluctuations. Consequently, there is a price range within which prices can be seen as natural. Pufendorf divided this range into three categories: generous, moderate and rigorous prices (Gaertner 2005, 240). All aspects mentioned here are already known from Thomas Aquinas, Molina and Antonin of Florence. The same applies, for example, to the demand for contractual freedom, which is already found in Antonin of Florence, Nicolas Oresme and others (Schreiber 1913, 161–193). The insight that the rarity of a good influences its price can be found under the price building factors listed by Konrad Summenhart and also Pufendorf's realisation that the shortage of goods in times of need can lead to a price increase of these goods (Gaertner 2005, 241) was by no means new, but was discussed in detail by the scholastics in the context of price taxes.

Here, Raymond De Roover's view is confirmed that the economic teachings of the scholastics were adopted to a considerable extent by their successors: 'Moreover, some of their important economic doctrines were taken over, with only slight modifications, by the philosophers of natural law, such as Hugo Grotius (1583–1645) and Samuel Pufendorf (1622–94) …' (Roover 1955, 162).

References

Blaug M (1971) Systematische Theoriegeschichte der Ökonomie, München: Nymphenburger Verlagsbuchhandlung

Deckers D (1991) Gerechtigkeit und Recht. Eine historisch-kritische Untersuchung der Gerechtigkeitslehre des Francisco der Vitoria, Fribourg: Academic Press

Dempsey B W (1943) Interest and Usury, American Council of Public Affairs, Washington D.C.

Eucken, W ([1952] 1990) Grundsätze der Wirtschaftspolitik, Tübingen: J.C.B. Mohr

Franco G (2017), Power and Weaknesses of the Idea of Natural Rights, in: Rendtorff (2017), pp 357–361

Franco G (2018) Von Salamanca nach Freiburg: Joseph Höffner und die Soziale Marktwirtschaft, Paderborn: Ferdinand Schöningh

Gabler-Wirtschaftslexikon (1988), Vol. 5, key word: Scholastik, Wiesbaden: Gabler, pp 1401

Gaertner W (2005) De jure naturae et gentium: Samuel von Pufendorf's contribution to social choice theory and economics, Social Choice and Welfare, 25(2/3), pp 231-241
Grice-Hutchinson M (2015) Early economic thought in Spain, 1177–1740, Indianapolis: Liberty Fund
Gundlach G (1964) Die Ordnung der menschlichen Gesellschaft, Bd. 2, Köln: J.P. Bachem
Hirschberger J (2000) Geschichte der Philosophie, Frechen: Komet
Höffner J (1941) Wirtschaftsethik und Monopole im fünfzehnten und sechzehnten Jahrhundert, Jena: Gustav Fischer
Höffner J (1947) Die Begründung der Völkerrechtswissenschaft durch die spanische Theologie des Goldenen Zeitalters, Trierer Theologische Zeitschrift, 56 (7/8), pp 193-200
Höffner J (1953), Der Wettbewerb in der Scholastik, ORDO-Jahrbuch, 5, pp 181-202
Höffner J ([1955] 2014), Statik und Dynamik in der scholastischen Wirtschaftsethik, in: Höffner J (2014), pp 251–287
Höffner J (1957) Die Funktionen des Privateigentums in der freien Welt in: Beckenrath E v / Meyer F W / Müller-Armack A (eds.) Wirtschaftsfragen der freien Welt, Frankfurt: Knapp, pp 121–131
Höffner J ([1959] 2015) Evangelische Soziallehren, in: Höffner (2015), pp 173–190
Höffner J ([1962] 2015) Sozialethik, in Höffner (2015), pp 215–225
Höffner J (1972) Kolonialismus & Evangelium. Spanische Kolonialethik im Goldenen Zeitalter, Paulinus, Trier
Höffner J (1975) Christliche Gesellschaftslehre, Kevelaer: Butzon & Bercker
Höffner J (2014) Wirtschaftsordnung und Wirtschaftsethik, Ausgewählte Schriften Bd. 3, Paderborn: Schöningh
Höffner J (2015) Perspektiven sozialer Gerechtigkeit, Ausgewählte Schriften Bd. 1, Paderborn: Schöningh
Honnefelder L (2012) Geschichte der Menschenrechte. Christentum und Mittelalter, in: Pollmann A Lohmann G (eds.) Menschenrechte. Ein interdisziplinäres Handbuch, Stuttgart: J.B. Metzler, pp 6–12
Illgner C (1904) Die volkswirtschaftlichen Anschauungen Antonins von Florenz, Paderborn: Schöningh
Keynes J M ([1936] 2013) The Collected Writings of John Maynard Keynes, VII, The General Theory of Employment, Interest and Money, New York: Cambridge University Press
Maddison A (2004) Die Weltwirtschaft. Eine Millenniumsperspektive, Paris: OECD
Melé D (1999) Early Business Ethics in Spain: The Salamanca School (1526–1614), Journal of Business Ethics, 22, pp 175–189
Muha M (2008) Kirchliche Friedensethik und Erziehung zu Gerechtigkeit und Frieden als gewaltlose Lösung der Konflikte und als Kriegsprävention, Dissertation Universität Passau, https://opus4.kobv.de/opus4-uni-passau/files/104/Muha_Maria.pdf, 14.04.2019
North D C / Thomas R P (1973) The Rise of the Western World, New York: Cambridge University Press
Popescu O (1997) Studies in the History of Latin American Economic Thought, New York: Routledge
Rauscher A (2007) Orientierung in Zeiten des Umbruchs. Im Gedenken an Kardinal Joseph Höffner, Kirche und Gesellschaft, 337
Rendtorff J D (ed.) (2017) Perspectives on Philosophy of Management and Business Ethics, Berlin: Springer
Roover R (1955) Scholastic Economics: Survival and Lasting Influence from the Sixteenth Century to Adam Smith, Quarterly Journal of Economics, 69(2), pp 161-190
Roover R (1957) Joseph A. Schumpeter and Scholastic Economics, Kyklos 10(2), pp 115-146
Schreiber E (1913) Die volkswirtschaftlichen Anschauungen der Scholastik seit Thomas v. Aquin, Jena: Gustav Fischer
Schumpeter J A (1954) History of Economic Analysis, London: Routledge
Sombart W (1916) Der moderne Kapitalismus Bd. 1, Leipzig: Duncker & Humblot

Starck C (2009) Verfassungen: Entstehung, Auslegung, Wirkungen und Sicherung, Heidelberg: J. C. B. Mohr

Utz A F (1953) Kommentar zu S.Theol. II–II 66,1 u. 2 in: Thomas von Aquin, Recht und Gerechtigkeit. Theol. Summe II–II 57–79, Bd. 18 der Deutschen Thomasausgabe, Heidelberg: F.H. Kerle, pp 423–571

Utz A F (1994), Sozialethik, Teil IV: Wirtschaftsethik, Bonn: WBV

Utz A F (2002), Ethik des Gemeinwohls, Paderborn: Schöningh

Weber W (1962) Geld und Zins in der Spanischen Spätscholastik, Münster: Aschendorffsche Verlagsbuchhandlung

Weber W (1967) Der Beitrag. Joseph Höffners zur Erschließung der spanischen Scholastik des "Goldenen Zeitalters", Jahrbuch für Christliche Sozialwissenschaften, 07/08, pp 11–19

Weizel H (2012) Die Naturrechtslehre Samuel Pufendorfs: Ein Beitrag zur Ideengeschichte des 17. und 18. Jahrhunderts, Walter de Gruyter: Berlin, New York

How to Approach Samuel Pufendorf's Economic Ideas?

Karl-Heinz Schmidt

Abstract The contribution reports on references to Pufendorf in German and English works in the history of economic thought. Thereafter, it addresses the question in which relation Pufendorf's oeuvre should be seen to be "modern" history of economic thought.

Keywords Pufendorf · Natural law · German history of economic thought · German Historical School

JEL Codes B11 · B41 · K10

1 Pufendorf's Academic Reputation

Pufendorf's academic appointments at the new universities of Heidelberg and Lund, as well as his position as "historian of the court" (*Hofhistoriker*) in Stockholm and finally in Berlin, enabled him to exert considerable influence on basic political discourses and documents. Review articles in dictionaries, historical studies, and books demonstrate the extraordinary impact of Pufendorf's oeuvre on the development of natural jurisprudence in Europe. He is acknowledged to have contributed significantly to establish a new direction of natural law. His doctrine is described to have been accepted in most of the European states; it had even dominated the way of thinking in terms of natural law around 1700. Especially, a relatively short publication of 1673, concerning the "tasks of man and citizen" ("*De officio hominis et civis*") became very influential, even more than his main important work about natural law and international relations ("*De jure naturae et gentium*"). The impact

K.-H. Schmidt (✉)
Universität Paderborn, Paderborn, Germany
e-mail: Karl-Heinz_Schmidt@notes.uni-paderborn.de

J. G. Backhaus et al. (eds.), *Samuel Pufendorf and the Emergence of Economics as a Social Science*, The European Heritage in Economics and the Social Sciences 24, https://doi.org/10.1007/978-3-030-49791-0_9

of Pufendorf's work decreased only during the second half of the eighteenth century, when a new version of natural law became more important. According to Jan Schröder's article on Pufendorf in the dictionary *Staatslexikon* (Schröder 1988, 620), Pufendorf's achievements also include his contributions to the renewal of the historical method.

2 Pufendorf in Major Works of History of Economic Thought

2.1 Paul Mombert (1927)

In his book on the history of national economics (*Geschichte der Nationalökonomie* Jena 1927), Mombert referred to Pufendorf in the chapter on mercantilism, when economic thinking was focused on economics of the state. Pufendorf elaborated on the changes of public policy by the central state orientated toward the private economy, emphasizing as supreme principle of that policy to support the political interest in the power of the state and to maintain strict guidance of the economy "from above," i.e., by the central state (Mombert 1927, 180). The ensuing changes in public thinking were identified by Mombert as consequences of the special versions of natural law of Thomas Hobbes and Hugo Grotius which had extended their influence into Germany and of Pufendorf's related activities and publications. According to Mombert, it was Pufendorf who "developed natural law into an independent science. His influence and his importance is to be seen with regard to the general orientation of social thinking, rather than in his specifically economic thoughts and teachings, although he had some achievements in this field too" (ibidem).

Furthermore, Mombert called Pufendorf the "the German founder" of an intermediate current of political thinking: partly liberal and partly determined by absolutism (p. 180). Following Mombert, Pufendorf mediated between different directions of natural law by reference to the absolutistic concept in Hobbes' works and by the impulse toward society and social life in Hugo Grotius' works. According to Mombert's interpretation, Pufendorf's intermediate position later was developed further by Christian Thomasius (1655–1728) to function as the fundamental basis of a "police state" ("*Polizeistaat*") and "enlightened absolutism." In a similar vein, the German philosopher and author Christian Wolff (1679–1754) also based his own concept of the state and society on Pufendorf's concept. Wolff's ideas and propositions exerted significant influence on governmental practices in German states during the eighteenth century (Mombert 1927, 181).

In Germany, Gottfried Wilhelm Leibniz (1646–1716) had prepared the ground for the philosophy of enlightenment: rational thinking should be orientated to the target of serving the general welfare (Mombert 1927, 181). Philosophical and economic thought were closely intertwined during the eighteenth century, as testified by the writings of Leibniz, which were popularized by Pufendorf.

2.2 *Othmar Spann (1930)*

In his book on "Theory of the Society" (*Gesellschaftslehre*, Leipzig 1930), Othmar Spann distinguished three basically different forms of individualism (p. 80 ff): (1) anarchism, (2) theory of government (or: "Machiavellism"), and (3) theory of contract or law of nature; in addition, (4) political forms of individualism based on natural law. According to Spann's comments on the theory of contract, this concept represents the most important form of individualism (p. 82). By means of the public contract (*Staatsvertrag*), the individual persons renounce to exercise their unlimited individual right to freedom. Spann concluded: "Thus (the individual persons) establish the State. Social State equals reciprocal shake hands (*Handreichung*) and mutual assistance (*Hilfeleistung*)" (p. 82). Consequently, Spann compared the State to an insurance company focused on mutual protection; the premium which has to be paid is seen to be incorporated in the limitation of inviolable rights of freedom ("*Beschränkung unverletzlicher Freiheitsrechte*"). He emphasizes that this is not an ethical concept of state, but only a utilitarian one. In Spann's original German words: "Auch dieser Staat ist nicht ethischer, sondern allein zweckmäßiger, nutzhafter (utilitarischer) Natur" (p. 83).

The author, yet, added a restriction, the more additional tasks are to be fulfilled by the state, the more the state develops toward an entity that is more than the total of individual persons (p. 83), therewith departing from the individual approach. Spann confronted his view with those of the original authors of the concept of natural law, like Grotius, Locke, Pufendorf, and others, i.e., authors who established the theory of the state on the basis of individualism (p. 83). Spann saw Pufendorf as opponent to his theory, whereas for most other authors Pufendorf aimed at a compromise between early individualism and enlightened absolutism. He probably foresaw that more time and more structural changes in economy and society would be necessary for a fundamental turn to liberalism.

2.3 *Karl Brandt (1992)*

In his book on the history of German economics (*Geschichte der deutschen Volkswirtschaftslehre*, Vol. 1, 57), Karl Brandt identifies Pufendorf as the most well-known author of early mercantilism. Brandt calls him "a strong representative of enlightened natural law" (*Verfechter eines aufgeklärten Naturrechts*), who had liberated the natural law from remnants of the scholastic period of law and culture. Brandt also emphasizes that Pufendorf's position was between Locke and Hobbes, like Locke, Pufendorf argued that the state was based on contract, but he followed Hobbes as far as active political power is concerned: the governing absolute sovereign should have the power of central decision making and he should determine the degree of freedom and self-initiative which should be conceded to the subjects of his principality.

With respect to Pufendorf's references to economic problems of his time, Brandt mentions his opposition to the consumption of luxury goods, to monopolies, and economic power demanded by gilds and other forms of concentrated economic organization. Brandt also emphasizes that Pufendorf strives for a new approach to explain the structure and development of prices. For the neoclassical economist Karl Brandt, this author of the seventeenth century is of great interest, because Pufendorf acknowledges costs as determining factor of prices, and he also embarks on a discussion of scarcity, with its effect on the prices of goods via changing quantities of goods and money. In Karl Brandt's words: "In der Preislehre geht er über die üblichen Erklärungsansätze hinaus, da er die Kosten als Preisbestimmungsfaktoren anerkennt und von der Knappheit spricht, die über die Warenmenge oder die Geldmenge preiswirksam wird" (p. 57). Thus, it appears that Pufendorf combined elements of different currents and concepts of economic thinking: mercantilism, absolutism, liberalism and classical, and even neoclassical thought.

2.4 Gerhard Kolb (1997)

In his history of economics (*Geschichte der Volkswirtschaftslehre*, 1997), Gerhard Kolb elaborates on the relations between the historical and philosophical background of the publications of Pufendorf and other contemporary and later authors. In an introductory paragraph of the chapter on physiocracy, where Kolb refers to natural law and the natural order (*natürliche Ordnung*) (p. 38 ff), he points to the different meanings of the word "nature" in the Greek philosophy and in the tracts of authors of the eighteenth century, e.g., Francois Quesnay, who had referred to several authors of the seventeenth century, especially to H. Grotius, Th. Hobbes and Pufendorf. Together with Christian Thomasius, Pufendorf had separated the concept of law from the concept of ethics (p. 32).

2.5 Joseph Alois Schumpeter on Pufendorf

Schumpeter devotes a special section on the philosophers of natural law in chapter 2 of his "History of Economic Analysis" (1954), with deliberate focus on few representative authors Grotius, Hobbes, Locke, and Pufendorf. As scholar of natural jurisprudence, Schumpeter considers the author Pufendorf "not much more than a follower of Grotius." At the same time, he gives high credits to Pufendorf's *De jure naturae et gentium, libri octo* as a treatise "that sums up and represents the whole structure of the science of the social philosophers much better than do the works of the greater men mentioned before. … It is the work to consult to get a general idea of the range and level of that type of social science" (Schumpeter 1954, 117). If Pufendorf "went much further into economics than Grotius, he still does not seem to have added much to the stock of knowledge and to the analytical apparatus of the late Scholastics." Schumpeter attributes this to the continued attachment of Pufendorf to theological thinking, who also approached social problems from a theological perspective in his tract *De habitu christianae religionis* ad vitam *civilem.*

2.6 Henry William Spiegel (1983)

This author mentions Pufendorf only marginally in his textbook "The Growth of Economic Thought," referring to Pufendorf and especially to John Locke, who had both emphasized the importance of personal liberty and property. Pufendorf acknowledged both values as two inviolable rights "... that are entrusted by the individual to the state simply for protection, (and hereby) the groundwork was laid for a future theory of purely individualistic economics." Spiegel cites this statement from a publication of the German author Otto von Gierke (1939, 108, cited by Spiegel 1983, 731). Spiegel's other reference is Leonard Krieger's book "The Politics of Discretion: Pufendorf and the Acceptance of Natural Law" (Chicago 1965), whose emphasis is on the relevance of Pufendorf's work for the social organization considering especially personal liberty and property of the individual.

3 Authors of the German Historical School

3.1 Wilhelm Roscher on Samuel Pufendorf

In his History of Economics in Germany (*Geschichte der National-Ökonomik in Deutschland)* Wilhelm Roscher writes extensively about Pufendorf under the heading "The Prussian National Economics during the reign of the Great Elector Friedrich Wilhelm" who ruled Prussia between 1640 to 1688, emphasizing the congeniality between the prince and the scholar of natural law. Roscher characterizes Pufendorf "as a most profoundly educated scholar of state science and economist of extraordinary importance" (Roscher 1874, 304 ff).

If in Pufendorf's approach as a scholar of jurisprudence state and society were tightly interlinked, compared to previous periods the organization of state and economy at his lifetime showed a tendency toward intellectual freedom liberty (p. 305). His intermediate position between demands for intellectual and economic liberty on the one hand and insistence on sovereign rights of the absolute state on the other hand, in order to promote economic and social development and enhance the power of the state and the country, is exemplified by Roscher under several aspects.

- Growth of population should be promoted, even by immigration of "innocent and harmless expellees," who can be rich or ambitious and industrious. The state may even compel citizens to get married, but only such persons who are suited according to their age and physical strength and able to support their family (p. 306). Concerning emigration, Pufendorf argued in terms of liberal natural rights.

- Differences of the social status between citizens are of minor importance in Pufendorf's view. He denied any privileges of the aristocracy. On the other side of the society, he accepted serfdom, partly as being founded on free service contracts, or on submission via a war (p. 307).
- With regard to property, Pufendorf argued that inherited property should not necessarily be distributed at equal shares among the children of a family, while preference for a child should be acknowledged for special merits or capabilities. Pufendorf's concept of property and heritage therefore has an "absolutely monarchic character," not constrained by natural law, but at the disposal of the sovereign (p. 309).
- Roscher devotes special attention to Pufendorf's price theory (pp. 309–311). It includes the distinction of value of use and value of exchange, and also the distinction of three kinds of economic goods: things (*res*), personal services (*operae*), and relations (*actiones*). Also free goods and scarcity of goods are explained (p. 310 f).
- Roscher also reports on Pufendorf's discussion of the economic functions of money. Not only precious metals can be used as money, but also leather, paper, and other materials, because it is convention among men or decree of the ruler which is decisive. Pufendorf emphasizes the importance of an unchanging value of money, by which he means purchasing power. As indicator of such stability he proposes the price of land, i.e., of real estates. He thought that the prices of estates would be stable, because they depend on the average of good and bad harvests, and because the prices of other goods depend on the prices of the estates, except the prices of luxury goods or extraordinary preferences of certain customers. Conclusively, the value of money will change, if money in relation to estates becomes more scarce or more abundant. Changes of prices may be the effect of the price of money or of the quantity of the supply of goods. Here Pufendorf's reasoning seems to resemble the quantity theory.
- Concerning capital and interest, Roscher locates Pufendorf's position somewhere between Calvin and Hume. According to Pufendorf it was not forbidden to charge interest, rather it was explicitly allowed (p. 312). But Roscher thought that Pufendorf was not an expert in the banking business.
- Pufendorf's ideas on "absolutism" followed to some extent from Hobbes' concept of law, state, and society (p. 313 f). He stressed the influence of the state through economic policy on the wealth of citizens. As regards property which citizens have acquired prior to the existence of the state, Pufendorf acknowledges only three rights of the state in relation to the citizens and their wealth (p. 314): to enact laws on the use of wealth, to impose taxes, and to apply special rights of government, the so-called "*dominium eminens*." For example, the state should initiate and sustain the citizens to strive for increasing wealth by saving money, to avoid the consumption of luxury products, and also, by specific mea-

sures, to sustain the development of new enterprises. He has a rather tolerant attitude toward privileges of gilds and monopolies in international trade (p. 315). He defends the privilege of staples and the imposition of customs duties on the transit of commodities. Transit of foreign goods must be allowed only for necessities of life (p. 316).

- Pufendorf's views on public finance were based on the system of "enlightened absolutism." This includes the right to levy taxes and customs, but taxation must be in due proportion to the benefits of the taxpayers from public services and social peace (p. 317). Overall, the structure of the tax system should conform to the principles of natural law (p. 318).

In the light of Roscher's encompassing account, it appears that Samuel Pufendorf's writings offer a comprehensive program of economic policy and public finance at the end of the seventeenth century. His academic and political activities in economics and public finance are still worth to be studied and reconsidered. Therefore, he may be recognized as part of "three historical stages of natural law" according to the scheme presented in the following table.

Historical stages of natural law Höffe et al. (1987).	
1. Stage:	Greek–Roman antiquity: Platon, Aristotle, Stoa
2. Stage:	Christian natural law: Church fathers/scholastics: Augustinus, Thomas Aquinas, Duns Scotus, William Ockham)
3. Stage:	Modern times (a) Enlightenment based on the principles of rationalism and liberty; authors of various European nations: H. Grotius, Th. Hobbes, S. Pufendorf, J. Locke, Chr. Thomasius, G.W. Leibniz, I. Kant (b) Criticism of natural law; G.W.F. Hegel, C.F. v. Savigny/Historical School of Law; in Germany: authors, who defended natural law–thinking, e.g., R. Stammler, and opponents of natural law, e.g., H. Kelsen and G. Radbruch
After the Second World War new tendencies of the concept of natural law emerged	

3.2 *Gustav Schmoller's Reflections on Pufendorf and his Time*

In his "Outline if general economics" (*Grundriß der allgemeinen Volkswirtschaftslehre*), Gustav Schmoller referred to Samuel Pufendorf mainly in a short chapter of the first volume. Summarizing the renaissance of sciences and the development of natural law during the seventeenth century, Schmoller points to a new current of thinking in philosophy and toward state and society, which prepared the ground for the emergence of economics as a social science and its emancipation and liberation from the dogmas of revelation and social thinking of the churches. (Schmoller 1923, Vol. I, 81). Consequently, a variety of new theories appeared simultaneously – concerning morals, the state (*Staatslehre*), national economics, and social policy (p. 82). It was natural law which provided the basic framework of intellectual developments during the seventeenth and eighteenth centuries, the age of Enlightenment (*Aufklärung*). Pufendorf's contribution to that development was significant.

According to the natural law philosophy, it is the "essence of humanity" ("*Wesen der Menschen*") upon which thinking about state, society, and economy has to be built. Scholars of natural law pursued the ambitious aim to derive a comprehensive overall concept for economic policy from the practical needs and desires of men (p. 84 f). At the same time, Schmoller emphasizes that during the eighteenth century, political ideas were dominated by the basic idea of absolutism, namely of increasing power of the state and the increasing number of its tasks and public rights (p. 85).

It appears that Schmoller's interpretation strongly reflects the political and economic scenery of the Prussian-dominated German Empire of the nineteenth century which attempted to seize Pufendorf for intellectual support.

4 Conclusions

1. Pufendorf's life and his scientific career and work are shaped by his strong will for independent thinking and personal international mobility. Therefore, he left Germany and moved to northern countries. Only toward the end of his life did he return to Germany, then honored as an important advisor and author of philosophical and political studies.
2. A variety of references in books on history of economic thought show that Pufendorf is still recognized not only as a philosopher, but also as an economist. Based on the concept of natural law dealt with subjects such as property rights, money, taxation, and costs and prices of goods and resources, the latter sometimes reminding of neoclassical thinking.
3. Pufendorf's importance for studies in economic and social development is highlighted in writings of the authors of the German Historical School, mainly by Wilhelm Roscher. In his detailed account, Roscher demonstrates that Pufendorf was one of the most important authors on political, social, and economic issues. Also, Gustav Schmoller found Pufendorf's oeuvre very broadly founded, in philosophical terms as well as in political and economic terms.

References

Brandt K (1992) Geschichte der deutschen Volkswirtschaftslehre, Band 1, Rudolf Haufe, Freiburg i.Br.

Höffe O/Demmer K/Hollerbach A (1987) Art. Naturrecht, in: Staatslexikon, 7th edition, vol. 3, Herder, Freiburg i.Br. 1987, p. 1296–1318.

Kolb G (1997) Geschichte der Volkswirtschaftslehre, Dogmenhistorische Positionen des ökonomischen Denkens, Vahlen, München
Krieger L (1965) The Politics of Discretion. Pufendorf and the Acceptance of Natural Law. Chicago
Mombert P (1927) Geschichte der Nationalökonomie, Gustav Fischer, Jena
Roscher W (1874) Geschichte der National-Oekonomik in Deutschland, R. Oldenburg, München
Schmoller G (1923) Grundriß der allgemeinen Volkswirtschaftslehre, Erster Teil, Duncker & Humblot, Leipzig, München
Schröder J (1988) Art. Pufendorf, in: Staatslexikon, 7th edition, vol. 4, Herder, Freiburg a.o. 1988, sp. 619–621.
Schumpeter J A (1954) History of Economic Analysis, Allan & Unwin, London Boston Sidney
Spann O (1930) Gesellschaftslehre, 3. Auflage, Quelle & Meyer, Leipzig
Spiegel H W (1983) The Growth of Economic Thought, Duke University Press, Durham, North Carolina

Why Pufendorf Matters

Dirk Ehnts and Erik Jochem

Abstract Modern economics evolves from (neo)classical political economy, which stresses the role of the individual and rationality. Using Kantian foundations, it is argued that *economic* is what concerns the individual urge to pursue personal wealth. Nature and the social sphere are both ignored. An alternative view can be based on the ideas of human nature that Samuel Pufendorf formed. According to him, man is sociable. His self-interest is often applied toward this end and not an end in itself. Also, nature plays a role as man can decide what to do with it. Last but not least, Pufendorf recognizes that individuals grow up in society, where they are formed through the use of language and the internalization of conventions. Man, without society, is not perfect and cannot hope to strive for happiness. He needs support from society to protect himself from his fellow man and to increase the chances of realizing this drive toward sociability. Economics could be rebuilt on stronger foundations as neuroscience seems to confirm Pufendorf's view of human nature in general.

Keywords Homo oeconomicus · Homo sociooeconomicus · Philosophy · Self-interest · Sociability

JEL Codes A1 · B1 · B4 · P16

D. Ehnts (✉)
TU Chemnitz, Chemnitz, Germany

E. Jochem
Pufendorf-Gesellschaft e. V., Leipzig, Germany
e-mail: jochem@pohleundklatt.de

J. G. Backhaus et al. (eds.), *Samuel Pufendorf and the Emergence of Economics as a Social Science*, The European Heritage in Economics and the Social Sciences 24, https://doi.org/10.1007/978-3-030-49791-0_10

1 Introduction

It is not natural to have something like *political economy*. The current version of political economy is called economics. It is, compared to earlier versions, a rather *un*political political economy – which is itself highly political. The current doctrine works through constitutions and treaties that make the State more and more impotent when it comes to political economy (Herrmann 2007). For instance, central banks move more and more toward an inflation-targeting approach, leaving little space for other considerations (Constâncio 2017). In the Eurozone, governments depend on the Euro, a currency that is created by the European Central Bank (ECB). The ECB is supranational and, as it stands, is not allowed take orders from national governments. On top of this, national governments in the European Union (EU) have agreed to follow the Stability and Growth Pact, effectively introducing the possibility of government default. Before that, the government was supported by its own national central bank, which ensured that the question of default would never arise. Today, Eurozone governments have to turn to the banking system in order to finance their spending (Ehnts 2016). If financial markets decide not to finance their spending, the Troika, an unelected and improvised body, will heavily influence the political economy of crisis countries (Blyth 2013).

Our thesis is that the way modern economics is practiced is fundamentally flawed. The resulting problems are by now obvious: the intrusion of the market into spheres where people don't want it, catastrophic climate change and the lack to address it, the overreliance on private enterprise and entrepreneurship to solve social problems, the misguided belief in the efficiency of financial markets in allocating resources, the naïve view that free trade can even exist when the role of government clearly implies that it can't, the unwanted rise in inequality, and a range of other issues. In this context, we believe that Samuel Pufendorf (1632–1694) can help us understand reality. All these problems have one thing in common: the policies that created them rely on a view of the world that builds on the individual and some notion of rationality, as embodied in the *homo oeconomicus*. Our goal is not to criticize the homo oeconomicus (Helmedag 2018, pp. 54–102; Kirchgässner 2008), but rather to rebuild some philosophical foundations upon which an alternative to modern economics can be created.[1] In this endeavor, we find the works of Samuel Pufendorf to be an important contribution. This is why Pufendorf matters.

[1] Our approach should be compatible with those arguing that uncertainty matters (Müller-Kademann 2019).

2 The Anthropocene

The *Anthropocene* is the age in which the domestication of nature started and – today – found a surprising limit. The agricultural revolution could be seen as the starting date, but a later date like the end of World War II is also possible.[2] What matters is that humans are changing the environment to an extent that it rather adjusts to us than forcing us to live within the limits that are good-natured.[3] The role of the environment has been mostly neglected in modern economics.[4] Principles of economics textbooks teach students that the supply curve is sloping upwards: more supply will be forthcoming at rising prices, but it will be forthcoming. There is no limit to supply. This way of looking at the world is based on Say's Law, named after Jean-Baptiste Say. Say (1852, 66) in his *Cours complet d'économie politique pratique* writes:

> The natural riches are inexhaustible, because otherwise we would not get them for free. Being unable to be multiplied or exhausted, they are not the object of economics.

So, there is no reason to examine nature more closely. Scarcity, *the* topic of economics, has to be solved through choice, since we cannot produce everything. However, in modern economics it is not the limits of nature that force us to choose, but rather the budget constraint. Money, in the form of income, is limited and forces us to choose. This view of man and nature is not undisputed. Many of the ancients, among them Pufendorf, understand obedience to the limitations of Nature as the very source of culture.[5] In *Of the Law of Nature and Nations*, Pufendorf (1672) writes about man and nature[6]:

> It is true that God allowed men to turn the earth, its products, and its creatures, to his own use and convenience, that is, He gave men indefinite right to them, yet the manner, intensity, and extent of this power were left to the judgment and disposition of men; whether, in other words, they would confine it within certain limits, or within none at all, and whether they wanted every man to have a right to everything, or only to a certain and fixed part of things, or to be assigned his definite portion with which he should rest content and claim no right to anything else.

As Tidemans (2010, 12) points out, for Pufendorf property should arise from human agreement. The extraction of natural resources could then be confined to "certain limits" or "none at all." This, compared to the position of Say above, is a very different approach to Nature. Pufendorf recognizes that the use of "the earth, its products and its creatures" has to be decided upon by the society and cannot be taken for granted. He thinks that law – property law – is the appropriate way for the Anthropos to deal with Nature.

---

[2] No official date has yet been set by any relevant institution.

[3] Humans have been influencing nature for millennia. For instance, the Amazon rainforest is a product of human intervention. See Mann (2005, Ch. 9).

[4] There are some alternative views at the fringes, like Georgescu-Roegen (1971).

[5] See Greenwood and Stini (1977, 393–408) for a modern interpretation of this view.

[6] Book IV, Ch. 4, Sect. 4.

In contrast, Modernity subjects Nature to the desires of men. We make use of the resources as we wish, mostly in the pursuit of profit. As a result, Nature – for the best and for the worst – has become the subject of man. With a global climate crisis under way, Nature, so far domesticated by man, now more and more domesticates man. Antoine de Saint-Exupéry (1943, ch. 21) writes in *The Little Prince* about this complicated relationship between man and nature:

> "Men have forgotten this truth," said the fox. "But you must not forget it. You become responsible, forever, for what you have tamed."

2.1 The Anthropos – Who Are We?

The Anthropos (Greek for human: ἄνθρωπος), according to Pufendorf, is deficient. Having lived through the Thirty Years' War, it is easy to understand how Pufendorf came to this conclusion. Hobbes (1642, 1651), who also lived in this period, assumed that the natural state would be war of all against all. The State would be needed to help tame the Anthropos. Pufendorf disagrees with this view. Man has always lived in groups, communities, and states. Therefore, community (the State) and the individual are not antagonisms – they constitute a necessary whole. In *The Whole Duty of Man According to the Law of Nature*, Pufendorf (1673) writes about the existence of communities[7]:

> The next inquiry we are to make, is upon what Bottom Civil Societies have been erected, and wherein their Internal Constitution does consist. Where, in the first place, this is manifest, That neither any Place, nor any Sort of Weapons, nor any kind of brute Creatures can be capable of affording any sufficient and safe Guard or Defence against the Injuries to which all Men are liable, by reason of the Pravity of Mankind: From such Dangers, Men alone can afford an agreeable Remedy by joining their Forces together, by interweaving their Interests and Safety, and by forming a general Confederacy for their mutual Succour; that therefore this End might be obtain'd effectually, it was necessary that those who fought to bring it about, should be firmly joined together and associated into Communities.

For Pufendorf, the State is more than an institution to stop us from killing each other. The State creates the possibility of furthering individuals' cooperation. We can rise above the sum of the parts for the benefit of the whole. Individuals do *not* grow up without society and later chose to sign something that resembles a social contract, as envisioned by Rousseau (1762). As Flint and Powell (2013, p. 270) point out, "society has never been constituted on a social contract." Individuals grow up in societies that predate the individuals. This view of the world is informed by Pufendorf's ideas about human behavior. The two driving forces that decide human action are self-interest and sociability.[8]

---

[7] Chapter 6.

[8] According to Saether (2017, 47), Pufendorf took the idea of self-interest from Hobbes and the idea of sociability from Grotius.

2.2 *Self-Interest*

According to Pufendorf, the Anthropos has a free will that allows him to follow his self-interest (Saether 2017, 68). In volume two of De Jure Naturae Et Gentium Libri Octo, Pufendorf (1934) [1688] writes:

> In the first place man has this in common with all beings which are conscious of their own existence, that he has the greatest love for himself, tries to protect himself by every possible means, and tries to secure what he thinks will benefit him, and to avoid what may in his opinion injure him. (II.iii.14: 205)

The pursuit of self-interest is the strongest force driving the Anthropos. That is "because man is so framed that he thinks of his own advantage before the welfare of others for the reason that it is his nature to think of his own life before the life of others. Another reason is that it is no one's business so much as my own to look out for myself" (ibid.: 207).[9]

2.3 *Sociability*

The second driving force of the Anthropos that Pufendorf identifies is that of sociability.[10] This is due to "the greatest weakness and native helplessness" (ibid.: 207). The Anthropos would feel punished if left alone by his fellows. According to Pufendorf, the Anthropos is "malicious, petulant, and easily irritated, as well as quick and powerful to do injury." This is why it is necessary for man to be sociable: "Every man, as so far as in him lies, should cultivate and preserve towards others a sociable attitude, which is peaceful and agreeable at all times to the nature and end of the human race" (II.iii.15: 207). Saether (2017, 69) points out that it is important to note that the Anthropos, according to Pufendorf, *must* be sociable. It would be wrong to conclude from Pufendorf's writings that the Anthropos is *naturally* sociable. We are imperfect beings, needing to cultivate a social attitude. If we do, with the help of (natural) law, the outcome can be quite acceptable:

> A man shall not harm one who is not injuring him; he shall allow everyone to enjoy his own possessions; he shall faithfully perform whatever has been agreed upon; and he shall willingly advance the interest of other, so far as he is not bound by more pressing obligations. (II.ii.9: 172)

The rule of law, according to Pufendorf, should be based on an understanding of the Anthropos as having an inclination for society. *Ordo amoris*, "rightly ordered loves"

---

[9] Saether (2017, 68) claims that Pufendorf rejects the possibility that people can act altruistically.

[10] To support this view Pufendorf quotes the Roman philosopher Seneca the Younger: "Man was born for mutual assistance" and the Roman Emperor Marcus Aurelius (121–180): "For we have come into being for cooperation" (ibid.).

in Latin, is an order of ethical values that individuals base their actions on in the years around 1700 (Vollhardt 2001, 67–94).

3 Neurosciences on Self-Interest and Sociability

The two driving forces of the Anthropos identified by Pufendorf have been investigated by neurosciences over the last years. Motivational system and aggression apparatus were identified as major components of our internal working. In a nutshell, our motivational system drives us toward sociable behavior while our aggression apparatus regulates violence as a means of protest against unacceptable social situations. According to Bauer (2011), "human behavior occurs in a neurobiological framework staked out by two fundamental systems. The first is the central drive … or motivation system. It aims – in addition to the satisfaction of basic needs (…) – on the attainment of attachment and social acceptance (…)." This connects to Pufendorf's idea of the Anthropos being sociable. It is probably not a wild guess that basic needs are satisfied through self-interest, and once that is achieved "social acceptance" is what is targeted next. A combination of scarce time and resources and/or money is the obvious ingredient to this.

Bauer continues: "The second system, the aggression apparatus, serves to ward off pain and social exclusion (…). The aggression apparatus is at the service of the motivation system: it becomes active when drive targets targeted by the propulsion system seem to be at risk (…)."[11] Note the stress on "social exclusion" as something to be avoided; unhappiness starts here, and not with underachieving the consumption targets of individuals as one might expect (Haller and Hadler 2006).

3.1 *Motivational System*

What is it that gives us satisfaction? Neoclassical economics assumes that it is the consumption of goods and services that increases our satisfaction. However, recent developments in the research of neuroscience point in a difference direction. Tabibnia and Lieberman (2007, 94) find "that people derive satisfaction from implementing justice and maintaining fairness by punishing unfair partners." So, there is much more to make us happy than consumption. Lyubomirsky and Ross (1997) find that happiness is affected by the presence and performance of peers. Unhappy people are much more effected by social comparison than happy people. So, not only is there more than consumption to make us happy or unhappy, but we are heavily influenced by our social surroundings when it comes to the happiness that we draw from our own performance. Surely, these results must be puzzling for everyone

[11] Own translation.

basing her or his thought on the homo oeconomicus. On the other side, those using the homo sociooeconomicus as a foundation will find their ideas confirmed. We are sociable and struggle for social position (Veblen 1899).

3.2 *Aggression Apparatus*

It is often assumed that the Anthropos is aggressive. However, "Man the Hunter" (De Vore and Lee 1968) or "The Selfish Gene" (Dawkins 1976) are myths that have been rejected (Lewontin et al. 1984; Sober and Wilson 1999). Our forefathers, instead, were vegetarians engaging in social cooperation (Robinson et al. 2017; Boyd and Richerson 2009). Even when they started hunting, there was no change. The Milgram (1963) experiments, often quoted to support the idea that humans can act aggressively toward other human beings, rather shows that humans are not willing to hurt others when unprovoked and not under pressure. The Neo-Darwinist ideas of "Man is evil" and "Man is a sinner" are also not correct, as there is ample evidence to the contrary.[12] Adding to this is the fact that Darwin himself was rather less Neo-Darwinist than many would think:

> A man who has no assured & ever present belief in the existence of a personal God or a future existence with retribution & reward, can have for his rule of life, as far as I can see, only to follow those impulses & instincts which are the strongest or which seem to him the best ones. A dog acts in this manner, but he does so blindly. A man, on the other hand, looks forwards & backwards, & compares his various feelings, desires & recollections. He then finds, in accordance with the verdict of the wisest men, that the highest satisfaction is derived from certain impulses, namely the social instincts. If he acts for the good of others, he will receive the approbation of his fellow-men & gain the love of those with whom he lives; & this latter gain undoubtedly is the highest pleasure on this earth.

Confirming this view, Eisenberger et al. (2003) find that rejection by others creates social pain that is comparable to physical pain.

4 The Individual and the State

Pufendorf recognized that community (the State) is an anthropological constant. Individuals would constitute the community, which would at the same time define them. One cannot exist without the other. This is one of the major insights of discussions in natural law (Dumont 1991, p. 85 ff.). Language is spoken by a com-

[12] In neoclassical economics, usually nothing is said about morality during classes in microeconomics or Principles of Economics. Following self-interest and maximizing profits is thought to be without any moral implications. Interpreting the silence as taboo, one might easily get the idea that homo oeconomicus could be evil or a sinner, especially in connection with popular books like *The Great Gatsby* or their respective movie adaption (usually starring Leonardo di Caprio as the young and rich "evil sinner").

munity, and the individuals adjust to the language spoken in the community. Individuals do not invent their own language. With language come certain ideas regarding ontology and epistemology that heavily influence the social reality of the individual (see Lawson 1997). The rise and development of individualism naturally depend very much on the use of language in the respective community. Heteronomy is a requirement for autonomy, as parents can easily verify when looking at their children.

In the modern West an opposite view of the world dominates. Society is assumed to be a contractual union of autonomous individuals, who signed this contract themselves. The relationship between individual and state is one of voluntary submission. The Hobbesian state has the monopoly of violence and has no further rule to play. Since the Enlightenment stresses autonomous rationality, individuals deal with their (self) interests without involving further parties. The state is the guarantor of these private contracts – its own role as a competent ruler with a view toward the public purpose is not seen as constructive. Values are relative. What leads to convergence of views between two individuals has legal power. Law is replaced by contract.

The society built on these arrangements will revive a feudal form of society. In the absence of public purpose as a concept of constructing reality, everyone seeks to maximize self-interest by subduing her or his own self-interest to that of another (self) interest or interests.

The success of neoliberalism has rested to some extent on being perceived as the embodiment of the Enlightenment. As this, it can be understood as an extension of the sad tradition of utopias in the twentieth century. With its focus on the so-called autonomous individual, neoliberalism supports the individual dreams of consumption of urban hipsters. In a world where individuals are only committed to self-interest, it is unproblematic to just follow one's ideas of consumption. A state that interferes with this can only be totalitarian. There is no better way to capture the Anthropos: consumption as the insignia of freedom.

4.1 The Enlightenment Versus Pufendorf

As we have seen above, Pufendorf understood community to be the institution that is needed to make individuals thrive. Protecting one from another against physical harm was only the beginning, as the community would play a role in supporting the Anthropos to be sociable and help to deliver common goods. This idea of the interconnectedness of the deficient Anthropos and the supporting community came under pressure during The Enlightenment – now the rational individual was all that we needed to get the best of all worlds – and it has been (almost) forgotten now that modern economics rules.

Saether (2017, ch. 5) sees Pufendorf as a "*Champion of the Enlightenment*," a characterization with which we disagree. Pufendorf saw the Anthropos as deficient, a view that was not shared by thinkers like Kant. The Enlightenment was based on the idea of rationality, a concept that was also used in Pufendorf's writings.[13] That rationality was the rationality of an individual, divorced from community. *Sapere aude* was addressed to this individual, not to a community. Hence, Pufendorf's deficient Anthropos did not fit into the new worldview. Thinkers now believed in the possibility of individual autonomy and perfection, in overcoming the self-inflicted immaturity through the effort of the intellect.

The rise of the natural sciences with their laws that were discoverable by the Anthropos led to a similar rise in self-confidence which stood in contradiction to the idea of a deficient Anthropos. The myth of the unstoppable progress of (Western) humanity started, continuing to this day. Pufendorf's imperfect individuals needed the help of society and the State, which is incompatible with the autonomous rational individuals that many thinkers of The Enlightenment envisioned.

4.2 Modern Economics and the Homo Oeconomicus

Political economy developed in the nineteenth century toward a discipline that would mimic natural sciences, with a strong focus on Newtonian physics. The concept of homo oeconomicus, the rational autist that contracts with others and consumes without any public purpose, was developed. The "economic man" acted in pursuit of self-interest, which was narrowly defined as the pursuit of wealth. Individual wishes (preferences), when satisfied, led to an increase in satisfaction (utility). Peace or the absence of aggression was taken for granted, justice and fairness ignored. Political economy became a narrow field of what used to be the state sciences (*Staatswissenschaften*), severing all ties that bound it with disciplines like the Law, sociology, psychology, philosophy, geography, and others. The distribution of incomes was justified by productivity alone.

Modern textbooks are still based on these old conceptions, and ideas coming from other fields or those that are not compatible with the framing of political economy are only introduced in an ad hoc manner at later times. In this way, one can talk about ecological economics with both feet in the neoclassical or neoliberal paradigm, arguing that taxation should change the incentives of the individuals so that markets can work best. No larger role for the state can be imagined within the neoliberal paradigm because of the deep foundations resting on the homo oeconomicus. In the last decades, the discipline has successfully reduced macroeconomics to a case of applied microeconomics, thus closing down the only part of economics where a larger role for the state could be imagined (Ehnts and Helmedag 2018). This surely has not been a coincidence.

---

[13] See Saether (2017, 53).

There exist now many intents to “rethink economics,” to reconstruct it, or to move toward a new economic paradigm. The project is perhaps larger than those that are working on the issue understand. In order to have progress in economics we need to go from a world based on the homo oeconomicus and the ideas of Enlightenment toward a new view of the Anthropos that could be called the homo sociooeconomicus. Since this change occurs at the foundation of modern economics, paradigm change is indeed called for. It would be worthwile to ponder how exactly this is brought about, but probably it will just happen as scientific change always happened. The older paradigm dies out, while young scientists intrigued by the new paradigm and by choosing to work within generate the conditions that will make it successful.

5 Conclusion

Since the Great Financial Crisis and the recent awakening to climate change, people have found economics to be deficient. Economics did not see it coming, did not use balance sheets as a methodology when it comes to financial crises (Bezemer 2009), did not discuss financialization or globalization with a critical attitude.[14] Economics did not even change the way that finance and macroeconomics is taught.[15] Instead, economics was widely perceived to be a force that argued in favor of more globalization and more financialization (Appelbaum 2019). Meanwhile, the two important topics of our time were almost completely ignored by textbooks and journals: Climate change and the fight to stop it and the rise in inequality.

While it is more or less understood why economics has not changed (yet), the question what it is that should replace it is still an open one.[16] In this chapter, we tried to lay down the argument that we should rebuild economics by abandoning the neoclassical superstructure – with the homo oeconomicus at the center – in favor of something that we’d like to call the *homo sociooeconomicus*. The *homo sociooeconomicus* is understood as a *social* being first, with *economic* motives playing a secondary role. Self-interest is used not only for economic, but also and perhaps more importantly for social gain.[17] Amassing wealth might be seen as a way to improve social status and position. Last but not least, the idea that the individual can exist without society has to be discarded. Learning language from his surrounding society, the individual can only think what is possible in that language and will internalize some if not most of the conventions.

---

[14] Giegold et al. (2016) provide a blueprint for financial reform from a policymaker’s perspective.

[15] The most convincing alternative seems to be Modern Monetary Theory (Wray 2015).

[16] See Slobodian (2018) for explanations of the persistence of the neoliberal regime and Schulmeister (2018) for a proposal to overcome it.

[17] The results of the discussion between Gigerenzer (2007) and Kahneman (2011) on the question of rationality versus decisions based on gut feelings are a separate issue.

References

Appelbaum, Binyamin (2019): *The Economists' Hour: How the False Prophets of Free Markets Fractured Our Society*, New York: Picador

Bauer, Joachim (2011): *Schmerzgrenze: Vom Ursprung alltäglicher und globaler Gewalt*, München: Heyne

Bezemer, Dirk (2009): No one saw this coming. Understanding financial crisis through accounting models, SOM Research Reports Vol. 09002, Groningen: University of Groningen

Blyth, Mark (2013): *Austerity: The History of a Dangerous Idea*, Oxford: Oxford University Press

Boyd, Robert and Peter J Richerson (2009): Culture and the evolution of human cooperation, *Philosophical Transactions of the Royal Society B: Biological Sciences*, 364 (1533): 3281–3288

Constâncio, Vítor (2017): The future of monetary policy frameworks, Lecture by at the Instituto Superior de Economia e Gestão, Lisbon, 25 May 2017, https://www.ecb.europa.eu/press/key/date/2017/html/ecb.sp170525_lecture.en.pdf

Dawkins, Richard (1976): *The Selfish Gene*, Oxford: Oxford University Press

de Saint-Exupéry, Antoine (1943): *The Little Prince*, New York: Reynal and Hitchcock

De Vore, Irven and Richard Borshay Lee [eds.] (1968): *Man the Hunter: The First Intensive Survey of a Single, Crucial Stage of Human Development—Man's Once Universal Hunting Way of Life*, Chicago: Aldine

Dumont, Louis (1991): *Individualismus: Zur Ideologie der Moderne*, Frankfurt/New York: Campus

Ehnts, Dirk (2016): *Modern Monetary Theory and European Macroeconomics*, Abingdon, UK: Routledge

Ehnts, Dirk and Fritz Helmedag (2018): The Present State of Economics: Errors and Omissions Excepted, in: Omar Feraboli and Carlo Morelli (eds.), *Post-Crash Economics: Plurality and Heterodox Ideas in Teaching and Research*, London: Palgrave Macmillan

Eisenberger, Naomi, Matthew Lieberman and Kipling Williams (2003): Does Rejection Hurt? An fMRI Study of Social Exclusion, *Science* 302 (5643), 290–292

Flint, John and Ryan Powell (2013): Individualization and Social Dis/integration in Contemporary Society: A Comparative Note on Zygmunt Bauman and Norbert Elias, in: Depelteau, F. and T. Landini (Eds.), Norbert Elias and Social Theory, New York: Palgrave Macmillan, p. 261–274

Georgescu-Roegen (1971): *The Entropy Law and the Economic Process*. Cambridge, MA: Harvard University Press

Giegold, Sven, Udo Philipp and Schick, Gerhard (2016): Finanzwende: Den nächsten Crash verhindern. Berlin: Wagenbach

Gigerenzer, Gerd (2007): *Gut Feelings: The Intelligence of the Unconscious*, New York: Viking Adult

Greenwood, David J. and William A. Stini (1977): *Nature, Culture, and Human History*, New York: Harper and Row, 393–408

Haller, Max and Markus Hadler (2006): How Social Relations and Structures Can Produce Happiness and Unhappiness: An International Comparative Analysis, *Social Indicators Research* 75(2), 169–216

Helmedag, Fritz (2018): *Warenproduktion mittels Arbeit – Zur Rehabilitation des Wertgesetzes*, 3rd ed., Marburg: Metropolis

Herrmann, Christoph (2007): Neoliberalism in the European Union, *Studies in Political Economy - A Socialist Review*, 79(1), 61–90

Hobbes, Thomas (1642): *Elementorum philosophiae sectio tertia de cive*, Paris: Parisiis

Hobbes, Thomas (1651): *Leviathan or the Matter, Forme and Power of a Commonwealth Ecclesiasticall and Civil*, London: Crooke

Jean-Baptiste Say (1852): Cours complet d'économie politique pratique, Paris: Guillaumin

Kahneman, Daniel (2011): *Thinking, Fast and Slow*, London and New York: Macmillan

Kirchgässner, Gebhard (2008): *Homo Oeconomicus - The Economic Model of Behaviour and Its Applications in Economics and Other Social Sciences*, Boston, MA: Springer

Lawson, Tony (1997): *Economics & Reality*, Abingdon (UK): Routledge

Lewontin, Richard, Steven Rose and Leon Kamin (1984): *Not in Our Genes: Biology, Ideology and Human Nature*, New York: Pantheon Books

Mann, Charles C. (2005): *1491: New Revelations of the Americans Before Columbus*, New York: Knopf

Milgram, Stanley (1963): Behavioral study of obedience, *The Journal of Abnormal and Social Psychology*, 67(4), 371–378

Müller-Kademann, Christian (2019): *Uncertainty and Economics: A Paradigmatic Perspective*, Abingdon, UK: Routledge

Pufendorf, Samuel (1672): *Of the Law of Nature and Nations*

Pufendorf, Samuel (1673): *The Whole Duty of Man According to the Law of Nature*

Pufendorf, Samuel (1934) [1688]: De jure naturae et gentium libri octo. Volume I, Photographic Reproduction of the Edition of 1688, with an Introduction by Simons Walter. Volume II, Translation, by Oldfather C. H. and Oldfather W. A., New York: Oxford University Press

Robinson, Joshua R., John Rowan, Christopher J. Campisano, Jonathan G. Wynn and Kaye E. Reed (2017): *Late Pliocene environmental change during the transition from Australopithecus to Homo*, Nature ecology and evolution, 1, article 159

Rousseau, Jean-Jacques (2014) [1762]: The Major Political Writings of Jean-Jacques Rousseau: The Two "Discourses" and the "Social Contract", Chicago: University of Chicago Press

Saether, Arild (2017): *Natural Law and the Origin of Political Economy: Samuel Pufendorf and the History of Economics*, Abingdon (UK): Routledge

Schulmeister, Stefan (2018): *Der Weg zur Prosperität*, Salzburg: Ecowin

Slobodian, Quinn (2018): *Globalists: The End of Empire and the Birth of Neoliberalism*, Harvard: Harvard University Press

Sober, Elliott and David Sloan Wilson (1999): *Unto Others: The Evolution and Psychology of Unselfish Behavior*, Harvard, MA: Harvard University Press

Sonja Lyubomirsky, Lee Ross (1997): Hedonic consequences of social comparison: A contrast of happy and unhappy people. *Journal of Personality and Social Psychology 73*(6), 1141–1157

Tabibnia, Golnaz, Matthew D. Lieberman (2007): Fairness and Cooperation Are Rewarding: Evidence from Social Cognitive Neuroscience. *Annals of the New York Academy of Sciences 1118*(1), 90–101

Tidemans, Nicolaus (2010): Property in a Utopian State, Informed by Ideas of Pufendorf and Locke, in: Backhaus, Jürgen (ed.) The State as Utopia: Continental Approaches, New York, Dordrecht, Heidelberg, London: Springer

Veblen, Thorstein (1899): *The Theory of the Leisure Class: An Economic Study of Institutions*, New York: Macmillan

Vollhardt, Friedrich (2001): *Selbstliebe und Geselligkeit: Untersuchungen zum Verhältnis von naturrechtlichem Denken und moraldidaktischer Literatur im 17. und 18. Jahrhundert*, Tübingen: Max Niemeyer

Wray, L. Randall (2015): *Modern Money Theory: A Primer on Macroeconomics for Sovereign Monetary Systems*, 2nd ed., London: Palgrave Macmillan

The manufacturer's authorised representative in the EU is Springer Nature Customer Service Centre GmbH, Europaplatz 3, 69115 Heidelberg, Germany. If you have any concerns regarding our products, please contact ProductSafety@springernature.com

Printed and bound by CPI Group (UK) Ltd, Croydon, CR0 4YY
30/09/2026
02225453-0013